BLOOD

on the

SNOW

———//———

Eyewitness Accounts of the Russian Revolution

BLOOD

on the

SNOW

—— // ——

by

Elisabeth Heresch

PARAGON HOUSE
New York

First American edition, 1990

Published in the United States by

Paragon House
90 Fifth Avenue
New York, NY 10011

Copyright © 1990 by Paragon House

Originally published in German as *Blutiger Schnee*.

Designed by Eve Kirch

Library of Congress Cataloging-in-Publication Data
Heresch, Elisabeth.
    [Blutiger Schnee. English]
    Blood on the snow : eyewitness accounts of the Russian Revolution
/ by Elisabeth Heresch.—1st American ed.
        p. cm.
    Translation of: Blutiger Schnee.
    Includes index.
    ISBN 1-55778-109-5
    1. Soviet Union—History—Revolution, 1917–1921—Personal
narratives. I. Title.
DK265.69.H4713   1989
947.084'1—dc20   89-3412
                                                        CIP

Manufactured in the United States of America

The paper used in this publication meets the minimum requirements of
American National Standard for Information Sciences—Permanence of Paper
for Printed Library Materials, ANSI Z39.48-1984.

CONTENTS

FOREWORD

This is not the one-thousand-and-first history of the October Revolution. There would certainly have been people more qualified to write that than I.

This is the mirror of those events as reported directly by the last living eyewitnesses, along with their memories of the chief figures of those times.

It all began with Tatyana Botkina. I was introduced to her in Paris in 1979. What she, the daughter of Czar Nicholas II's personal physician (who was shot along with the czar), told me, gave a more vivid picture of events than any historical account could, and moreover, it showed how old the phenomena of anarchy and revolution, which seem to us to be unique to our times, really are. I asked myself whether other witnesses from the period around 1917 might be able to provide their own subjective reports based on their experiences, which could be put together to form an objective mosaic of those historic events. This mosaic might in turn come close to the truth—or at least to reality.

I found little in what had already been written that corresponded to my idea: There were fascinating memoirs by individuals who depicted their journey through the jungle of those years, but there was no compilation of experiences from many viewpoints that complemented each other to make up a total living pattern.

The generation of eyewitnesses had all but died out by the end of the 1960s. During my trips as a journalist or interpreter to Paris (the haven of the Russian emigration), to other European cities, to the United States, and also to the Soviet Union, I tried to find those people who were still alive who could report on these events from first-hand experience, and who were willing to do so.

Unfortunately, such people were hard to find in the country that now looks back proudly on its achievements in 1917 as the historical origin of what it has become today. Therefore, reports from Bolsheviks and Social Revolutionaries are in the minority compared with reports by those who considered themselves then, and still consider themselves, to be *Russian patriots*.

This book attempts to bring to life the mechanism of the February and October Revolutions of 1917 by means of eyewitness reports organized chronologically. At the same time, it shows models of political and human behavior under similar circumstances—models which are, as is well known, not resticted to time or location. Some light is also shed, however, on the historical myths surrounding idealized or damned figures, whenever eyewitnesses report on *their* impressions of the czar or the revolutionaries. Was Lenin really an unerring genius and Czar Nicholas II a cruel autocrat?

I translated most of the personal reports from Russian but have left them unchanged stylistically in the context of the interview. The reports are complemented by documents from the time and depictions of German and even American financing for the Bolsheviks.

My thanks go to the eyewitnesses, who entrusted their memories with me so that their memories last.

History is made by a few, and carried out by their followers, but it is borne on the shoulders of everyone, no matter what political opinions they may have.

On the shoulders of *all* eyewitnesses to history.

Elisabeth Heresch

INTRODUCTION

—*++*—

The Revolution(s) of 1917: Necessity or Accident?

Was the Russian "October Revolution" a historical necessity? Was it the uprising of a people, the inevitable result of political and social developments as was the "February Revolution" which preceded it in the same year?

It most certainly was not, and nor was the hasty abdiction of the Czar. According to the eyewitnesses who report on Russian reality at the time, what has gone down in history as the October Revolution was in no way carried out or desired by the masses. Rather, it was a carefully planned putsch organized by a small group and aided by the fact that resistance was insufficiently organized. In contrast to the real uprising that had taken place in February 1917, the success of the October coup lay less in the conditions affecting Russia, especially its capital Petrograd, than in the ability and resources of the revolutionaries who were able to make use of those conditions. One of the chief factors here was the First World War, which caused unresolved social tensions to escalate and offered the Bolsheviks a foothold for propaganda and similar operations that coincided with the interests of the German General Staff, the Bolsheviks' chief financiers.

Russia at the beginning of the First World War was a nation well on its way to transforming itself from an agricultural to an industrial nation. In view of its economic and territorial potential and its inexhaustible human resources, other powers, especially Germany and England, were beginning to develop respect, and at the same time they showed increasing concern. All of this was reinforced by the strong financial and political support of Russia by France, which had long seen Russia as a logical ally in the fight for preeminence in Europe. Extensive foreign loans had been brought in from France, above all thanks to Minister Kokovzov. Russia's industrial production in 1916 rose to an impressive 34 million tons of coal and almost five million tons of steel.

The country's social climate was relatively promising. As a result of the reforms in the 1860s, the peasants had been guaranteed legal equality within the population. Moreover, the founding of the *Semstvo* had given them independence from their plot of land and the chance to buy their own land, take out loans, join a cooperative, etc. If Stolypin's reform plans—which were to have been carried out at the latest by 1922—had been realized, and if a step-by-step attempt had been made to deal with the country's problems, including making plans for settlement and land use, peaceful conditions might have been preserved in the country. This would have meant the creation of a great power that would have been strong enough to survive even the events of the war. Such a country would have been anything but fertile soil for revolutionary propaganda.

Of course, the forced industrialization and the recruitment of workers from the peasantry, all made necessary by increased arms production, had brought an industrial proletariat into being. The czarist state, however, seemed blind to the needs of that fledgling class. The brutal response to the uprising of 1905 can be explained only in this way. Though Czar Nicholas II had a more or less fatalistic attitude towards power, he nevertheless felt himself bound to maintain an "unsullied" crown, in the sense of unlimited government power, and in this he was probably influenced strongly by his advisers and, above all, by his wife. The institution of the First Duma—the Russian parliament created in answer to the events of 1905—did give the promise of shared government through elected representatives, but it did not *de facto* lead to effective action, although such action was theoretically possible under the law. To top it all off, competent ministers who had succeeded in making progress in Russia's domestic or foreign policy frequently had to give way to incompetent successors. This was the result of intrigues and protectionism and—last, but not least—of the Czarina herself, acting irrationally under the influence of Rasputin. This proved to be the decisive factor preventing the Duma from acting positively and thwarting any real cooperation with the Czar as the highest decision maker. All this made for a weak and disunified government and state power that was not particularly difficult to destroy. In no way did it offer protection shied against a programmatically and financially well-supplied group of revolutionaries intent on using the problems of the war for all they were worth.

Revolutions in Russia were not necessarily a phenomenon coming from unsolved problems. Alexander II, for instance, whose government had called into being and partially realized the already mentioned social and economic reforms, was torn apart by a bomb. In contrast to the revolutionaries of February and particularly October 1917, the Russian revolutionaries of the nineteenth century were inspired by residual and unbridgeable gap between a dissatisfied population and a state that reacted to the demands of that population in too authoritarian a manner. They were led on by the ideas of idealistic philosophy, electrified by the thought of Marxism as an (imported) theory of salvation that could be applied in Russia. Their discussions occurred not in peasant cottages, workers' quarters, or centers of industrial misery but rather at the coffee tables of intellectuals, who, especially in avant-garde circles in the capital city of Petersburg, found sympathizers open to progressive ideas and interested in creative changes. The pamphlets of the demonstration led by Gapon and Kalayev in 1905—which was essentially peaceful and did not aim to destroy the czarist regime—make clear demands for attention to an improvement of social problems, but they are free of the ideological, revolutionary, and class-conscious coloring of the revolutionary group in 1917. In view of this, at least, the thesis that the revolutions of 1917 were in some way the delayed outcome of the events of 1905 is indefensible. The strikes and uprisings of February 1917 were certainly the manifestation of social despair and must be understood in the context of the misery of the time. In contrast to this, though, the subsequent propaganda campaign by the red revolutionaries, which called on soldiers at the front to lay down their weapons and on the population in general to rise up against the government, ultimately leading to the overthrow in October, was characterized solely by the slogans of ideology and class hatred.

Paradoxically, it seems that what allowed the revolutionaries to act and prepare for the putsch in October 1917 in relative calmness was less a lack of democratic spirit than a failure of vigilance and realistic assessments of the situation by the government. Even for critical observers, the political climate of the time has to be viewed as liberal. Newspapers of all political stripe (with the exception of those against a continuation of the war) were allowed to be published. In the Duma, all the parties were represented, though the majority of representatives—in accordance with the will of the people—were conservative. Out of 422 seats, 266 were held by representatives of conservative or right-wing parties, while the Social Revolutionaries (Trudoviki) had 10 and the Social Democrats—including the Bolsheviks—only 5. In spite of this, conservatives, monarchists, and Constitutional Democrats (Cadets)—although loyal to the Czar—switched over to the liberal or leftist camp again and again in protest against the prevailing situation at the czar's court during the era of Rasputin.

Finally, the foreign policy situation once again proves itself to be a lever working in tandem with domestic political considerations. The Bolsheviks under Lenin were able to concentrate their propaganda on the idea of ending the war. They were able to do this because the people were tired of the war and thus open to such ideas. At the outbreak of the war, the population had been patriotic and put domestic tensions on the back burner in order to work on unifying efforts. But after it became clear that the army was not prepared for its confrontation with the enemy, the populace became depressed and demoralized. Hence it viewed the government's continuation of this costly sacrifice critically—even though the Czar had not wanted the war. On the other hand, the war aims represented by conservative Foreign Minister Milyukov in the Provisional Government even after the February Revolution seemed absurd to average citizens, and certainly to soldiers. These aims for military conquest (for instance, to secure the Straits of Constantinople, etc.) offered an easy target for peace propaganda.

Even Milyukov's successor, Tereshchenko, though seemingly more liberal on the outside, continued his policy of aiming for military conquest disguised as defense. Though one can admire his flexible formulations to the population on the one hand and the forum of the Duma and the allies who wanted to continue the war on the other, his basic policy could not remain hidden for long.

Several times, Lenin suffered setbacks that put his success in seizing power or keeping it once he had achieved it into question. In the summer of 1917, there was the discovery of the help Germany gave him—which dated back to 1915. Reacting with great presence of mind, his comrades were able to carry out a lightning action that prevented the publication of the incriminating material sent out by the interior minister to the newspapers. Because the government was acting with such little cleverness, the revolutionaries were warned in time and were mostly able to escape arrest. Meanwhile, the damage done to Lenin's followers was made good again through well-aimed denials and attacks. Then there was the Constitutional Assembly, scheduled for fall 1917, which would have tended to disqualify Lenin's party as not strong enough. And there were more and more open offers for peace negotiations (from Austria-Hungary, among others). This would have pulled the rug out from under the Bolsheviks' feet with respect to their main arguments for peace. Hence Lenin had to act against the convictions of his own comrades, who had grown cautious, pushing through an immediate overthrow of the Provisional Government. Finally he ordered the Constitutional Assembly, which might have compromised his party, to be militarily dispersed. Then there was the peace treaty of Brest-Litovsk and its conditions. Accepting them was catastrophic for the Bolsheviks and their followers. But Lenin's biggest setback, which he himself saw as the end of his power, was the military situation of 1919. The "White" armies had gotten so close to Moscow that it looked as if they were going to take it. At the last moment, Russia's former allies withdrew their help, Trotsky took concerted action inside the Red Army, and the "White" resistance army itself made mistakes. Only this made it possible for Lenin to keep power and for Russia to remain Soviet.

BLOOD
on the
SNOW

Chapter One

//

War or Peace?

The outbreak of the war of 1914 as seen by the Russians and peace as a propaganda issue.

The opening shot of what was later to go down in the history of Russia and of the world as the Russian October Revolution did not fall in Russia itself. It fell elsewhere.

In Sarajevo.

The event was the assassination of the Austro-Hungarian successor archduke Franz Ferdinand and his wife on 28 June, 1914 that brought about the weighty chain of events that was to involve Russia in the war then beginning—a war that the leading politicians of Russia believed to be a threat to Russia itself, which had been going through a period of reform. As early as 1905, the then prime minister Count Witte had warned against what the revolutionaries were hoping for: a debilitation of the country brought about by military events. Six years later, Stolypin warned against the same thing shortly before he was assassinated, and even as late as February 1914 Interior Minister Durnovo had issued a similar warning. The destabilization of the country was precisely the thing that could give the revolutionaries a chance to seize power.

The threats of war and the ultimatums, notes, and telegrams that were now exchanged among the governments of Austria-Hungary, Serbia, Germany, France, and Russia also pushed forward the events at a time when Russia itself was unprepared for a military conflict. It would have been hard to find a more unsuitable time for the fulfillment of Russia's alliance obligations such as those to Serbia. Nevertheless, Russia was tied to Serbia not only politically but also as the defender of Slavic unity in the Balkans. Moreover, Russia was tempted by the enticement of Constantinople. Hence the Russian military had little enthusiasm when Prussia dispatched a military mission to that city.

The following protocol was written in French in the Petersburg Ministry for Foreign Affairs. It gives one an idea of the tense succession of events in those summer days of 1914:[1]

Thursday, 23 July:
    18:00: Delivery of the Austro-Hungarian ultimatum to Belgrade.
    19:30: The president of the Republic[2] and the Czar toast each other on board the *France.*

Friday, 24 July:
    13:00: Lunch at the French Embassy (in Petersburg). Present: Paléologue (the French ambassador), M. Sasonov (the foreign minister) and Sir George Buchanan (the British ambassador).
    15:00: A routine ministerial meeting occurs under the chairmanship of M. Goryomkin (prime minister). Sasonov issues a request to the Viennese Cabinet for an extension of the Austro-Hungarian ultimatum, so that the great powers will be able to form an opinion on the legal situation. They have all been requested to declare their position on this.
    20:00: M. Paléologue pays a visit to M. Sasonov, who tells Paléologue that the council has decided to withdraw Russian funds on deposit in Germany.

Saturday, 25 July:
    Telegram from the prince regent of Serbia to Czar Nicholas, dated 24 July.
    Communiqué from the Russian government:

    "The government is carefully following the development of the Serbo-Austrian conflict, in which it cannot be disinterested."

In the morning, an emergency meeting of the Council of Ministers takes place in Krasnoye Syelo under the chairmanship of the Czar. His Majesty decides on principle to mobilize thirteen army corps to be used if necessary against Austria.

Count Pourtalés, Germany's ambassador, presents Minister Sasonov with the following note:

"As an ally of Austria, Germany naturally supports what it considers the legitimate demands of the Viennese cabinet against Serbia."

M. Sasonov advises the Serbian government to request mediation by the British government.

18:00: Decision to reschedule the promotion of young officers to an earlier date.

18:30: The minister of war and the chief of the general staff confer with the Czar, who orders that preparatory measures for mobilization be taken in the military districts of Kiev, Odessa, Kazan, and Moscow, as well as certain secret measures in Warsaw, Vilna, and Petersburg. Moreover, in the cities and districts of Petersburg and Moscow a state of siege is declared.

22:00: The training camp at Krasnoye Syelo is dissolved, and troops are ordered back to their normal quarters immediately.

Sunday, 26 July:
Partial mobilization of the Austrian Army. Sasonov invites the Austro-Hungarian ambassador to an open and frank discussion. He suggests to Count Berchtold (the Austro-Hungarian ambassador) that direct talks be initiated between Vienna and Petersburg about the changed situation and the way it relates to the ultimatum.

The minister of war summons the military attaché in order to explain to him that at the moment Russia is restricting itself to preparations for mobilization, whereas the mobilization order itself will not be made public.

Monday, 27 July:
Telegram from the Czar of Russia to the prince regent of Serbia:

"Your Majesty may be sure that the fate of Serbia can under no circumstances be a matter of disinterest for Russia."

Sasonov, who had sought direct mediation for negotiations with Vienna, accepts the English suggestion for a conference among the Four, or any other way to settle the conflict peacefully.

Tuesday, 28 July:
General mobilization of the Austro-Hungarian Army and declaration of war on Serbia by Austria.

15:00: Meeting of (Foreign Minister) Sasonov with (German Ambassador) Count Pourtalés. At the meeting, Sasonov asserts that Germany is supporting Austria in its inflexible attitude.

Meeting of M. Paléologue with Count Pourtalés and Count Szapary in the Foreign Ministry. A disquieting atmosphere results.

15:45: Visit by M. Paléologue to Foreign Minister Sasonov. The Russian government stresses that it is in principle open to all suggestions by France and England to save the peace.

22:45: Telegram from Kaiser Wilhelm to Czar Nicholas:

"I do not overlook how difficult it is for your government to withstand the pressure of public opinion. In view of the heartfelt friendship which has bound us together for so long, I want to use all my influence on Austria-Hungary to move it toward an honest consensus that is acceptable to Russia."

Wednesday, 29 July:
13:00: The answer of Czar Nicholas to Kaiser Wilhelm:

"In order to prevent the kind of catastrophe that a European War would mean, I beg you in the name of our old friendship to undertake everything in your power to prevent your ally from going too far."

15:00: The ukase (order) for partial mobilization, ready since the 23rd of July, is now signed. Count Pourtalés informs Foreign Minister M. Sasonov of the decision of the German government to mobilize if Russia does not cease its military preparations. Sasonov suggests to Count Pourtalés the following formulation:

"In recognition of the fact that Austria's conflict with Serbia has taken on the character of a European problem, if Austria will declare its readiness to eliminate from its ultimatum the claims that amount to an attack on Serbia's sovereignty, Russia promises to cease its military preparations."

18:30: New telegram from Kaiser Wilhelm to Czar Nicholas:

"I believe that a direct understanding is possible and desirable between your government and Vienna—an understanding that my government is seeking with all its resources to achieve, as I have already telegraphed to you. Of course, the military measures that have now been taken by Russia, and which the Austro-Hungarian government feels to be a threat, could bring about the catastrophe that we both wish to prevent, making it impossible for us to fulfill the mission as intermediary that I would so gladly have accomplished in view of your appeal to my friendship and assistance."

23:00: M. de Basily, assistant director of the chancellory of the Ministry for Foreign Affairs, visits the French Embassy to inform Paléologue that the secret preparations for the general mobilization are being carried out.

A half hour later, Czar Nicholas informs the War Ministry and the Foreign Ministry that in view of the most recent telegram from Kaiser Wilhelm he has decided to put off the general mobilization.

Thursday, 30 July:
News of the artillery bombardment of Belgrade reaches Petersburg in the morning.

Mr. (René) Viviani of the (French) Foreign Ministry telegraphs Paléologue: "France is determined to fulfill all of its commitments as an ally."

The same afternoon, Czar Nicholas receives the following telegram from Kaiser Wilhelm:

"Austria-Hungary has mobilized only part of its army against Serbia. If, as seems to be the case, according to both your warning and that of your government, Russia now mobilizes against Austria-Hungary, then the intermediary role with which you have so graciously entrusted me, and which I undertook in response to your express wish, will become difficult, if not impossible."

13:20: The answer of Czar Nicholas:

"The military preparations that are now being undertaken had already been decided on five days ago and are merely a defensive measure against the preparations on the part of Austria-Hungary. I hope with all my heart that these measures will have no effect on your role as an intermediary, to which I attach the greatest importance."

15:00: M. Sasonov is received by the Czar in Petrodvorets.
16:00: M. Sasonov relays by telephone to the chief of the general staff the order to proceed speedily with the general mobilization.

Friday, 31 July:
The order for the general mobilization of the Russian Army is made public in the early morning. Telegram from Czar Nicholas to Kaiser Wilhelm:

"As long as the negotiations between Austria and Serbia are continued, my troops will refrain from any act of provocation. I solemnly give you my word on this."

14:00: Telegram from Kaiser Wilhelm to Czar Nicholas:

"Peace in Europe can still be saved if Russia decides to cease the military preparations that are now threatening Germany and Austria-Hungary."

M. Sasonov accepts a modification of his formulation for conciliation in the way suggested by England.

A State of Emergency is declared in Germany.

15:00: Count Pourtalés is received in audience by the Czar in Petrodvorets.

23:00: Count Pourtalés urgently requests to be received by M. Sasonov.

24:00: Count Pourtalés declares to M. Sasonov that if Russia does not begin to demobilize within twelve hours Germany will be forced to mobilize its entire army.

Saturday, 1 August:

14:00: Telegram from Czar Nicholas to Kaiser Wilhelm:

"I understand that you feel yourself forced to mobilize; nevertheless, I would gladly have the same assurance that I gave you—specifically, that these military measures do not mean war, and that we will continue to negotiate for the well-being of our two countries, which is so dear to our hearts."

17:00: Kaiser Wilhelm orders a general mobilization. Within the hour, the French government takes the same measure.

18:00: Count Pourtalés delivers the declaration of war to M. Sasonov.

18:30: Sir George Buchanan requests an immediate audience with the Czar in order to deliver to him a telegram in which King George V makes a solemn plea for moderation.

22:45: Sir George Buchanan delivers King George's telegram to Czar Nicholas. The Czar dictates an answer to him.

Sunday, 2 August:

1:45: Czar Nicholas receives a final telegram from Kaiser Wilhelm:

"An immediate, clear, and unambiguous answer from you is the only way to fend off an incalculable catastrophe. Until I receive such an answer, I deeply regret that it is impossible for me to deal with the subject of your telegram. I must categorically ask you without delay to give your troops the order under no circumstances to make the slightest move at our borders."

By the time the telegram reaches Czar Nicholas, seven hours have gone by since Germany's declaration of war on Russia. Hence Czar Nicholas lets the telegram go unanswered.

With Russia's entry into the war against Germany, the German name of the capital city is russified. Petersburg is now called Petrograd.

Czar Nicholas II signs the manifesto on the declaration of war on 20 July (2 August). He then proceeds from the Malachite Hall of the Winter Palace to the Nicholas Hall, where the manifesto is read publicly:

The Czar's Manifesto on the Entry Into War

By the Grace of God
We, Nicholas the Second,
Emperor and Sole Ruler of All Russia,
Czar of Poland,
Grand Duke of Finland,
etc., etc.
declare to all Our subjects:

In accordance with Our historic mission, Russia has never stood by passively and watched the fate of the Slavic peoples with which it is united through faith and through blood. In complete unanimity and with great strength, the fraternal feelings of the Russian people for the Slavs have been raised to new heights in the last few days, during which Austria-Hungary made demands on Serbia that were obviously unacceptable to a sovereign state. Despising the conciliatory and peace-seeking answer of the Serbian government and rejecting the friendly mediation of Russia, Austria proceeded without delay to an armed attack, subjecting the defenseless city of Belgrade to its artillery.

Owing to the situation thus brought about, We are forced to take the necessary preparatory measures. We have therefore ordered the mobilization of the army and of the navy. At the same time, nevertheless, since the blood and the dignity of Our subjects are dear to Us, We have offered to do everything in Our power to work for a peaceful outcome to the negotiations that have now been started.

In the midst of friendly relations, Germany, which is allied to Austria, has acted against the hopes We had entertained on the basis of Our centuries-old good neighborliness, and in spite of Our assurance that the measures taken in no way pose a threat to Germany, it demanded the immediate cessation of the measures. After the refusal of this demand, Germany immediately declared war on Russia.

Now We are faced not only with the defense of Our unjustly insulted homeland, which is so dear to Us but We are also called upon to preserve the honor, dignity, and sovereignty of Russia, and its position among the great powers.

We are unshakable in the belief that all Our loyal subjects will rise unanimously and confidently to the defense of Russian soil.

May all inner discord be forgotten in this difficult hour of trial.

May the bond between Czar and People become ever closer, strengthening Our unity, and may Russia rise up as one man to defend itself against the shameful attack of the enemy.

In the deep belief that Our cause is just and in humble faith in Almighty Providence, We ask and pray for God's blessing on Holy Russia and on Our troops.

Given at Petersburg
on the twentieth day of July
in the Year of Christ One Thousand Nine Hundred
    and Fourteen
in the twentieth year of our reign.

NICHOLAS

Many eyewitnesses report on the atmosphere at the Winter Palace and at the great square where a mass of people waited for the appearance of the czar. Their impressions generally agree with one another. The president of the Duma, Rodsyanko, was in the palace and also outside:

On that day, a huge mass of people had gathered in front of the Winter Palace. The Czar spoke a few words after the worship service and closed with the solemn promise not to end the war as long as even a single foot of Russian soil was occupied by the enemy. A thundering "Hurray!" pierced through the halls of the palace, and the crowd outside on the square joined in enthusiastically. The Czar stepped out onto the balcony, followed by the Czarina. The mass of people was crowded so thickly into the immense square that they even streamed out into the neighboring streets, and when they saw the czar it was as if an electric spark had gone over to them, engulfing them all. Shouts of "Hurrah!" that never seemed to come to an end filled the huge space under the open sky. Flags and signs with slogans like "Long Live Russia and the Slavic Essence!" surged to and fro, and everyone kneeled down before the czar.

When we left the palace, we mixed in among the crowd. I joined in with a group of workers and reminded them that they had just gone out on strike. "Those were our own personal problems—we thought that the Duma's reforms were being put off again—but now it is a question for all Russia! We have gathered around our czar as we would gather around our flag! We will follow him and achieve victory over the Germans!"

Events in Petersburg proceeded favorably. With the mobilization, the workers' revolts ended suddenly. In the Putilov factory, the workers refused to stop work even for a moment. They worked day and night, and the army's orders were filled not in twenty-three days, as had been promised, but in eleven days.

Tatyana Botkina, daughter of the personal physician to the Czar's family, Yevgeny Botkin, remembers the hours that preceded this day:

On the evening of the eighteenth, father brought us from the palace the news of the terribly insulting German ultimatum: Russia must nullify its general mobilization within twelve hours. The next evening, we learned that our czar had refused to give in to the insulting demand. At 7:00, the German ambassador had delivered the declaration of war to Foreign Minister Sasonov. The Czar received the news as he was returning from the evening worship service in the Fyodorov Cathedral, where he had prayed for peace. He had just sent a telegram to his cousin Wilhelm II asking him to avoid conflict, and he hoped with all his might that reason would prevail. "I have done everything in my power to avoid this war" is what he is said to have confided to the teacher Gilliard later on. " 'I have never had to bear such agony.' " During the subsequent dinner, the czarina and the princesses could not hold back their tears when they heard that the irreparable harm had occurred after all. "Prussia is Germany's bad luck," the czarina said later. "The German people have been filled with feelings of hatred and revenge. The fight will be horrible and terrible, and all of humanity is moving toward great suffering."

On the day after Germany's declaration of war, the Czar went to St. Petersburg to attend a Te Deum. Officers and important personalities, but also people of more modest standing, were invited into the Winter

Palace to celebrate the solemn ceremony. The police did not have any kind of security controls, and a huge mass of people poured onto the square and the palace steps. In the front rows, the participants held up large portraits of the ruling couple, and many banners were fluttering in the wind.

In the interior of the Winter Palace, a deacon read a manifesto on Russia's entry into the war after the Te Deum was over, and then the czar turned to the gathering in the hall. He brought back again the old formulation that Alexander I had used in the year 1812, when he appealed to the Russian soldiers "to fight with the sword in hand and the cross in the heart." He blessed his army and added, "I will not sign any peace as long as a single enemy soldier is standing on Russian soil."

These words by the Czar caused an immense storm of enthusiasm. Thundering cries of "Hurrah!" arose, and then came the hymn "God Save the Czar," and the whole congregation joined in. Ignoring protocol, people encircled the ruling couple, kissing the hands of the ruler and the dress of the Czarina, who could no longer suppress her tears. After the ceremony, the Czar appeared on the balcony, with the Czarina behind him. The crowd gathered on the square fell to their knees and lowered the banners with the coat of arms of the Romanovs; as from a single throat came the prayer "Spasi Gospodi, lyudi tvoyi" (God, save your people). After a heartfelt call to ensure Russia's victory, everyone made the sign of the cross.

General Lukomisky, like many Russians, saw Germany rather than Austria as the real cause of war.

Germany's declaration of war was greeted by all of Russia with enthusiasm. I say Germany's because we did not speak much about Austria-Hungary; we were not angry at that country, because everyone believed that "the German" was responsible for everything.

The appearance of the Czar after the Declaration of War and the demonstration on the square in front of the Winter Palace mirrored the feelings of all the Russian people. No one can assert that the people were forced to go to the Winter Palace or that "the police" had organized the demonstration. No, one could sense that the entire population had become a single organism, and that in its general excitement it wanted to throw itself upon the enemy that was threatening its independence.

The mobilization and the gathering of the troops went well and on schedule. It is true that in some districts of Siberia and the Volga there were delays and even disorder. In Barnaul in Siberia there were even serious disturbances, but on the whole they had no influence on the course of the mobilization.

The appointment of Nicholas Nikolayevich as the commander in chief was greeted positively by all.

In the following eyewitness report—that of the Social Revolutionary and later chairman of the Provisional Government Alexander Kerensky —one can see not only the unanimity of the people described above but also the idea of taking Constantinople, which will later seem absurd and hardly justified to the demoralized army:

Then came the declaration of war, and a miracle happened. Nothing remained of the barricades and the street demonstrations, the strikes—of the revolutionary movement at all, neither in Petersburg nor in the entire vast empire. Within one hour, the morale of an entire population was transformed. The general mobilization was carried out with a punctuality and orderliness that surprised everyone. Here, in order to prevent misunderstandings, I have to stress something that is very important for understanding the period of war and revolution in Russia: The unanimous patriotic mood that seized large masses of the people in the first days of the war has nothing to do with the warlike aims that had been circulating for a long time in the higher echelons of Russian society.

Neither the idea of raising the cross in Constantinople nor the destruction of German militarism, nor any other ideological invention, played a role in the people's mood. According to Russia's position in the midst of powers fighting for world hegemony, the people saw the war as an evil forced on them from outside. They felt that they had to free themselves from it as soon as possible in order to return to peaceful work. The goal of the war for nine-tenths of the Russian people consisted of a single task: defense.

Nina Burova:

It was an unbelievable mood change. A certain national pride broke through. It wasn't hatred of the enemy. There was a feeling of enthusiasm, but no evil thoughts about the enemy. When the people knelt down on the square in front of the Czar and sang "God Save the Czar," there was not a single thought about revolution, strikes or anarchy.

Vasily Oryechov, an officer at the time:

> At the time of the assassination, Russians sympathized with Austria-Hungary and offered help in prosecuting the crime of the assassination. Of course, later on we found the conditions imposed on us by Germany to be deeply humiliating. Our Czar offered mediation and assistance for a peaceful solution to the conflict. When these offers were refused by Austria-Hungary and Germany, and when the Germans refused to take back their diplomatic note, we went into war with a bitter pride, but at the same time with patriotic enthusiasm for Russia and Serbia. We looked more at Wilhelm than at the Austrians as the guilty party.

In addition to the early promotion of officers that had already occurred before the official declaration of war, front soldiers who had been recruited as volunteers were also promoted earlier.

It was not just monarchists who volunteered for the front. The offspring of liberal families did the same. Gleb Struve, the son of the liberal Petersburg journalist Pyotr Struve, was one of them:

> In 1914, I was sixteen years old. I hadn't yet finished high school. My family was very patriotic, and I wanted to volunteer for military service, but my mother was against it. As a compromise I volunteered for the so-called land-city association. This was an organization under the leadership of Prince Lvov, who was later to play an important role in the Provisional Government.
>
> Because of problems with my heart, I was not allowed to enter military service even after I had finished school—I was attending a progressive school where girls and boys were mixed together. I ran the supply center for workers in the Carpathian Mountains in an unpopulated area where no one but lumberjacks and uneducated construction workers lived. My job was to arrange their provisions of food and see to their transportation. Since I had my own horse, I was able to ride around. Thus I was there until 1916, when Rasputin was murdered. All of this was not far from the Romanian border. Once, when I had a vacation, I rode home, which took a couple of days and nights by horse. I could already see that the supply situation was terrible then. Not even the horses of the cavalry regiment had enough to eat.

But in 1914 everything still looked all right. Tatyana Botkina reports on the optimistic mood:

In that year, the summer was terribly hot and hard to bear. Fires from the forests and in villages resulted in a piercing, clinging smoke that hung in white clouds in the streets of Tsarskoye Syelo, which were normally so enchanting.

Most conversations were about the political developments. Right up to the last moment, Uncle Peter had been in favor of an alliance with Germany. Russia could only lose in a war, he said, since its industrialization was just beginning.

We sat in the garden, the evening was mild, jasmin and lilac floated magically in the air, and in the miraculous quiet that surrounded us we heard from afar the evening prayers that were being sung together by the troops. First the "Our Father," then the hymn "Spasi, Gospodi, Lyudi Tvoyi."

We loved these melodic prayers sung by hundreds of male voices that traveled all the way to us, and as the choirs grew silent in the dusk, father turned to Uncle Peter and said, "Such people deserve only victory!"

In our youthful recklessness, we were absolutely fanatical: Our brave army, in alliance with France and England, would soon put an end to German imperialism. We did not have the slightest doubts about victory. Highly excited, Yury declared to us that he would volunteer. He rushed into the room where father was telephoning the latest news to Uncle Sasha. When the conversation was over, Yury told father what he wanted to do: to go to the front as a simple foot soldier. Father gave him a kiss. "That is good," is all he said. "You are brave, and I fully agree with your intention."

When I saw how Yury was transformed, elevated by the decision to fight, I felt with bitterness the fact that, unlike him, I was a woman and would not be allowed to take part in the wonderful test that was being put to holy Russia.

Even areas far away from the capital Petersburg—now Petrograd— were infected by the patriotic will to defend the country. In the southern town of Taganroz on the Asov Sea, the feeling seemed the same. Tatyana Neklyudova, fifteen at the time, remembers:

My two brothers Sergei and Vasily volunteered immediately. Even I had the desire to fight. But I was turned down.

The female population, on the other hand, helped to collect money and produce goods for the various needs of the army and the hospitals.

Subsequently, even Tatyana's brothers and their friends became infected with the first wave of enthusiasm and idealism and volunteered for the cavalry or the infantry. Certain of victory, the young men wondered whether or not they should pack along their parade uniforms for the victorious entry into Berlin right away. Everyone counted on a quick and victorious return. The first successes at the front seemed to support the slogan about a "three-month war."

The war seemed to have hit the population as a total surprise. The unusual situation worked its way into people's daily routine even before the war had really begun. Maria von Meiendorf remembers:

> Back then, when the war with Japan broke out, the population had been gradually prepared. Volunteers who wanted to enter the ranks of the defenders of the fatherland went through preparatory officer training courses; in all the cities there were crash courses for Sisters of Mercy.
>
> 1914 was different. The decree for immediate mobilization came at about the same time that the Germans crossed our border.
>
> We had spent the summer at our grandmother's. Since I was already grown-up enough, my mother told me to go to Petersburg in order to go to the Court Bank and have our receipts entered and verified there. That was before the declaration of war. All the necessary papers were already at the bank. All I had to do as the agent for my mother was to pick them up. I went to Petersburg for several days and stayed with Uncle Bogdasha. When I arrived at the bank on the given day, I was amazed at the unusual business and haste that filled the entire building. Bank employees rushed by me in all directions. When I asked why, I was told, "Excuse me, but you will have to wait a bit." When my turn finally came, without comment they pressed a mountain of financial papers into my hands and went on immediately to the next person. I sensed that something must have happened, but I did not know what. The next day the war was declared. I quickly went back home to my family.
>
> On the way, I met a teacher who had just come back from his vacation in Yalta. He had been in the mountains for a few days, and upon his return he had asked at the post office in Yalta for letters from his wife. But there were no letters for him there. Uneasy, he wanted to send her a telegram. But they were not accepting private telegrams! When he insisted on some sort of explanation, they answered him with the question: "Don't you understand that we are not in the mood for private telegrams now?" But he did not understand. "Do you come from the moon, or why don't you know that war was declared on Germany yes-

terday?" He had not come from the moon, but only from one of the mountains around Yalta.

The mobilization proceeded quickly but in an orderly fashion. Two of my brothers were also affected. One of them was an agronomist, the other a communications technician. What did they know about military matters? People were even allowing schoolboys to volunteer in those days. One year as a foot soldier and they were eligible to take the examen for officers and be called a reserve officer. Many young men knew nothing about military service and quickly wound up at the front. I still remember that this was precisely the weak point in our mobilization that caused some criticism among the population. It was particularly hard for my brother Yuri's children to say good-bye to their father, since they had lost their mother two years earlier. The nine-year-old Maka clung in despair to her father and had to be forcibly separated from his feet.

Princess Katharina von Sayn-Wittgenstein describes in her diary the general mood and the first rumors and reports about the fighting:

Monday, 14 August 1914
Japan has given Germany an ultimatum: to clear Japanese and Chinese waters of German warships, or to disarm them, and to give up Kiauchou to Japan without compensation. All of this has to be done within a month. The ultimatum runs for seven days. The Japanese cannot exist without being insulting, but this time the insults are of use to us. But it's a good thing for the Germans to experience what it is like to get diplomatic notes in the same tone as the ones they gave to Austria to pass on to Serbia.

6 August, 1914
The Austrians have taken Kamenez. Tomorrow at dusk we will go toward Rochny.

8 August, 1914, Kiev
We slept wonderfully in the train and were in the best of moods because the officer told us that a decision had been made to take back Kamenez, that the Austrian troops near Ushitzky had been beaten off, and that there was no bad news with respect to Mogilyev. We are encountering war trains everywhere: train cars with machine guns, automobiles, trucks and, provision wagons with horses. Some soldiers sleep in the hay, drink tea, and eat bread. Everyone seems to be in a good mood. It's hard to believe that war is so terrible when one sees them like that.

10 August, 1914—on the train to Moscow

The trains are packed full. There is only one per day. The others are needed for military transportation. In Broniza, everything is all right. There are rumors that we have taken Krakow and Lemberg!

From a report in the Kiev newspaper *Kievskaya Mysl*:

The mass of booty that has fallen into our hands in the last few days proves how far the Austrians have retreated before our troops, who have pursued them. Strewn across paths, in forests and marshes, our troops found goods discarded by fleeing rich people: treasure chests, weapons (sometimes even ammunition), bullets, and various war materiel. There are masses of wounded people in the hospitals. Solitary Austrians from various battalions wander through the forests and surrender voluntarily.

Rumor has it that the Austrians will not resist greatly when Przemysl is taken. The area along the Western Dnyepr is being held by our troops near Cernovitz. The enemy has withdrawn to the mountains and is occupying the mountain passes of the Carpathians.

An appeal to the population for help in the newspaper *Russkie Vyedomosti* points out the "significance of the current war with Germany."

On 14 August clever tricks led to the success of an attack by Baron Wrangel. The first Crosses of St. George were awarded. Winning back Kamenez on the way to Cernovitz was easy. The great event in the initial wave of success occured on 22 August. The newspaper *Russkoye Slovo* screamed in a banner headline at midnight:

"LEMBERG TAKEN!"

The men waiting for news that night in front of the newspaper building bared their heads. The heart of Galicia was now back in the hands of the Slavs, people said in Russia.

A new wave of patriotism, assistance initiatives, and contributions surged. The population increasingly began to volunteer to work for the army. Women and girls from noble families—Katharina von Sayn-Wittgenstein, for instance—had themselves trained as nurses. Not only the Russian wounded were given aid. The enemy, too, received assistance:

Today our responsibilities have already begun. Countess Bobrinskaya telephoned us to come to the Alexandrovsky train station. Two trains with the wounded and prisoners of war were supposed to be coming: 1,200 men. We had to prepare a large slice of bread with sausage and a glass of tea for each of them. That was hard work. Most of them were lightly wounded—those who had been badly wounded stayed in Kovno. Most were cheerful. They said that we would attack Konigsberg. The prisoners said the same thing. They all came from the German border, the area around Gumbinnen and Soldau. They are almost all Poles. They speak a little Russian and seem to be in good spirits. Strong, tall, handsome fellows. There are also some Prussians among them, with helmets, covered with khaki-colored rags. They behave quite arrogantly and demand more bread. The Poles are quieter and thank us when we give them something to eat. Today I gave a badly wounded German officer something to eat and drink. He moved with difficulty and groaned all the time. All the wounded prisoners look pitiful. Is it their fault that their Wilhelm has decided to take over the world? The wounded and the prisoners are living newspapers: They report on what they have seen and felt. These are the soldiers about whose heroism we read in the newspapers. I can only be amazed at their willingness to go back to the front right after they recuperate.

"We have been attacking the entire time, and they've been retreating."
"Do the Germans fight well?"
One of them: "Yes, but we fight better."
Others: "What do you mean by better? They're running away from us!"
"Are you afraid of the Germans?"
"No, in two days we will have chased them eighty versts."*

Our soldiers have a strange attitude toward the prisoners: not even a bit of animosity. They treat the prisoners with tolerance, gently, as friends. We give out tea. One volunteer sits on the running board and says, "Thank you, we all have enough, but give our little German there a bit more, he's a nice guy!"

Again and again, one is astounded at how little enmity and how much comradeship the Russian soldiers showed for the enemy at the front in those years. Among the Austrians captured in the first war years was Count Xaver Schaffgotsch. Because of his ancestry and

---

*A verst = ⅔ of a mile

education (he had grown up in Laibach, today's Ljubljana, and Trieste and hence spoke not only German and Italian but also a Slavic language) it was easier for him to make his way in Russia. Because of his calm, cheerful disposition, he was well liked—by the Russians too. Through personal connections, he was even able to have his shot-out teeth replaced:

> I was immediately sent from the camp to Irkutsk, escorted by a non-commissioned officer. In the hospital, I was greeted in an almost royal fashion and given my own room. Even the chief doctor came to visit me: a wonderful general practitioner. I was treated fantastically there. They actually repaired my fourteen shot-out teeth. That means that above and below they made two gold bridges each. They looked wonderful. All the children had fun with it later on: when I laughed, they called me "Uncle Goldmouth." But of course they didn't last long, because they were far too soft. But no matter—in the hospital in Irkutsk I was wonderfully cared for.
>
> There were also Russians there, who were very friendly. I still re-member quite clearly, on 26 November 1916, when news came that our old Kaiser Franz Josef was dead, a delegation of Russian officers came to us to give us their official condolences. They asked us, "What will your Kaiser now be called in history? The Great?" Well, we had great respect for our old Kaiser. After all, he was our commander in chief. But as for the Russian idea that he could go down in history as "the Great"—we were doubtful about that.

Of course, few prisoners of war were as fortunate as this one. Nevertheless, it is quite true that in civilian situations, the Russians were free of animosity toward the enemy, and they did not give evidence of a class-conscious rejection of dynastic hierarchies. In the hospital mentioned above, Schaffgotsch advanced to become the assistant to the coroner, due to the chronic shortage of doctors. At first he was ordered back to the camp by the hospital inspector, but several weeks later he appeared again in his new position.

In the meantime, however, the situation at the front began to turn against the Russians. The first attacks by the Russians were victorious, partially because of cleverly planned surprise maneuvers at the German front, and partially because of tactical mistakes by the Austrians. But sobriety soon set in. As early as the 18 August, when the Russians were thirty kilometers into East Prussia and only five days from Berlin, suddenly the Russian advance was halted. Hindenburg destroyed the Second Russian Army at Tannenberg. Two weeks later, the First Russian Army under Rennenkampf was beaten at the Masurian Lakes. Some 250,000 men were unable to fight—some were wounded, some taken prisoner, some killed. The Russian Northern Army retreated to Kovno and Grodno.

The failures then beginning at the front were later to lead to demoralization, battle weariness, and ultimately to the preparation of the ground on which revolutionary propaganda thrives so easily. But these failures had, among other things, causes that could easily have been corrected from within Russia's own ranks. At first, the absolute military elite had been taken from Petersburg, and some had been sent to the French front in order to help Russia's ally. They were replaced by poorly trained and sometimes idealistic volunteers recruited from among schoolboys or farmer's children. Some of them who came from the farther regions of the country had no understanding of what the fighting was all about, nor of the patriotic goals for which the young people in Petersburg were ready to sacrifice themselves. Finally—and this was a fatal problem that gradually began to spread across the entire Russian front—the supply situation got progressively worse: first with weapons and war materiel and then even with food. The supply and transport system deteriorated, and in the provinces the source of materiel and also initial enthusiasm and readiness for sacrifice began to slow down. The soldier Yuri Oskin remembers the consequences of fighting among poorly equipped and trained troops:

> Our situation was made worse by the fact that at least one-third of the men in our corps were without weapons. As a result, we were unable to hold the line anymore. As soon as the Austrian ranks had been deci-mated by our artillery, the Second Division stormed out of the trenches and used the confusion of the enemy to seize fifty prisoners. Immediately, their weapons were distributed to those of us who didn't have any.

> Not only weapons, but also ammunition was lacking. Shortly before, marching through Galicia in constant anticipation of running up against the enemy, every soldier was supposed to carry much more than the required 120 rounds. That was a heavy burden for the long marches, and therefore on the way through Galicia we had frequently thrown many rounds of ammunition into the trenches. At night, many of us unscrewed our rifles in order to make a fireplace with the butt ends to warm us and to boil water for tea. In this way, many valuable weapons were senselessly

destroyed. Later we missed them bitterly, and we were able to replace them only by taking them from the fallen or wounded.

In addition to the disorganization of untrained units, there was sometimes a reckless stupidity of superiors—like regimental commander Colonel Samfarov, who, instead of trying to strengthen the fighting capability of his troops, chose instead to criticize the improvisation of field equipment such as boots. He did not look into the cause of this improvisation: the dysfunctional supply system for winter uniforms.

In October 1914, General W. M. Besobrasov, of the Cavalry Guard Regiment, wrote in his diary:

2 October, Friday
The regiment gathers on the right bank of the Vistula in Yusevo in order to fashion a bridge to cross to the left bank. To my right, the Third Cossack Corps of General Ivanov; to my left, General Krusenstern's Corps under the cover of a forward guard brigade that has pushed ahead toward Opatov. In the garden of the house in which I am put up, Austrian soldiers and officers are buried.

5 October
In the night, I received a telegram with the command to pull back the troops and demolish the bridge—no reasons given. As early as four o'clock in the morning I went to the bridge. It was raining hard. There I encountered a mass of refugees, women and children with packs and domestic animals, in the midst of the soldiers. First I established order, sending the civilian population back, then the Vosnesyensk-Ulans, then a couple of squadrons of Alexandrian Hussars, cossacks from various regiments, and at the end I had the Finns and Pavlovians come over. The enemy was nowhere to be seen. At three o'clock in the afternoon, we began to disassemble the bridge. I received no reason for the retreat. It wasn't until later that I heard about the losses that our guards had suffered, and about their retreat.

8 October
Received distressing news about the heavy losses of our guards near Otapov on 21 September. They were almost completely surrounded by the far superior enemy, and lost nine cannons.

9 October
Cannot see the enemy, but shots are heard from the opposite bank.

11 October

Occasional shots from the opposite bank. The uninterrupted rain has made the road impassable.

14 October

Received new directives. Dismiss General Leshitzky from the 9th Army and create a reserve army under the personal command of the high commander [Author's note: Archduke Nicholas Nikolayevich]. I am relieved to get rid of General Leshitzky. Lieutenant Levshin and Count Dimitri Grabbe have arrived to join my cavalry general staff.

15 October

The shift from the guard by parts of the 18th Army Corps has begun. The exchange was carried out at night, for security reasons. The weather is getting better.

16 October

The replacement is continuing. From the north: heavy shooting. No reliable information, only rumors that the Prussians are sixteen versts from Warsaw.

One week later:

23 October

All day long fierce battles with the Austrians. The Hungarian infantry fought particularly hard. We had to use our bayonets. The Finnish Bodyguard Regiment seized two machine guns. Archduke Nicholas Nikolayevich arrived. Toward evening, we fended off the enemy with our bayonets. I rode the length of our position on the right flank. The intelligence reports of Mannerheim's cavalry army contradicted General Schwarz's view that the enemy is retreating.

In the early morning we opened full fire. Ordered artillery attack on Polichnovo. First, artillery reported it had already been taken by the 75th Infantry Division. As far as I knew, however, it was in the hand of the enemy. General Pototzky asserted that we were shooting at our own people. This proved to be untrue. After a huge loss of time, we continued with the attack. At two in the afternoon, little time was left for an attack in late fall. I telephoned the order to attack along the entire front. From the hill, I was able to observe how our soldiers stormed into battle with bayonets and cries of "Hurray!" The enemy broke apart, began to flee. Some gathered together again in little groups, threw their weapons away, and raised their hands. I sent Mannerheim's cavalry army to Polichnovo to pursue the enemy. The enemy gave up all of his positions. Unfortunately, the pursuit was abandoned because of nightfall. The Austrian rear guard tried to stop our attack near Adamov but was defeated by Mannerheim and the sharpshooters from the Guard. The enemy's airplanes appeared.

28 October
Received order to attack immediately in the direction of Krakow. I am worried about the availability of supplies. . . .

The Duma's report to the Czar at the beginning of 1915 says that the Russian Army was retreating primarily because of unsatisfactory supplies, thus giving up hard-won territory. Artillery, howitzers, cannons, etc. were all lacking. Indeed, one city after the other, Przemysl, Lemberg (Lvov), Warsaw, Kovno, Grodno, and Brest-Litovsk on the western front, had to be abandoned again by the Russians. Gradually, even the capital Petrograd was threatened by the German approach. In Petrograd, there were reports of a conference of the parliamentary delegates in Kiev, where Viktor Adler stressed the heavy sacrifices demanded by the war while at the same time emphasizing the need to continue with the war and try to achieve immediate peace negotiations. Of the 170 million inhabitants of the Russian Empire, a total of 13 million were in the army. By 1916, 2.5 million of them had died and 4.5 million had been wounded.

Despite all the patriotic enthusiasm at the beginning of the war, the "three-month victory" seemed to be a long time in coming. In the beginning, the Russian Army fought relatively well at the front, considering its state of unpreparedness, but here too—dependent on the generals in a front line that extended for thousands of kilometers— success alternated with failure.[3]

Supporting the war effort no longer seemed worthwhile to the simple soldiers, who had now been separated for years—instead of months—from their families and their land. Finally, the supply problem at the front and in the capital city became drastically noticeable. A police report to the Ministry of the Interior at the beginning of 1917 notes:

The problems with food supplies that have arisen in the empire are the result of the destruction of the transportation system and other effects of the war, which are getting worse and worse and threaten to create a serious situation. Compared to the situation during the price increases of the previous year, which were protested chiefly by the lower classes, the increases and food shortages since January of this year could lead to huge problems which might cause a "Hunger Revolt" against the government. On the one hand many small businesses have had to close because of these shortages, and on the other hand the big wholesalers are manipulating their deliveries—partially in order to protect themselves against government collection measures—and this artificially raises the prices for goods that are in short supply. Because of the uncertainty of the situation, the banks are withdrawing capital from some trade and industrial companies, thus further harming economic life.

Even foreign traders who are begging to fill these holes are also partially to blame for the fifty to one hundred percent price increases, in part because of the low exchange rate of the ruble.

From farmers and landowners who are taking advantage of the situation for their own profit to merchants who are taking illegal measures for their own benefit, many individuals are responsible for the catastrophic situation, which could very soon become dangerous.

In view of the hunger that necessarily affects part of the population already, the "Progressive Bloc" is trying to take advantage of the dissatisfaction with the government that is frequently expressed in the capital and even in conservative circles. Its public speakers want to convince the inhabitants of the city, who do not understand the deeper causes and connections of the crisis, that only a reorganization of the supply system into the hands of the people's representatives can save the country from general starvation. Leftist radical groups have joined in this sort of argumentation and are planning a "Revolt of the Hungry," the effects of which must not be underestimated, if it should succeed. Massive disturbances could then lead to revolts against the government throughout the country.

The report went on to recommend immediate measures—the creation of a central distribution organization for supplies, the organization of food shipments, and a listing of all the goods available in Petrograd. These measures, as the report suggested, would have removed the population's principal worry and might perhaps have put an end to the unrest.

For the population, the war is the cause of all their problems. The war's goals (for instance, the taking of Constantinople) make the many sacrifices of what had originally been a defensive war look more and more questionable.

Peace—that was the new slogan! Liberals, the dissatisfied, and above all revolutionaries made use of this slogan. The time for the sowing of Bolshevik seeds had come. War or peace, that is the question.

Arkady Petrovich Stolypin, son of the minister Pyotr Stolypin (who was murdered in 1911) remembers:

> There was relatively a lot of freedom of the press. Lenin sent his newspaper *Pravda*, which was published in Paris, to Petrograd by train. This was the Bolsheviks' newspaper. The Mensheviks had *Svyesda*. The two newspapers represented and supported two contradictory positions. *Pravda* argued that we shouldn't fight anymore and should make an alliance with the Germans—Lenin had by that time already gotten money from the German General Staff. *Svyesda* stood for defense. But even then there were contradictory positions: Fight on at all costs to victory, or not? At any rate *Pravda* was quickly banned due to its weakening effect on military morale—but only for that reason, and not because of its ideological position, because there was a liberal political climate. The peace propaganda reached its first peak in 1916 at a time when the Russian Army still had a good chance. Germany was exhausted, a fact one can find confirmed in the memoirs of General Ludendorff. Austria could still have been beaten if it hadn't been for the tactical errors we made. We had already crossed the Carpathians, Bulgaria and Turkey had suffered enough defeats. But the peace for which Lenin propagandized was not a just peace. It was a peace in which the enemy could dictate his conditions. Which is precisely what happened later. Because everyone was tired of the war, and in the capital's barracks and headquarters the officers who were fighting at the front had been replaced by workers who were open to revolutionary ideas. And no one, no one at that time had any idea who the Bolsheviks really were and what they would do later.

NOTES

1. The protocol, translated here from the French, was evidently taken according to the Western calendar, introduced in Russia only in January 1918

2. French President Poincaré happened to be in Russia for an official state visit.

3. As a reminder: The original successes against the Austrians were weighted

against the strategically unnecessary defeat near Tannenberg on the German front in the northwest. As a result of this defeat, General Samsonov shot himself. Przemysl, which had been conquered in March 1915, was quickly lost again. The allies were able to send war materiel only by way of Archangelsk or Vladivostok. In 1916, the situation improved for a while.

Chapter Two

———//———

Czar Nicholas II: Ruler or Ruled?

The personalities of the Czar and his most influential advisors from various viewpoints.

At first I thought that a mistake had been made, and that a third-class passenger had somehow gotten into the first-class compartment. The man was dressed like an ordinary peasant. He had hair like a bird's nest and a long beard which bore the traces of his last meal. His hands and face were badly in need of washing.

I got out at the station in order to stretch my legs. My traveling companion did the same, and I noticed that the people on the platform showed him a great deal of respect and crossed themselves when he went by. I asked one of the valets who this man was.

He answered, "Gregory Rasputin."

This was the impression British journalist Jones Stinton got of the man who, from 1914 to 1916, was said to play a far greater role in the decisions of the Czar's court than would normally have been imaginable. Was this an indication of the lack of an intelligent, reasonable, and well-balanced leadership, of its weaknesses? The situation was in fact the result of something else: the determination of the Czarina on the one hand and the easily influenced personality of the Czar on the other. Alexandra Fyodorovna, born in Hessen, seemed not only able to influence the Czar in his decisions but also to press him into making decisions. Her efforts in support of her husband in political matters were massive and probably well meant, but she lacked competence and vision. She based her help firmly on two principles: a mystically oriented belief in God (and in beings blessed by God on this earth); and in a purely autocratic form of government for Russia. The latter principle was focused on the preservation of the Czar's throne and unrestricted exercise of power by Nicholas II, above all with respect to the transfer of power to successor Alexey.

In 1914, Czar Nicholas II was forty-six years old, had ruled Russia for twenty years, and was the father of four daughters and a long-awaited but sick son ten years of age.

Nicholas's approach toward power seemed marked by something almost like resignation. Strengthening of his will seems to come again and again from outside—from his closest advisers and above all from his wife. Moreover, Nicholas II felt himself bound by his oath to pass on the throne intact. It has been proven that in the first war years Nicholas II succumbed in his ministerial and advisory appointments to the pressure of the Czarina, who was sometimes falsely led by her own advisers, and who was also concerned that a minister might be too liberal with respect to democratic tendencies. Her correspondence shows that she was responsible for the removal of Grand Duke Nicholas Nikolayevich as commander in chief of the Russian forces. He had held this position since the beginning of the war and threatened to become more popular with the troops than the Czar himself. On 23 August (5 September) 1915, the royal order appeared:

Most High Command to the Army and the Navy:
    As of today We Ourselves have taken on the highest command of all land and sea forces currently in the theater of war.
    In the firm belief in God's grace and with unshakable confidence in final victory, We will carry out Our holy duty to defend Our homeland, and We will not dishonor Russian soil.

Imperial Headquarters, 23 August 1915

Nikolay

But this meant that the Czar would frequently be absent from the capital, since he was now personally at headquarters in Mogilyev on the Dnyepr. Of necessity, he left Petrograd to its own fate. Subsequently, Czar Nicholas was to be held responsible not only for the successes but also for the failures at the front. Moreover, Foreign Minister Sasonov was replaced by the unpopular Stürmer, of German descent, and War

Minister Polivanov, who at the beginning of the war had still been in office with Finance Minister Witte, was replaced. The Czarina felt it was her duty to remind Nicholas constantly of his role, at least as she saw it, and whenever there was a danger that he might give up some of his power to the democratic machinery of the Duma (letter dated June 17/30 June 1915):

> Never forget that you are and must remain the autocratic emperor. We are not yet ready for a constitutional government.

Who was Rasputin?

Gregory Yeyfimovich, called Rasputin, came from the Siberian village Pokrovskoye near Tobolsk. Because of his intuitive prophecies and successful healings, for which he used not only natural herbs but also his own obvious power of suggestion, he was able precisely in these critical moments to achieve an improvement in the condition of the hemophiliac successor, for whom traditional medical help had failed. Under these circumstances, it becomes clear how a man gifted with religious charisma, a magical aura, and an impressive stature was able to win the trust of the Czarina, who was primarily concerned with the health of the successor. It is only logical that this position of confidence went on to give Rasputin the authority that can only belong to a favorite of the court.

Aron Simanovich, who was assigned as Rasputin's secretary and told to see to his material well-being, analyzes the man:

> His female admirers—it would be more correct to say: his venerators—can be divided into two groups. Some believed in his supernatural abilities, his holiness, and his divine mission; others were simply bowing to fashion, or they hoped through him to achieve benefits for themselves or their kin.

> Rasputin himself seemed to enjoy his position and to bask in the veneration accorded him with the archaic ease of a pasha. It is possible that even men, who tended to believe less in the earthly mission of this man than to cling to the influence that Rasputin had won, used Rasputin for their own purposes.

The question of whether Rasputin was paid by the Germans is addressed by the Swiss Pierre Gilliard, tutor at the Czar's court:

"All the News That's Fit to Print."

The New York Times.

THE WEATHER
Increasing cloudiness, rain by tonight and tomorrow; moderate shifting winds, becoming southeast.
For the full weather report see Page 16.

VOL. LXIV...NO. 20,922.

NEW YORK, FRIDAY, MAY 7, 1915.—TWENTY-TWO PAGES.

ONE CENT In Greater New York. | TWO CENTS Within 200 Miles. | THREE CENTS Elsewhere.

RUSSIANS ARE BEATEN, LOSE TARNOW; RETREATING FROM MOUNTAIN PASSES; AUSTRO-GERMAN ARMY SWEEPING ON

Three Rivers Crossed and Gorlice, Jaslo and Dukla Also Taken.

MAY CAPTURE FLEEING ARMY

High Mountain That Protected Great Base at Tarnow Taken by Storm.

LINE SMASHED BY NEW GUNS

Czar's Legions Wither Under Terrific Fire of Austrian 42s and Smaller Howitzers.

TWO BALTIC PORTS MENACED

Russian Foreign Minister, Through Washington Embassy, Denies Foes Are Victorious in Carpathians.

VIENNA, May 6. (via London, May 7.)—The victorious advance of the Austro-German armies in West Galicia continues. The Northern wing has captured Tarnow. The southern wing has crossed the Wisloka River and the Russians are retreating eastward of the Lupkow Pass. An official communication issued late this evening by the War Office says:

At 4 o'clock this afternoon the last Russian positions on the heights east of the Dunajec and the Biala Rivers were gained by our troops.

Tarnow was captured by us at 10 o'clock this morning.

The strategic achievement of rolling up a hostile battle front by a flanking attack, of which Chancellorsville is one example in modern history, is now in full progress in West Galicia. Favored by continued good weather, mile after mile of the Russian Carpathian front has been rendered untenable by the steady, unchecked Austro-German advance.

The Austrian cavalry and infantry followed the Gorlice turnpike. The supporting artillery dropped shells on the road from Zmigrod to Jaslo, one of the principal lines of the retreat for the Russians in the Kukla region.

The Russian forces have been in full retreat since dawn on May 5, and are being closely followed by the victorious Carpathian army, according to official

German Armies Operating on a Scale Unparalleled in the History of War

LONDON, May 6.—The Germans, in consort with their Austrian allies, are putting forth an effort, the extent of which has never been approached in the history of war. Throughout virtually the whole length of the eastern front they are engaged with the Russians, while in the west, in addition to their attacks around Ypres, they are on the offensive at many points. At other points they are being attacked by the French, British, and Belgians.

Far up in the Russian Baltic Provinces, heretofore untouched by the war, the Germans are attempting to advance toward Libau and Riga. On the East Prussian frontier they are engaged in a series of battles, and with a big gun are bombarding at long range, as they did Dunkirk, the Russian fortress of Grodno. In Central Poland they have had to defend themselves against a Russian attack. In Western Galicia they are attacking with all their strength the Russian flank and compelling the Russians to abandon the Carpathian passes which were gained at such cost during the Winter.

advices reaching here. More than 50,000 prisoners have already been captured by the Austrians in West Galicia.

Think Russians Can't Escape.

Field Marshal von Hoetzendorf's plan is working out with precise regularity with respect to this section of the front. Confidence is expressed by headquarters that the principal portion of the Russian army under General Radko Dimitrieff, which is attempting to defend positions in the Carpathians to the west of Lupkow Pass, cannot make good its retreat. Detachments of this army may work their way out, but it is declared that the bulk of the army, with the heavy artillery and baggage, can scarcely succeed in avoiding capture, in view of Field Marshal von Hoetzendorf's rapid advance through the Gorlice breach in the lines.

On the northern front the Russians held on desperately to Tarnow and Wal Mountain—a fortified crest 1,500 to 2,000 feet high between the Biala and Dunajec Rivers—to enable them to get great quantities of stores accumulated behind Tarnow away and cover the retirement of the armies to the southward. The Russians fortified this mountain until it was a veritable Gibraltar, but the Archduke's men attacked it with a desperate valor and were well served by their artillery. This struggle may go down in history with that for Putiloff Hill, to the south of Mukden, in the Russo-Japanese war.

The question as to whether the Russians can make a successful stand on the line of the Wisloka River is the important one from the Austro-German military viewpoint. If they cannot, the breach in the Russian line is considered complete, and the situation for the Russian Carpathian armies will undoubtedly be critical.

Great Mortar Fire Overpowering.

The heaviest artillery was employed in these operations. The 42-centimetre mortars in action were, however, not the noted German guns, but of Austrian make. They were designed originally for coast defense purposes, but have been found exceedingly valuable for land warfare. They fire projectiles 680 pounds heavier than the German mortar and are understood to be comparatively mobile and quickly set up. The effect of these mortars during the artillery preparations for battle is described as overpowering. Shells from them have reached the supply depots behind Tarnow.

The Austrians are also equipped with highly effective smaller howitzers of a new type, which were put into the field during the later stage of the war.

The fighting is taking place in the difficult country of mountain spurs and foothills of the Northern Carpathians, and the successes of the Germanic forces are not being won without the hardest efforts. All hills and bridges in the rear of the original Russian lines had been fortified with triple rows of trenches, in preparation for such an emergency, and the Russians, with all the advantages of prepared trenches and gun positions, are putting up a stubborn resistance.

Many unverifiable rumors concerning the number of prisoners taken by the Austrians are in circulation. Some report say that the total number of prisoners reached between 100,000 and 150,000 today and yesterday, but the authorities themselves warn against credence being placed in any particular set of figures. Probably they themselves do not know within thousands how many Russians have been taken prisoners.

The text of the War Office announcement of the operations issued today follows:

Forces of the Teuton allies are advancing successfully along the entire front in West Galicia. Troops of the enemy, still intact, are attempting, by taking up favorable defensive positions, to cover their hasty retreat.

The strong Russian forces in the Beskid region are being seriously menaced by the flank attack of our victorious armies. Already we have forced the fighting in the regions of Jaslo and Dukla, and the engagement now in progress will complete the annihilation of the Third Russian army.

The number of prisoners in our hands has been increased to more than 50,000.

On the remainder of the front the situation remains unchanged.

In the Orova Valley a strong Russian attack on the hill of Ostry has been repulsed with great slaughter of the enemy.

Berlin Cheered by Victories.

BERLIN, May 6. (via London.)—The military developments of the last week have had a visible effect on popular feeling in Berlin, which is decidedly more optimistic. Operations in the Russian province of Courland, on the Bal-

tic; in Galicia, and in Belgium indicate that German forces are rolling the offensive on a large scale, and that greater events are to be expected.

Further developments in Galicia are awaited with breathless interest, as it is believed that the events in this section of the front may give a decisive turn to the entire Eastern campaign. The view held here is that the whole Russian position in the Carpathians has now become precarious.

The operations of the Austro-German force which is now threatening the Russian lines between the Dunajec and Biala Rivers is regarded as a first-class performance, from a German military standpoint, particularly as it is the result of a frontal attack against strongly fortified positions.

The Austrians crossed the Dunajec near its confluence with the Vistula, although the Russians were strongly protected behind a dike on the eastern bank.

The Austrians, behind a dike on the west shore, advanced pontoons by night, cutting through the dike and depositing the pontoons among high reeds along the shore. They refilled and remodded the cut each night. In this way a sufficient number of pontoons was concealed in three nights for effecting a crossing of the stream. When these preparations had been completed a terrific artillery bombardment enabled the Austrians to bridge the stream with comparatively little loss.

The Austro-German attack near Gorlice is described as an unparalleled artillery performance. The Russians believed their position to be absolutely impregnable. The number of the allies, from 42 centimeters down, so completely overwhelmed the Russians, however, that the Austro-German infantry was able to take the opposing positions at the first rush.

Attack on the Nida a Blind.

These operations were veiled by a heavy bombardment of the Russian positions along the Nida River last week, the Germans and Austrians meanwhile bringing up a powerful force, including an enormous amount of artillery, to the Dunajec for the great push eastward toward Lemberg.

The Russians still hold one strong position on a range of hills, more than 1,000 feet high, near Tuchow, but this position is now threatened from both the north and south. Artillery is already preparing the ground for an attempt by infantry to dislodge the Russians.

In view of this situation it is generally believed in Berlin that the operations in Galicia during the next ten days will yield big results.

The War Office report of the latest operations thus follows:

In the war area to the east of Tarnow and to the north of that place as far as the Vistula River, and on the right bank of the Dunajec River, fighting continued far into the night. The number of prisoners so far taken has reached to more than 40,000. It is worthy to note that this is the Russian front.

In the Beskid Mountains, on the Lupkow Pass Road, an attack is being made by the forces under General of Cavalry Von der Marwitz simultaneously with an attack made by the Austro-Hungarian army which is co-operating with the Germans. These attacks are progressing favorably.

The bulletin concludes: " We not only forced a crossing of the Wisloka at several points, but firmly put our hands on the Dukla Pass, the road and the place."

GERMAN GAINS NORTH AND SOUTH

Allies Lose Two Positions Near Ypres—Retake Hill 60 Trenches.

LONDON, May 6. Several successes along the western front are recorded in today's official German statements. Berlin reports that the Kaiser's forces have made progress southeast of Ypres, but makes no mention of the recapture

Czar Nicholas II and his family.

zar Nicholas II.

Grand Duke Nicholas Nikolayevich, supreme commander of
the Russian forces at the beginning of the war.

eneral Kornilov as an Austrian prisoner
war in Galicia.

Czar Nicholas II and Grand Duke Nicholas Nikolayevich at the general
staff quarters.

rand Duchesses Maria and Anastasia in the army hospital at Zarskoye
yeto.

Czar Nicholas II and Czazevich Alexey inspecting the front; major general Drosdivskiy on horseback.

Пребываніе въ Москвѣ ИХЪ ВЕЛИЧЕСТВЪ.

Czar Nicholas in front of the Alexandrinian military academy in Moscow, December 1914.

Czar Nicholas II.

Moscow: The Red Square before the revolution.

Czar Nicholas II inspecting a company.

ar Nicholas II and French officers in an army training field.

oscow: View of the Kremlin from river Moscow before 1914.

Group of Russian officers and sergeants.

stival parade of the Russian equestrian artillery.

valry parade.

Austrian-Hungrian infantry in Russian Poland.

Russian soldiers on the western front.

ar Nicholas II watching a parade on the army training at Zarskoye Syeto.

ar Nicholas II during maneuvers.

Czar Nicholas visiting the front.

Five hundred ruble bill from 1912.

Rasputin's house was protected by the Imperial police from possible attacks by the enraged population—but also by the Social Revolutionaries, who understood that he was working for them. I do not believe that Rasputin was an agent paid by Germany, but he was certainly a respected instrument in the hands of the German general staff, which had an interest in the security of such a valuable ally. Thus he was also surrounded by their spies, who also served as his bodyguards.

Prince Felix Yusupov, on the other hand, a young, loyal monarchist married to the niece of the Czar, Princess Irina, was fully convinced that Rasputin was being financially supported by the Germans:

> I can be all the more certain of it, because he even told me himself. I repeat his own words. Rasputin was in favor of a separate peace with the Germans. He was paid by the Germans. This man was an enemy agent; he even wanted to introduce me to the most important spies. His position at the court and the dependency in which he kept most of the ministers and generals gave him exact knowledge of the position of the armies and troop movements. He kept the Germans informed about this, which naturally meant defeats for the Russian Army that could possibly have been prevented.

As will be seen later in the scene of Prince Yusupov's last encounter with Rasputin, Rasputin is not in fact the "man sent from God" for which his admirers—including the Czarina—took him. Further suspicions are justified.

According to Simanovich, Rasputin's claim to the Czar that failures and supply difficulties in the army were nothing more than disinformation intentionally distributed by High Commander Nicholas Nikolayevich led to Nikolayevich's removal and transfer to the Caucasus —just as the Czarina had wanted.

In political circles and in the population, dissatisfaction with the situation at the court grew. Observations as to the dissolute and decadent life-style of the favorite Rasputin led to doubts about his integrity, and this in turn gave a basis to speculation and worry about his influence on the Czarina, and, through her, on the Czar himself. Fears that Alexandra Fyodorovna might, moreover, think more like a German than like a Russian resulted in many rumors and anecdotes. Her image in the population is illustrated by the following scene— perhaps apocryphal. Alexey is said to have told a servant at the court:

"Every time the Russians lose, Papa cries. When the Germans lose, Mama cries. When should I cry?"

French diplomat Maurice Paléologue sums up the clouded political decision making in Petrograd during these years:

> There can no longer be any doubt that Russian politics is led by the intriguers around the Czarina. But who embodies this group of people? From whom do they get their programs and directions? Certainly not from the Czarina. The people, being more inclined toward simple thoughts and clear ideas, are not right in their judgment of the Czarina's role. It exaggerates and falsifies her position. Alexandra Fyodorovna is too impetuous and unsteady—in a word, too mentally unbalanced to design a political plan and carry it out. She is the political tool of a conspiracy the existence of which is constantly perceivable in these environs: however she is nothing more than a tool. So too are those around her: Rasputin, Vyrubova, General Voyekov, Taneyev, Sturmer, Prince Andronikov, etc. are all subordinate lackeys, obedient intriguers, or stooges. If the interior minister, Protopopov, gives the impression of having a bit more persondality, this is in fact only due to his diseased excitability.
>
> If I were to draw conclusions from the contradictory answers and suspicions of the people I have asked, I would say that the disastrous policies for which the Czarina and her clique will be held responsible by history are being given to them by four men: the chairman of the far right in the Imperial Council, Shtsheglovitov, the patriarch of Petrograd Pitrim, the former director of the police department Byelyetzky—and finally the banker Manus.
>
> With the exception of these four men, I see nothing more than a play of anonymous, mutual, disparate, and sometimes unconscious powers, which perhaps shows only one thing: the centuries-old effectiveness of Czarism, its instinct for self-protection—everything that has remained of its organic power and the dynamism it has achieved.

What do members of the government think about the phenomenon —or problem—of Rasputin? Many conservatives had joined the opposition party in protest against his influence at court. In March 1916, the president of the Duma, Michail Vladimirovich Rodsyanko, requested an audience with the Czar. On 8 March, he was received by the Czar in Zarskoye Syelo. The conversation lasted for one and a half hours:

I told him everything. About the intrigues of the ministers working against each other with Rasputin, about the lack of a goal-oriented policy, about general misuse of offices, about ignoring public opinion, and about the fact that an end to the population's patience was in sight. I reminded him about Rasputin's contacts with dubious people, his excesses, and his orgies. I told him that Rasputin's close relationship to the Czar and his family and his influence in affairs of state in those war years enraged the population and upright men in the government. I left no doubt about the fact that Rasputin was a German spy.

"If Your Majesty's ministers really had only one goal in mind—the well-being of our country—then the presence of a man like Rasputin would be insignificant for affairs of state. But the problem is that the ministers are partly dependent on him and include him in their intrigues. I have to inform Your Majesty that things cannot go on this way. No one is opening your eyes to the role this man plays. His presence at Your Majesty's court undermines faith in the most high power of the state and could have terrible consequences for the fate of the dynasty, because it turns the hearts of the people away from their emperor."

While I recounted these unpleasant truths, the Czar was silent or showed amazement, but he remained friendly and polite. At the end of my comments, he asked, "How do you think the war will end—in our favor or not?" I responded that we could count on the army and the people, but that it was the military leaders and internal politics that stood in the way of a victory.

My report was successful. On 11 March came an order that Rasputin should be sent back to Tobolsk; however, several days later the order was rescinded—at the request of the empress.

Meanwhile, Rasputin pulled another trick: In the absence of the Czar, who was at the front, Protopopov became interior minister at Rasputin's intervention. This happened in September 1916. Advisers to the Czar wrote him a note begging him not to take over the high command of the army in Nicholas Nikolayevich's place, thus leaving the court almost entirely to the Czarina, under the influence of Rasputin. But the events feared by Charitonov, Krivosheyn, Sasonov, Bark, Shtsherbatov, Samarin, Ignatyev, and Shachovskoy continued to take their course.

Nina Alexeyevna Krivosheyna, née Meshtsherskaya, remembers the attempt by several members of the czar's family to intervene and open

Czar Nicholas's eyes. She learned about the result of this attempt while she was helping to prepare packages for the military hospital installed in the Marble Palace on the Neva with other girls from the nobility:

> One day in December, while Natalya Ivanovna[1] was there, the door suddenly opened and in rushed Yelena Petrovna—wife of Prince Joan Konstantinovich and daughter of the dead Serbian King Peter I (Kara-georgevich), sister of the Yugoslavian king Alexander. She was sobbing loudly and ringing her hands, and she threw herself into the arms of Natalya Ivanovna: "Mon Dieu! C'est fini! C'est fini! Il ne les a pas reçus, il n'a pas voulu. C'est la fin! C'est la fin! Nous sommes perdus!" (My God! This is the end! This is the end! He did not receive them, he didn't want to. This is the end! This is the end! We are lost!)
>
> At first we were rigid with shock, then we were sent out of the room. It turned out that the Grand Dukes Nicholas Michaylovich, Pavel Alexandrovich, and Nicholas Nicholayevich had written the Czar a letter pointing out to him the general dissatisfaction of the people and the dark shadow that Rasputin was casting on the Czar's family—above all on the Czarina. They asked him to remove the Czarina from Zarskoye Syelo[2] and send her to a monastery,[3] but send Rasputin back to Siberia. The next day, they appeared personally at the Alexandrovsky Palace in Zarskoye Syelo and requested to be received by the Czar. But they were refused and informed that the Czar did not wish to see them.

Soon afterward, on 17 December 1916, Rasputin was murdered by Felix Yusupov with the help of his friends. This was a desperate attempt by patriotic monarchists convinced that they were saving Russia from a dreadful evil and thus from collapse.

Prince Felix Yusupov himself remembers the murder very well. In many ways, it was not an easy undertaking. His depiction also says something about Rasputin's personality:

> Rasputin was a very distrustful man. Therefore, he rarely accepted invitations to private houses. Above all, he knew that the nobility in Petersburg did not like him, a fact which he attributed to his origins as a Siberian peasant now privileged with access to the highest social circles and even with political influence. I tempted him with the prospect of getting to know my wife, something he had always wished for.
>
> I picked him up at his house—at the back steps, as he had desired.

As agreed upon, he had sent away his bodyguards and the secret police who guarded him day and night. Rasputin had put on a silk shirt tied around with a raspberry red girtle. I had never seen him so fine, hair and head carefully barbered and smelling of soap. It was already after midnight, but Rasputin asked if we shouldn't stop by at the gypsies' on the way. I promised him we would do this later. "Is no one else in your house?" he asked, worried. I said no. He expressed his concern by saying that the Czarina herself and her protégé Minister Protopopov had warned him against going out in the next few days, because people were seeking to take his life. "But they won't succeed," he concluded, as if to calm himself. Suddenly, I was overwhelmed somehow by a feeling of pity for this unsuspecting man. I was ashamed of the sophistication to which I had resorted in order to carry out my intention. At that moment, I despised myself for being able to come up with such a crime. I did not understand how I had been able to decide on it.

I looked grimly at my victim, who was standing calmly and trustingly in front of me. What had become of his gift of prophecy? How was it helping him, now that his own future lay in the balance? Of what use to him was the ability to read other people's minds when at the same time he was blind to the death trap into which he was about to step? If fate had already muddled up his consciousness, then we ought to let mercy go before justice.

But suddenly every stage in the despicable life of Rasputin struck me like a bolt of lightning. My pangs and worries disappeared and made way for the decision to carry out my plan.

No one saw us as we were driving along the Moyka; the streets were dead. Once again, we entered my house via the back door.

As we entered, we could hear the gramophone music that my friends were playing especially for Rasputin.

"What does this mean?" asked Rasputin. "Is someone here giving a party?"

"No, no, my wife is merely entertaining a few guests. They will go soon. Let's drink tea in the dining room in the meantime."

While he was examining the tiny wooden chest here on the bottom floor, pushing its drawers in and out, I gave him his last chance. Didn't he want to leave Petersburg? It would be better for him. His negative response to this idea sealed his fate. I offered him wine and tea; to my great disappointment, he turned both down. What was making him suspicious? Now I was determined: He would not leave the house alive.

We began to talk about this and that, of course about common acquaintances, the court, Anna Vyrubova, and Protopopov, who had warned Rasputin that he might become the victim of a conspiracy.

"I am not afraid," he repeated as before. "I am protected against danger. There have already been a number of attempts on my life, but God protected me. Disaster will befall anyone who lifts up his hand against me."

These words rang ominously through the room. My only thought now was how I could get him drunk as soon as possible.

Finally Rasputin asked for tea. With the tea, I also immediately brought a plate of cookies. Why was it that I began with the ones that were not poisoned? I was still hesitating when I brought him the ones with cyanide. At first he shoved them away: "They are too sweet."

But then he took one, and then one after another. I was watching him with horror in every limb. The poison was supposed to work immediately, but to my surprise Rasputin continued quite calmly with his conversation. Again I suggested to him that he should try some of our Crimean wine. Again he refused. As with the cookies, I did not pay any attention to him and simply filled two glasses full—time was going by, and I had become quite nervous. Again, for some reason I used the glasses that did not contain cyanide. And again Rasputin changed his mind and went for the wine. He liked it a lot, and he was amazed when I reported that we had an entire wine cellar full of this estate wine from the Crimea.

"Give me some Madeira," he now demanded. This time, I finally wanted to pour it into one of the prepared glasses, but he protested, "I want to keep my glass."

"That is impossible," I protested. "Grigoriy Yefimovich, you cannot mix two kinds of wine."

"It doesn't matter, I will use the same glass," he insisted.

I couldn't do anything about it, but I did succeed in letting the glass fall down unnoticed, so that it did not look like I had intended to do so. Immediately, I poured wine into a poisoned glass.

I remained standing in order to watch him as he immediately emptied the glass expecting him to collapse at any moment.

Despite this, he continued to tip his glass pleasurably, like a connoisseur. Even the color of his face did not change. The only change was that from time to time he felt at his throat, telling me when I asked him that he was having problems swallowing.

Finally, he got up and paced up and down the room. He demanded more Madeira. I filled up another poisoned glass. He emptied it without any effect. In the meantime, I had filled myself a glass too, in order to induce Rasputin to drink the next poisoned glass. It was the last remaining glass with cyanide.

Silence came on. We were sitting across from each other.

He looked at me. In his eyes, there was a malicious expression, as if he intended to say, "Look, you are just wasting time, you can't do anything to me."

Suddenly, his expression changed to wild anger; I had never seen him look so fearsome. He fixed me with his wide open eyes, and at this expression I felt such disgust that I would have dearly loved to strangle him with my bare hands.

The silence became ever more threatening. I had the impression that he now knew why I had brought him to my house. We were both fighting a strange and terrible battle with ourselves at that moment. The next moment, I could be crushed like nothing by his hand. It was as if I were dozing.

When I could think clearly again, he was still holding his head in both hands and sitting across from me. I had myself under control again and offered him tea. In a raw voice, he requested it, saying that he was thirsty; his eyes had become dull. Again he began to pace up and down. His sight fell upon my guitar.

"Come and sing something merry, I like to hear you sing so much."

At that moment, I felt like anything but singing, especially something merry. I wanted to say no. But then I took the guitar after all and sang a Russian song. At first, I thought that he had fallen asleep in his chair, but when I had finished he looked up somberly and demanded another song. I obeyed, but I no longer knew my own voice.

Time passed; the clock already showed half past three in the morning. My friends must have gotten impatient; the nightmare had gone on for two hours already—what would happen if they suddenly rushed in?

Rasputin raised his head: "What is the meaning of the noise up there?"

"Probably the guests are leaving. I will go see."

One floor above, my friends Dimitri, Purishkyevich, and Suchotin rushed up to me: "Have you done it? Is it over?"

"The poison did not work," I replied.

Everyone stared at me. "That is impossible!" the Grand Duke finally said. "With the entire dose?" I nodded.

At first, everyone wanted to rush down together with me, overpower him, and strangle him. Finally we decided it would be better if I acted alone again. I put Dimitriy's revolver in my pocket and went down again.

Rasputin was still sitting at the table. Somewhat faint and complaining about a headache and burning pain in his stomach, he demanded some more Madeira again. This did indeed seem to give him new strength, and now Rasputin suggested that we drive to the gypsies. He didn't want to listen to my objection that it was already very late:

"They are used to that. I always come late. Sometimes I am delayed in Zarskoye Syelo or at prayers, then I go directly to them. The body, too, needs recreation, isn't it true? All of our thoughts belong to God, but our bodies belong to ourselves, isn't it so?" he said with a wink. I would have expected anything else but that from a man who had just swallowed such a tremendous dose of poison. I was particularly surprised by the fact that a man with his instincts did not understand how close he was to his own death. And his piercing look had not picked up the fact that I had a revolver hidden behind my back?

I now began to look at the cross on the wall.

"Why are you looking at that?" asked Rasputin.

"It is so beautiful," I replied.

"It is beautiful; it must have cost a bundle. How much did you pay for it?" he asked, and finally made the steps I had expected in that direction, adding, "But I like the chest better."

"Grigoriy Yefimovich," I now said, "it is better for you to look at the cross now and say a prayer."

Rasputin was so surprised, almost shocked, as I had never imagined that he could be. Now he came closer to me and looked directly into my eyes. Evidently, he was looking for something that he had not expected, but he couldn't find it. Now the decisive moment had come. There was no way around it.

"Oh Lord," I prayed, "give me the strength to do it now and put an end to it." While Rasputin stood there motionless, I slowly raised my right arm—should I aim at his temple or at his heart? After a brief hesitation, I pulled the trigger. Rasputin gave a wild cry and collapsed onto the bearskin.

For a moment, I was struck by how easy it is to kill a person. One finger movement—and a live man had become a dead puppet.

When the shot rang out, my friends stormed in. One of them had brushed against the light switch in his haste, and thus the light had gone out. And someone pushed against me in the darkness and screamed. One of them turned the light on. Rasputin was pulled off the bearskin and examined. The bullet had hit near the heart. No doubt about it, he was dead.

Our hearts filled with hope, with all those thoughts that had driven us to this plan: Now the dynasty would be saved and freed from the shame of this man. Those who wanted to rule the land reasonably would be given a chance. Could we have known that no one was willing or able to do this?

Thus we left the bottom floor, which we closed off, and went upstairs. As had been arranged, we wanted—one of us in Rasputin's clothing—to drive to his house and pretend to bring him home, in case anyone had seen him drive away with us. Then someone else was supposed to drown his body at Petrovsky Island. While we were speaking about this, I followed an inexplicable impulse and went downstairs to look around. Rasputin was lying exactly as we had left him. I felt his pulse. Nothing. I propped up his torso and shook him. He fell dully back. I turned around to leave, but then I froze, scared to death. His right eyelid began to twitch, and little by little his whole face began to do the same. Suddenly, his eyes were wide open, and he was staring at me with hatred. My blood froze in my veins. I wanted to run away and call for help, but my legs failed me, and so did my voice. It was as if I were caught in the middle of a nightmare, unable to free myself. I stood there petrified.

And then something terrible happened: Rasputin stood up to his full height, gazed at me with his bulging eyes, gasped out my name, and grabbed for my neck. He clawed his other hand into my flesh.

No words can express the horror that I felt. There began a fight between us. This devil, who had deadly poison inside him and who had been hit by a bullet—he must have been saved by the power of a devil. There was something frightening in this existence and its diabolical refusal to die. I understood who Rasputin was. He was the embodiment of Satan himself, holding me in his claws and not letting me loose.

I strained myself to the utmost and freed myself. He fell back onto his back and lay there motionless, still holding in one hand the epaulets he had ripped off of my coat during the struggle. Now I got the strength to rush up and cry, "Hurry, he is still alive!" At the same moment I heard a dull noise behind me. I went to the stairway, followed by Purishkyevich with his revolver. We saw Rasputin, who was trying to climb the steps. He was doing it on his hands and feet, groaning like a wounded beast. Finally, he gave himself a last desperate push and landed at the entrance to the courtyard. I knew that this was locked and quickly loaded my revolver. But to my shock the door was open, and Rasputin disappeared outside! Purishkyevich behind him. Two shots fell. In order to prevent the unbelievable—that even in this condition the man might escape—I

ran out the main exit into the street, in order to cut off his path from the
Moyka in case Purishkyevich missed him. The courtyard had three chain
gates to the street, but only the middle one was unlocked. I saw Rasputin
just trying to pull himself up on it when a third shot fell and then a fourth.
Rasputin reeled and then fell onto a pile of snow. Purishkyevich ran to
him and looked at his body for a few moments. Certain that this time it
was the end, he ran into the house. I called to him, but he didn't hear
me.

I reassured myself that no one was there who could have heard the
shots. When I was sure of it, I came closer. Suddenly, two of the servants
came running from the side, and a policeman too.

"Your Excellence, I heard shots. What happened?"

"Nothing of importance." I turned my back to the gate so that the
view toward the dead man lying behind the pile of snow was cut off.
"One of my guests drank too much and shot into the air. If someone
questions you, tell them that."

Then I walked into the courtyard. Rasputin had now somehow
changed his position. My God, was he still not dead? I was at the end of
my strength. All I could do was drag myself to the house, where I met
Purishkyevich. He was getting ready to carry away the corpse. Then the
servants again announced the visit of the policeman. His explanation was
not satisfactory for the officers of the district who had heard the shots.
He thus wanted to learn more from us.

When he entered our room, Purishkyevich explained in a loud voice:

"Have you ever heard of Rasputin? The man who was about to ruin
our country, the czar and your brothers in the army? The man who
betrayed us to Germany?—Did you hear me?"

Not understanding what was expected of him, the policeman was
silent. "Do you know who I am?" Purishkyevich went on, "I am Vladimir
Mitrophanovich Purishkyevich, member of the Duma, and the shots that
you heard killed Rasputin. If you love your country and your Czar, hold
your tongue."

Rigid with fright, I listened to this unexpected confession, which was
such a surprise that I couldn't even interrupt. Purishkyevich was so excited
that he did not understand what he was doing.

Finally, the policeman said, "You did the right thing, and I will not
tell anything unless I have to give evidence under oath. Then I will have
to tell the truth, because lying would be a sin."

In the meantime, Dimitriy, Suchotin, and Doctor Lasovert packed up
Rasputin's corpse and took it to Petrovsky Island, where they sank it.

After a brief fainting spell on my part, my friends brought me to my room, where I fell into a deep sleep. This gave me the strength for the interrogations and everything else that awaited me the next morning as a result of this deed.

Amid the population, the news of the assassination of Rasputin was greeted with euphoria. In the army, too. The head of the French military mission in army headquarters, Janin, reports:

> Everyone is talking about Rasputin's murder. A victorious battle with 100,000 prisoners taken could not have caused more joy and excitement. Even Colonel Basarov said joyfully than even Wilhelm's death would not have brought him such pleasure. Many people believe that now the Czar will finally have to send the Czarina to a cloister.

The writer Konstantin Paustovsky was witness to an episode at a train station:

> A freight train gets closer. Purishkyevich is working on the platform. He had just set up food tents—hence one can forgive him for a lot. Soldiers and officers get off of the car. Among them a Cossack major, quite large, certainly over three hundred pounds. He sees Purishkyevich, stands still, stares at him, mutters something, and slowly approaches him:
> "Purishkyevich, is that you?"
> "Yes, it's me."
> "Allow me in the name of the Russian Army to shake your noble hand. You have killed Rasputin."
> "But."
> "No false modesty. All Russia knows it. To Purishkyevich and all those who killed the damned dog, hurray!"
> And a thunderous hurrah echoed all over the platform.

The Czar learned about Rasputin's murder at the front. According to eyewitness reports, he was more relieved than dismayed, thus encouraging the impression that he had been freed from a nightmare that had operated on him through his dominating wife and that led to decisions that he himself had objected to. Even when looked at from a different point of view, the picture of Czar Nicholas II as a person proves to be the same. Sofia Ivanovna Caruso, née Stavrakova, saw him when she was seventeen. She had been born in Yalta, the daughter of a Ukrainian landowner. She remembers:

> He was certainly a weak person. He was wonderful, gentle, and noble, but in no way cut out for the role of Czar. More for that of a landlord concerned only with his family and his land. Moreover, he worshipped his wife and was completely under her influence.

The tutors of the Czar's family report that Czar Nicholas II was at his happiest and most relaxed as a pater familias. Above all, he spent as much time as possible with his son Alexey. In Zarskoye Syelo, he and the Czarina preferred the more intimate Alexander Palais to the large palace. Usually, he wore a simple soldier's uniform. In the evening he used to read to his family from the works of his favorite authors— Tolstoy, Turgenyev, and above all Gogol. On beautiful days, he went boating with his children on the lakes. When the crown prince was sick and the Czar had time, he carried him into the garden himself—as at the end of his life, when he was a prisoner in Yekaterinburg. Nicholas had his son in his arms when he and his family were killed by the bullets of the Cheka.

Nina Fyodorovna Burova, born the daughter of a field marshal in Vilna in 1894, remembers a visit by the Czar around 1913 or 1914 for the festival of Ostrobranskaya Matka Boska. Afterward, she was introduced to the Czar, as protocol demanded for the wife of an officer on the Russian General Staff. Nina Burova was surprised by the simplicity of his behavior, but she was even more impressed by something else:

> He had such eyes that—when one had seen them—one couldn't forget them ever again. I think that he had a premonition that he would die as a martyr one day. Again and again, he said, "For my homeland, I will do everything that is necessary." He truly sacrificed himself for Russia. For us, he is a holy man. He has recently been pronounced a saint.

Members of liberal emigré circles view the Czar less sentimentally. Gleb Struve, born in 1898, later became famous as a philologist in emigration. He was the son of a lawyer and a liberal historian:

> I was never a follower of Czar Nicholas II, and my father wasn't either. We had more of a negative attitude toward him, something like

ke Felix Yusupov shot Rasputin in his house on December 16, 1916.

Guest house of the restaurant "Ville Rode" where Rasputin's parties took place

Rasputin surrounded by ladies of the Russian court.

Rasputin, Grigoriy Yeyfimovich

Caricature of Rasputin:
he Russian Reigning Family."

Czar Nicholas II and his daughters Olga and Tatiana.

Card with Easter greetings from the imperial family.

The four grand duchesses: Olga, Tatiana, Maria and Anastasia.

katerina Alexandrovna countess Vol-
nskaya.

Nina Fyodovovna Burova.

other, aunt and uncle of Countess Bob-
skaya.

The Czar mother Marie Feodorovna.

Czar Nicholas II (center right) visiting the Petersburg military academy, und
the command of General Sacharov (see center left).

Czar Nicholas II in uniform.

Handwritten letter dated August 22

Ceremonial greeting of Czar in the field; in the middle General Sacharov; to
left the Cossack bodyguard.

...from Czar Nicholas II to General
...eyev.

GERMANY PLEDGES HUMANITY AT SEA;
WILL ALSO PAY LUSITANIA INDEMNITY;
AUSTRIA AND TURKEY TO JOIN IN PLEDGE

INCLUDES THE PERSIA CASE

If German U-Boat Sank Liner Commander Will Be Punished.

LUSITANIA DISAVOWAL NEXT

Only the Wording of the Agreement in That Case Now Believed to be at Issue.

FRYE SETTLEMENT AT HAND

Washington Regards the Whole U-Boat Problem Near End—Safety for All Noncombatants.

Special to The New York Times.

WASHINGTON, Jan. 7.—The whole aspect of the complicated and grave situation caused by Teutonic submarine attacks on merchant ships in the Mediterranean changed late this afternoon when Secretary Lansing announced that new written assurances had been received from the German Government regarding its attitude.

Equally important is the information, unofficially made known, that similar assurances will be furnished by the Government of Austria-Hungary and Turkey. Incidentally, the German guarantees apply to the Persia case in such a way as to dissipate the international crisis over the sinking of that vessel.

These assurances were contained in a note which Count von Bernstorff, the German Ambassador, received from the Berlin Foreign Office this morning, and which he delivered in person to Secretary Lansing during a conference later in the day.

According to these assurances no German submarine will be allowed to sink an enemy merchant vessel in the Mediterranean until after safety has been accorded to passengers and crew—unless the vessel offers resistance or attempts to escape. This new pledge, broader than any previously given by the German Government to the United States, applies to freight as well as passenger vessels.

Additional assurances are given that any German submarine commander who

Germany's Pledge of Safety in Mediterranean and Promise to Punish Those Violating It

Special Dispatch to The New York Times.

WASHINGTON, Jan. 7.—After a visit of Count Bernstorff to the State Department today Secretary Lansing issued the following statement, comprising the text of the new written guarantees from the German Government:

The German Ambassador today left at the Department of State, under instructions from his Government, the following communication:

"(1) German submarines in the Mediterranean had, from the beginning, orders to conduct cruiser warfare against enemy merchant vessels only in accordance with general principles of international law, and in particular measures of reprisal, as applied in the war zone around the British Isles, were to be excluded.

"(2) German submarines were therefore permitted to destroy enemy merchant vessels in the Mediterranean—i. e., passenger as well as freight ships as far as they do not try to escape or offer resistance—only after passengers and crews have been accorded safety.

"(3) All cases of destruction of enemy merchant ships in the Mediterranean in which German submarines are concerned are made the subject of official investigation, and, besides, subject to regular prize court proceedings. In so far as American interests are concerned, the German Government will communicate the result to the American Government. Thus, also, in the Persia case, if the circumstances should call for it.

"(4) If commanders of German submarines should not have obeyed the orders given to them they will be punished; furthermore, the German Government will make reparation for damage caused by death of or injuries to American citizens."

sinks a vessel in violation of the pledge thus furnished will be punished, and the German Government will make reparation for damage caused by the death of or injuries to any American citizen.

Pledges Germany's Allies.

Germany's guarantees are to be observed likewise by the Austrian and Turkish Governments. While this is not set forth in the communication delivered by the German Ambassador, it is understood that the German, Austrian, and Turkish Governments have confidentially come to an understanding among themselves agreeing to the rules under which submarine, flying their respective flags are to conduct their warfare against merchant craft in the Mediterranean, and that the Berlin Foreign Office has taken the initiative in bringing about a common line of conduct between the central powers and their allies for observance in submarine warfare.

The pledge of the German Government is regarded as all the more important because it was given voluntarily by the Berlin Foreign Office without waiting for a request from the United States Government for information as to the manner in which German submarine warfare would be conducted in the Mediterranean. And particular significance is attached to the fact that the assurances thus given by

the Berlin Government are a direct outcome of the Ancona and Persia cases.

SERBIAN RETREAT A HEROIC TRAGEDY

Flight to Sixth Capital in Two Months Through Albanian Mountains Described.

GUNS AND CONVOYS LEFT

Officers and Soldiers Wept as They Destroyed Them—Army Harassed by Guerrillas.

PARIS, Jan. 7.—Hardships encountered by the Serbian Army in its flight through the mountains of Albania are described in a letter to the Temps sent from Scutari on Dec. 11.

"This is the sixth capital Serbia has had during two months," says the writer. "After Nish it was Kraljevo, then Ras-

ka, Mitrovitza, Prizrend, and finally Scutari.

"As a tourist I am acquainted with the Alps, the Carpathians, and the Pyrenees, but I have never seen such paths for roads running along the edge of terrible precipices and the sides of peaks in the clouds. The officials of the Serbian Government rode little mountain ponies, but often they had to abandon their mounts and go on foot. I have seen their horses slip and fall into abysses. Sometimes one had to go on fours. Some, to avoid vertigo, had to be guided with closed eyes.

"Then there was snow, which caused fresh suffering. Roads were we through the snow a yard deep. Albanian guerrillas were taking pot shots at us from behind rocks high up or from opposite sides of the canyons.

"The army could not bring its guns and convoys through such country. When we began to enter it we had to destroy automobiles, wagons, vehicles, and every sort of gun. Officers and soldiers wept as they demolished the guns, those pieces of steel which they called their 'French friends,' the ordnance having been made at Creusot. The men had become attached to them, and many artillerists served the same gun four years. Some officers refused to destroy their pieces, saying they preferred to use their last bit of strength in trying to save them, and some of them have succeeded and actually have brought their guns across.

"After all these sufferings from cold, hunger, and fatigue, many soldiers being barefoot, we are here.

"Altogether there have arrived various routes 11,000 women and children. The tragedy of the situation is that the army has almost nothing to eat. The soldiers had no bread for four days, but small quantities of flour were kept for the women and children

Germans May Have Sunk Persia.

During his visit to the State Department Count von Bernstorff also informed Secretary Lansing that an official dispatch from Berlin brought the information that the German Government only knew of the Persia disaster through the newspaper reports and was not aware that any German submarine sank the liner. That a German submarine may have sunk the Persia is inferred from the statement that the circumstances in the case if the circumstances should call for it. The American Government also is to be notified of any facts as are obtained. From this admission to the Persia it is now believed here that should a German commander report that he attacked the Persia, and if it should be shown that the Persia neither tried to flee nor offered resistance, Germany would punish that commander and make reparation to the United States.

Similarly, the dispatch from Ambassador Penfield at Vienna stated the Austrian Government had not been notified that any of its submarines sank the Persia, but that any information that the Vienna Government obtained from its commanders would be communicated to the United States. It was pointed out at the State Department today that neither from Vienna, Berlin, London, Malta, Cairo, Alexandria, nor Marseilles has the United States Government been able to obtain any facts regarding the sinking of the Persia that could be regarded as evidence that the steamer was torpedoed, or upon which this Government could act.

During his conference with Secretary Lansing, Count von Bernstorff also discussed the Lusitania case. While neither would disclose the result of the conference, there is authority for the statement that these discussions have made such progress that the Lusitania question soon will be settled to the satisfaction of both Governments. Germany will pay an indemnity for the loss of American lives in the destruction of the Lusitania. There will be some form of disavowal, but the wording of this has not been finally determined, and the understanding to be the only cause of the delay in the settlement. That there will be a prompt settlement is conceded.

Secretary Lansing would not today state the character of the note from Germany on the Frye case. He said the note would be made public tomorrow. It is understood that in this communication Germany grants what the United States asked. The note is declared to be satisfactory.

pity. He was a weak man. Our pity was actually a reaction to the fact that he died so tragically with his family.

Yekaterina Alexandrovna Volkonskaya, born in Petersburg in 1896 as the daughter of a general of the cavalry, was invited—thanks to the position of her father—to a ball at the court in honor of the three hundredth anniversary of the Romanov Dynasty in March 1913:

> I still remember the festive day, when the ruler accepted people's best wishes in a hall in the Winter Palace. In the Nikolayevsky Hall, we could look through the window at the Neva. It was a beautiful winter day, and snow was falling. I still remember quite clearly that we had to wear Russian court clothing, made to specific proportions. We were introduced to the Czar one by one. He gave each of us his hand. He said a couple of nice words to everyone. He was quite simple and modest in his manner. He was modest in general. It was well known that he didn't like French cuisine but preferred Russian. He liked borscht, cabbage, and Russian kasha, and he was simple in other ways, too.

The royal couple also wore Russian court clothing during their subsequent tours through the old Russian cities that had played a role in the history of the Romanovs. In Moscow, where the Czar rarely stayed, the reception was pompous and enthusiastic. But the image of the popular crown prince Alexey, who because of his condition was carried by a cossack of the imperial bodyguard behind the Czar and the Czarina, was greeted by rumblings among the people, as Minister Kokovzov reports:

> How sad to see the heir to the Romanov throne so weak, sickly, and helpless.

Kokovzov further remembers the festive parade in Moscow:

> In all the glitter and jubilation, the royal couple was completely unaware of the reality and the danger that threatened Russia from within and without.

In Moscow, too, there was a chance to observe the Czar's family privately. Alexander Vladimirovich Bulgakov, a sergeant, was a guard in the Kremlin Palace:

I was ordered to stand in the palace in front of the private chambers. Of course, it was difficult to stand totally motionless for two hours, surrounded by a lot of mirrors, movement, and life all around—but we had specific orders about how we were to stand, as we had been trained in the Alexandrian military school in Moscow.

Toward evening, when the changing of the guard came, we knew that the grand duchesses were coming: Olga, Tatyana, Maria, Anastasia. They looked around, they were bored, they ate grapes and sweets and behaved in a very natural and unpretentious manner. And then the crown prince, Zarevich Alexey, came from the city gate. Someone was holding him by the hand. Later he came to me and said that I should see to it that when he wanted to build an oven with bricks, I should make sure that his mama and papa would not see it.

We were so prepared for our task that, had the order come, we would naturally have been ready to give our lives for them.

Colonel Dubenzev, who was stationed with his bodyguard regiment in Rovna (near Kiev), saw the Czar frequently when he was in the headquarters after the replacement of Nikolas Nikolayevich:

Our division consisted of four regiments—the Ulans of His Majesty, the Hussars, the Cossack Bodyguard of His Majesty (to which I belonged) and the Ataman Regiment. In each squadron, there were one hundred men. Everyone had the royal initials N II on their shoulder patches.

Sometimes the Czar came to parades or exercises. No matter whether the people judged him well or not, there was nevertheless an untouchable respect for the dignity of the Czar. Czar Nicholas II was well respected, although he was not as popular with the soldiers as Grand Duke Nicholas Nikolayevich.

He always wore the uniform of our bodyguard regiment. I still remember an episode in February 1915. During one of his unexpected informal visits, one of the soldiers became embarrassed—on an earlier occassion, he had taken the monarch to be a double and, much to the Czar's amusement, refused to let him pass; this time, the soldier recognized the monarch, but in his embarrassment he stuttered his salute and stopped suddenly in the middle of a sentence. The Czar smiled at him and smoothed over the embarrassment: "Married? Children?" The soldier nodded. "Then kiss them from me."—"Certainly, your Imperial Highness."

The Czar was simple, warm, and human. As soldiers, we were unconditionally subordinate to him. Later, when the unrest in Petrograd broke out, our commander telegraphed to him our readiness to stand by him at any moment and fight to the last drop of our blood. But our deployment was called off by General Alexeyev. When we then heard about the incomprehensible abdication of the sovereign, our commander took his pistol and shot himself.

Like Colonel Dubenzev, other eyewitnesses also report that Czar Nicholas II changed significantly during the war years and above all shortly before the revolution. Count Stenbock-Fermor suspects:

> We were convinced that Badmayev, a tartar homeopath who was the Czar's second doctor, was giving the monarch a drug that weakened his will power. In the course of time, he became so strangely apathetic, and one can assume that there was a connection there to the despicable activities of Rasputin: It was in his best interest to see to it that the Czar was less and less able to make his own decisions.

Long-time finance minister count Kokovzov seems to confirm this view. After a one-year interruption caused by the absence of the Czar, who was in the military headquarters, Kokovzov paid a visit to Zarskoye Syelo in January 1917:

> On 19 January (1 February), I drove to Zarskoye Syelo. During this year, nothing had changed in the Alexander Palace. The guards, lackeys, everyone was the same. And yet I can never forget this visit.
>
> The sight of my ruler deeply shocked me. In that one year that we had not seen each other, he had changed so much that I almost didn't recognize him. His face was sunken, his eyes dazed, and—in contrast to earlier, when he had always looked at people calmly—his eyes wandered nervously here and there. Strangely enough, he received me at the door and remained there during our conversation, something he had never done earlier. The door to his office was also open, contrary to usual custom, and I could not get by the thought that someone was standing behind the door. Spontaneously, I asked him about his well-being. The ruler brushed aside my concerned question as to whether he was sick or tired. With a tortured smile, he explained that he had recently had less occasion to be out in fresh air than he was used to. To my great amazement, he became embarrassed when I suggested that I should now give him my opinion about a matter discussed with him two days earlier by his foreign minister. He, who had always had an excellent memory before, seemed at the

moment not to remember what the matter was about. Again with a tortured smile, he asked me what it was about, and when I explained he answered, "Yes, I spoke to Pokrovsky[4] about that, but I am not prepared for this question now. I will write to you." Upon which—again with a sickly smile—he opened the door as a signal for me to go. I left destroyed, convinced that the Czar was seriously ill and that his sickness might have affected not only his nerves but also his mind.

The British ambassador Sir Buchanan, incidentally, made a similar observation.

Adoration of a father figure and of his likable, natural children (who were, however, forbidden by the Czarina to speak with people outside the court); empathy for the simple character and human warmth of the Czar toward the people that he had to deal with, all described by the court tutors Gilliard and Gibbes and the daughter of the Czar's personal physician Botkin; the peaceful, collegial behavior when Nicholas spoke with officers and soldiers at headquarters wearing his simple soldier's uniform, as Colonel Dubenzev recalls; the calmness and dignity with which later on the ex-Czar bore the insults of the red guards as a prisoner with his family in Tobolsk and Yekaterinburg, as the same guards were later on to report with increasing amazement: All of this and the worship of Russian patriots did little to narrow the gap between the Czar and his people, which resulted from a communication and information vacuum, and which had become unbridgeable because of a series of wrong decisions.

Arkady Petrovich Stolypin, son of the former minister and adviser Arkady Petrovich Stolypin, sums up the fatal constellation:

> He had a weak will for making decisions, so he was easy to manipulate—from every side. I do not like to criticize him—but I had the impression that whoever was last in his study had changed his opinion again. Nevertheless, he was the only one to support my father in his unpopular reforms, and without his support my father could have done nothing.
>
> Around 1916 and the beginning of 1917, the country was in a state of chaos. Nicholas allowed himself to be forced into abdication because he believed that he would be preventing more bloodshed that way. But the unity of the people was destroyed and torn apart by the fractions in the government.
>
> Finally, he was a broken man—broken by governing through all those

many years when he didn't get enough support: when the liberal intelligentsia, the Cadets, most of the Duma—where the most educated people were—did not want to work together with the government. The Czar came to Petersburg only occasionally, and the Czarina began to concern herself with too many things. She was certainly an honest woman, but she understood absolutely nothing about politics and gave advice. There began a series of reassignments at the top of the government and above all in the Ministry of the Interior, and when people told the monarch that all this would lead to a bad end, he didn't believe them.

Much of this could have been avoided, but many serious mistakes coincided. A large part of the blame lies with the unfortunate empress, even if she did end as a martyr. Rasputin's advice and her influence made Protopopov interior minister after all. Though he was a member of the Duma, he was absolutely unsuited for this position. For instance, most of the garrison in the capital city should not have been filled with unreliable reservists at this time during the war—they fell completely under the influence of enemy propaganda. That's what happened, thanks to the minister of the interior. All of this could have been avoided.

But it all seemed to happen inexorably, as if to spite us, as if to prepare ground for the February Revolution, which then actually happened.

On 18 August 1916 the British ambassador in Petrograd, Sir George Buchanan, had written laconically to his superiors: "If the Czar continues to keep his current advisers, I fear that a revolution will be unavoidable."

NOTES

1. Natalya Ivanovna Sergeyeva, wife of the Russian ambassador in Sweden and then in Serbia, was the director of this charitable action.

2. The Czar's family spent most of its time at the summer residence in Zarskoye Syelo.

3. In Russia this is a traditional and relatively mild measure taken by czars with unwanted family members.

4. Foreign minister at the time.

Chapter Three

⧸⧸

Farewell to Yesterday

The February Revolution of 1917 and the circumstances accompanying the Czar's abdication as the prerequisite of the autumn's events.

From my report, Your Grace will be able to see that I consider the situation in the empire now to be more serious than ever before. The mood in the country is such that one can expect the most serious unrest. There are no more parties; all of Russia is of one mind in demanding a new government and the appointment of a responsible prime minister who enjoys the trust of the people. On the basis of mutual trust, the legislative bodies and the public organisations must work together to achieve victory and bring order to the country. To our great discredit, we must admit that the country is now being seized by general decay.

At a meeting to discuss the situation at the front, I reminded the Czar that in the year 1915 I had already implored him not to take over the high command, and that now, after the defeats on the Rumanian front, people would hold him completely responsible. "Do not let it come to that, Your Majesty," I said. "Do not force the people to choose between yourself and the fatherland! Until now, the concepts Czar and fatherland have been inseparable. In recent times, however, people have begun to separate the two!"

Then the Czar covered his face with both hands and said softly, "For twenty-two years I have only been trying to achieve the best. Can it be that for twenty-two years I have erred?"

That was the memory of Duma president Michail Rodsyanko of his meeting with Czar Nicholas II in Zarskoye Syelo on 7 (20) January 1917.

What was the relative distribution of the various factions in the Duma which had an influence on the course of events at the time? At the beginning of 1917, Russia was governed by the Fourth Duma, which had been in office since November 1912. The complexion of the various legally permitted parties was liberal. However, due to the voting law passed under Prime Minister Stolypin, who had been murdered in 1911, the composition of the various estate representatives in the Russian parliament was in fact quite random. This was true less because of reactionaries trying to maintain feudal privileges than because of pan-Russian principles.[1] None of this changed the fact that the Social Revolutionaries, who since the initiation of the Duma had been legally allowed, had nevertheless gone into the illegal terrorist underground after the Second Duma because of unbridgeable differences of opinion with the conservative forces in the Duma. They were not to return from illegality until the fall of the Czarist government and the rise of the Provisional Government, when they again became part of the public parliamentary process. The opposition liberals and socialists in the Duma made up only one-fourth of all representatives in 1917, shortly before the February Revolution, while the conservatives were strengthened by the addition of right-wing radicals such as the Russian People's Federation and the Federation of the Archangel Michael. Meanwhile, ministers Protopopov, Sturmer, and others, who belonged among the conservatives and had been appointed during the Czar's absence by his irrational wife—using specious criteria—were incapable even of seeing the pressing problems of the time, let alone of solving them. Not only this, but they also committed serious errors that made even conservatives begin to criticize the government and switch to the liberal camp.

But events took their own course—as if to prepare the way for the revolutionaries who were in exile waiting for their moment to begin. The revolutionaries were looking to seize control of a situation that has gotten out of hand, pushing the needs and demands of a despairing population in the direction of ideological propaganda.

Bad news had come from the front—and with it hordes of deserters. The promising victory of the Russian Ninth Army in the middle of 1916 under General Bryusilov against the strong forces of the Austro-Hungarian Seventh Army had been the last big success. After they had changed fronts and gone against their own Austrian partners, the Italians pressed General Alexeyev to move against the Austrians with the Russian west flank in order to take pressure off of Northern

Italy. The Austrian Army had fought well and bravely there in spite of great losses—until Conrad von Hotzendorf came up with the unhappy idea of attacking during the winter in the midst of bad weather.

Bryusilov's attack pushed the Austrians behind the Dnyestr line. But other generals did not follow. Ewert and Kropatkin hesitated on the northwestern and southwestern fronts, to the latter of which badly prepared soldiers under the leadership of equally poorly trained reserve officers had been sent to die pointless deaths. This time, the army leadership was failing where there were actually enough munitions to continue the war successfully for the Russian side. Thanks to the countless weapons that had fallen into the hands of the Russians from dead and captured Austrian soldiers, it was even possible to cut down Russian weapons production for a while. Nevertheless, the tide of success had turned. In addition to growing rejection by the troops of their own military leadership, there were now increasing transportation problems, which occasionally brought all military actions to a standstill. Ludendorff and Hindenburg exploited Russian weaknesses in their tactics, attacking from two sides, a method which had already proved successful for the German Army at Tannenberg. This was the last straw. Hardly anyone believed anymore in a final victory for Russian troops.

The population of a hinterland that now found itself in the truest sense of the word in a state of chaos was less and less willing to take on the burdens of war for questionable successes. It is said that existence determines consciousness. The consciousness that caused despair, hatred, and rejection of the responsible government was called hunger. Hunger ruled above all in the capital. In the country, the peasants still managed to get by with the bare necessities and had not yet been affected by the worsening transportation problems. The capital was the traditional place for a climate of revolution, spiced by the intellectual and progressive ideas of a largely leftist "intelligentsia" in Petrograd. This intelligentsia had always been more liberal and less conservative in Petrograd than in Moscow—and certainly more so than in the countryside. The city was also the center of the new factory proletariat on the edge of town. Antiwar sentiment was strong in the Putilov factory, which produced weapons. The keepers of law and order were no longer able to suppress expressions of dissatisfaction. The armories in Petrograd were filled with reservists who had hardly been trained, recruited from among the peasantry and poorly motivated to defend the ruling system. The armories had lost career soldiers to the front.

Gradually, protests begin: first a demonstration in commemoration of the anniversary of "Bloody Sunday," which had been observed since 1905. The sparks fly. New, spontaneous protest groups begin to form. There are calls for bread. People shout, "Down with the war!" and "Down with the government!"

The smell of revolution hangs in the air.

On 13 (26) February 1917, the Petrograd secret police writes in a report:

> Since this morning, there have been unsettling rumors in Petrograd about the possibility of massive unrest: Around one o'clock in the afternoon, news spread in the factory areas (Narva, the Kolomer, and the Alexander Nevsky Rayon) that the supporters of a strike on 14 February had gotten the upper hand over those who were against such a step, and that they had persuaded them to take part in a protest against the war. At about two o'clock in the afternoon, unrest began in many places. It was started by soldiers who had been called up today; crowds of up to five hundred people marched through the streets singing the Marseillaise and shouting. "Down with the war, down with the police, beat up the marauders!" Storefront windows were broken, policemen were chased away from their posts, and one officer was beaten up as he tried to pacify an angry crowd. Until seven o'clock, there were reports everywhere—in the streetcars, in stores, etc.—of clashes between workers in the Putilov factory and the police.

Vasily Vasilyevich Oryechov, an officer since 1915, had been decorated with the Cross of St. George after his participation in the East Prussian campaign. He was just coming home from the front and remembers this day in Petrograd:

> On 23 February (8 March), I arrived with a small commando of military technicians from our batallion. I was to look at a particular tank train for use on the western front. I had just been named commander of this train. The moment I arrived, I noticed clear indications that there were problems here. At first, we were shocked by the lines in front of the bread stores. More than that, there was a nervous atmosphere in the population that we could sense. But no one was thinking of a revolution. On 26 February, when we were done inspecting the tank train, I went to report to the Petrograd command post for military transports before my departure. The officers were complaining that no measures were being taken to

subdue the protests and disorder that had begun in the capital. But the commander of the Petrograd military district, General Chabalov, with whom I spoke personally, humiliated one officer, a bearer of the Cross of St. George, in front of the eyes of his fellow officers, when this gentleman offered him his tank patrol from Gachina in order to help maintain order and prevent excesses. The general explained that there was no reason to worry, that the police were prepared; under no circumstances could regular troops be transferred to the capital and used for purely police functions—this would go against the honor of officers. "And in general: Leave, and do not disturb us in our work."

On 25 February (10 March), Czar Nicholas ordered the cancellation of the Imperial Duma session, which was put off until April due to the country's desperate situation. Chabalov sent a cable to General Alexeyev, the high commander, in General Headquarters:

I hereby report that as a result of the shortage of bread many strikes broke out in our factories on 23 and 24 February. On 24 February, about 200,000 workers went on strike and violently drove out those who were working. Traffic was disrupted by the workers. On 23 and 24 February at noon, some of the workers broke through to the Nevsky Prospect, where they were driven away. Store windows were broken, as well as windows in streetcars. The troops did not make use of their weapons. Four police officers suffered wounds. A band of demonstraters was broken up by cossacks. In the morning, the police chief of the Vyborger Rayon had his hands broken and suffered head wounds. Officer Krylov was killed while trying to drive away a crowd. Besides the Petrograd armory, five squadrons of the Ninth Cavalry Reserve Regiment from Krasnoye Syelo were involved in putting down the unrest, as well as one hundred members of the Pavlowsky Cossack Bodyguard Regiment and five squadrons of the reserve guard cavalry regiment.

Nina Alexeyevna Meshcherskaya, later Krivosheyna, remembers:

My cousin, who was living with us in those days and going to an officers' course at the Pavlovsky Military School, called up his superior and reported that he could not come to class, because there were rebellious soldiers surrounding our house. They had spread out all over Liteyny to the Nevsky Prospect. What was he ordered to do? The director of the military school answered, "Are you drunk, maybe? What nonsense are you talking, what kind of soldiers? Where? The whole city is peaceful and quiet. I advise you not to spread any stupid rumors!" And with that he hung up.

Indeed, masses of soldiers were waltzing by under our windows, and also through the parallel streets Furshtatskaya and Sergeyevskaya. There were even officers among them.

We were standing at the window of the large living room in the second story, and the picture we saw was unforgettable: A mighty mass of soldiers was moving quite purposefully toward the Taurian Palace, the seat of the Duma, screaming and shouting as they went. Our housekeeper Jenny Grauding, who had been serving my mother for many years, came running up and reported that soldiers had come into the courtyard and were hiding there. There were about twelve men, and they had thrown away their rifles there; they explained to the doorkeeper that they had been forced to march along with everyone, and some of them added that since that morning completely unknown officers had suddenly started surfacing in their barracks and giving them orders.

Somewhere there were shots—I think from the Nevsky and the Nikolayevsky train station, but that was very far away from us.

The February Revolution had begun.

Duma president Rodsyanko called for an extraordinary session. The Czar had meanwhile gone to the headquarters of the General Staff, the "Stavka" in Mogilyev. Aware through reports of what was going on, he telegraphed to the commander of the Petrograd military district, General Chabalov:

> We order the liquidation of the unrest in the capital by tomorrow, since in this difficult time of war with Germany and Austria it cannot be tolerated.

> Nicholas

The writer Viktor Shklovsky was a journalist at the time:

> Soldiers in the barracks, who had lost their belief in the old regime, were only held back by the hard hand of their superiors. But the superiors were already growing unsure of themselves. Everyone was in an uproar. At this time, career soldiers—indeed, any soldiers at all between the ages of twenty-two and twenty-five—were rare. They had all been slaughtered

like animals, pointlessly, at the front. The Petersburg soldier of those years was a dissatisfied peasant or a petit bourgeois.

These men were not even dressed properly; people simply tossed them gray military coats, and they were put together in bands, crowds and dhordes that were then called reserve battalions.

Igor Krivosheyn, son of a liberal minister under the Czar:

The day the February Revolution began, I was at home in Petrograd's Sergeyevskaya Street. This street went from the Neva to the Tavrichesky Dvoryez (Taurian Palace), a chiefly aristocratic district. My father, by the way, was the one who had suggested changing the name of the city from Petersburg to Petrograd.

I watched the revolution from the windows of our home. Suddenly, the streets had filled with soldiers. But they were not marching in lines and blocks. Rather, they formed a disordered mass of people. I watched the rebellious soldiers from my window. They were guard soldiers from various regiments. As far as I can remember, there were no major incidents on that day, no officers were killed, but people were already listening to revolutionary agitators. In the days that followed, soldiers' committees were formed, and the officers, who for the time being were staying mostly in their quarters, had hardly any power over them anymore. The soldiers were mostly reservists. Reserve regiments whose soldiers were at the front had ordinary soldiers as substitutes. These soldiers easily came under the influence of enemy propaganda.

Did we consider all this to be merely a passing incident? No—we had the feeling that Russia was approaching its end. My father said back then: "Maybe Russia will once again become large and powerful. But this Russia which I have served and loved—it will never exist again."

On 26 February (11 March), the Volhynian Regiment shot at demonstrators. Duma president Rodsyanko sent a telegram to the Czar:

The situation is serious. In the capital there is anarchy. The government is crippled. Traffic, supplies, and heating are in a chaotic condition. General dissatisfaction is growing. There is pointless shooting in the streets. Troops are shooting at each other. It is unavoidable and urgently necessary to immediately entrust a person who enjoys the country's confidence with the formation of a new government. It is impossible to wait any longer. Any hesitation would mean death. I pray to God that in this hour no guilt will fall upon the bearer of the Crown.

Rodsyanko

Marily Markovich reports:

Every passing hour is bringing us closer and closer to the inevitable. The army is beginning to go along with the people. One can no longer even be certain of the loyalty of the police. Everywhere, crowds of people are gathering and shouting, "Bread, bread!"

Highly dramatic scenes are taking place everywhere. A battalion of the Semyonovsky Guard Regiment received the order to clear the Nevsky Prospect. It hurries to the scene and encounters a battalion of the Wolhynian Regiment, which has gone over to the side of the people. The two regiments threaten each other, there is uncertainty: What will happen? And suddenly something completely unexpected happens. An old officer who is commanding the soldiers and the guard straightens up in his stirrups and turns to his men: "Soldiers, I cannot give you the command to shoot at your brothers, but I am too old to act against my oath!" He draws his revolver and shoots himself. His body is covered with a flag, and his soldiers go over to the side of the people.

General Chabalov was forced to telegraph to the Czar that battalions from what until then had been model regiments—such as the Pavlovsky, the Wolhynian, the Preobrashensky, and others—were now refusing to obey commands and shoot at rebels. Of course, these were only reservists, but that did not change the fact that the general was not capable of restoring order to the city. Chabalov demanded reliable troops from the front.

Rodsyanko demanded more. On 27 February (12 March), he saw the situation even more dramatically:

At the command of Your Majesty, the Imperial Duma's session has been interrupted until April. The last bulwark of order has been pushed aside. The government is completely powerless and cannot master the disorder. The troops in the armories are unreliable. The reserve battalions of the guard regiments have become infected by the spirit of rebellion. They are killing their own officers. They are making common cause with the masses and the people's movement and marching on the center of the

Interior Ministry and the Imperial Duma. A civil war has begun. Give
the command immediately to form a new government on the basis of the
suggestions that I made to you in my telegram of yesterday. Do not
hesitate, Majesty. If this movement catches on in the army, too, then
Germany will triumph, and the collapse of Russia and of the dynasty will
be unavoidable. Tomorrow it may already be too late.

All of this is confirmed by the diary entries of Katharina Sayn-
Wittgenstein:

27 February 27, 12:00 Noon
The time has come. For four days now, there has been unrest in Petrograd; the machines in the factories are at a standstill, the trams are
not running, everyone is on strike. Today almost all of the marching
divisions of the guard regiments rebelled. Next door to us, in the barracks of the Wolhynian Regiment, there have been mutinies since early
today; beneath our windows there is a division of the Preobrashchensky
Regiment, and they have pointed their machine gun at the barracks.
From minute to minute, we can expect that there will soon be shots.

Five o'clock in the afternoon
Uncle Kolya came back all right. He says that there is shooting on the
Liteyny Prospect. Beneath our windows, the mass of people is getting
thicker and thicker, and the shouts are getting louder. Too bad that
they took away the machine gun. We are watching the street from the
bay windows in our room, from which we can see all of Basovskaya
Street with the barracks, Baseynaya Street, and part of Liteyny Street.
On the streets, masses of soldiers and "comrades" are surrounding the
officers and removing their sables. We saw how a soldier on horseback
rode right up to an officer and shot directly into his face. Cars full of
soldiers with rifles and red flags are driving through the streets. The
crowd rushes toward them and shouts, "Hurray!" On Sacharevskaya
Street, the district court is in flames; the chief administration building
of the artillery has been destroyed.

Tatyana Botkina:

There was no more sunshine, and snow had begun to fall in thick
white flakes. The house in which we had made ourselves at home was
located in the barracks district, and toward evening we heard shots from

the streets and the whistle of bullets. Something unbelievable was happening on the street. Drunken soldiers without belts, dressed sloppily, with or without rifles, were running here and there and stealing everything from the stores that they could get their hands on. Some took bolts of cloth, others a pair of boots. Some were already drunk and took bottles of wine or vodka along. Still others had wrapped themselves in colorful bands. During the night, one of the largest wine warehouses went up in flames, and the drunken soldiers who were in the cellar were burned to death.

Mrs. Giovanni was an art student with Rerich:

I enjoyed every day of class. It was already my last year of study. And suddenly one day—there was still snow on the ground, but somehow it was beginning to melt, and it was not particularly cold—the other students rushed into our class and shouted, "Hurry up, come to the street! Terrible things are happening there!" Of course, we all ran outside. Our school was only two steps away from the Nevsky. I was living on Senate Square—where the Moyka River flows. That was not very far from school. The teachers wanted to hold us back and said that we should not go outside under any circumstances, because armed cossacks were hunting up and down the Nevsky in order to drive away the crowds. They had cossack whips in their hands. From time to time, we heard shots. But I believe that they were only warning shots fired into the air.

Andrey Borisovich Nolde, the son of a legal historian in Petersburg, was twelve years old:

There was a fire in the court building on Liteyny Prospect. We could see it from our apartment on the sixth floor. We were living about five hundred meters away as the crow flies. We children did not know what this meant, but our parents explained to us that the city court was burning. Then our mother declared that all three of us were sick, so that we would not go outside the house. We stayed in bed for three days, because my mother insisted that we were so sick that we were not allowed to get up. Finally, we were allowed to go outside. I still remember that there were already long lines in front of the bakeries. There was a rumor that there was not enough bread, so many people rushed to the stores in order to go shopping. On the corner of Furshtalskaya Street and Liteyny Prospect was the well-known delicatessen "Cherepynik." People had been plundering there. The casks of wine had been rolled out of the cellar, and all the wine had been poured out onto the street. A red river was flowing down the street. Afterward, I can still remember the seventh of March, when the victims of the revolution were buried. There were about one hundred and ten dead. It was a very emotional moment. I was there because my entire school had been sent to the burial. The coffins were red, not black. Everyone was buried on the Marskoye Polye (the Field of Mars), where they are still resting to this day.

We were always led from school to the demonstrations—and later on to the events where the agitators spoke. We had to go there, for instance, on May First, the "Day of the Workers." School students, according to the direction of the school, also belonged to the "workers." The schools were run by members of the intelligentsia, who were liberal in their orientation, which at the time meant that they were Social Revolutionary. That was before the Bolsheviks, whose propaganda only really began in the early summer, with the return of the revolutionaries. But the liberals were leftist and hence in favor of the revolution. They believed that the czarist government was unable to master the problems of the country. People wanted to have a Constitutional Assembly, but this kept on being put off. Finally, it was to happen in October, but the seizure of power by the Bolsheviks put an end to that. My father left office by May, after the resignation of Foreign Minister Milyukov. The difference between the socialists, who were not identical with the later Bolsheviks, and the Party of the Cadets, was chiefly that the latter, as members of a bourgeois Constitutional Democratic Party (abbreviation: Cadets) were on the side of the ruling constitution and order and thus more in favor of an evolutionary solution than of a revolutionary one.

Vladimir Semyonovich Averino was thirteen years old at the time:

In those days, every sort of order seemed to have collapsed. There were also constant arrests, and we had the impression that chaos and randomness ruled everywhere. Our teachers were Englishmen, and I believe that they were satisfied with the revolution—after all, people wanted some kind of a change back then. My Swiss tutor even believed that this was a good development, and he put himself on the side of the revolutionaries. In October, when we finally made the decision to emigrate, he did not want to go with us. He wanted to stay there. Later, I met him again in Lausanne. He had become a commander of the Swiss police. So it is apparent that his convictions quickly evaporated.

Question: "Was there more chaos before, during, or after Kerensky?"[2]
Averino: "Before, during, and after him."

Yelena Sacharova was already twenty-three years old and married when she experienced the February Revolution:

At that time, I was in Petersburg, where my son was born. I lived at number 12 Kiroshnaya Street. There I saw the beginning of the horrors of the revolution. My mother and I were dumbfounded when the soldiers marched by with their flags. We could sense that a new age was on its way. I had already experienced the first revolution in 1905. Back then, though, I was still very young. In 1917, it was a question of the leftist party and the whole situation in the country, the supply problems, exhaustion with the war. My mother sent flour to the countryside, where I was living—we had an estate in the Tversk District—and I was surprised about it. I could not know that because of poor supplies there was hardly anything to eat in the city. We had certainly been good to our peasants, and I believe it to be untrue that any kind of uprising came from that direction. But there were a number of revolutionary people in the city always, and it was only a question of the precise moment in order to make the powder keg explode.

My father, who was serving in the military at the time—he was general adjutant of the Czar in his entourage official visits in Moscow or abroad —was asked by the Czar to go to Saratov when there was unrest there. Back then, Stolypin was still alive. He was the governor there.[3] My father stayed at his house during this time. One day—it was before breakfast —the servant announced that someone wanted to speak with my father. A woman was led in. She had a letter of recommendation in her hand. She gave it to my father. The moment he began to read it, she shot him dead. She was a young revolutionary. Her name was Bisenko. Later on, she was taken to court and sentenced to twenty years in Siberia. But when the revolution of 1917 broke out, she was—like many others in internal exile—able to come back. Later she was sent by the Soviets as an official delegate to Brest-Litovsk.

Between the first and the second revolution, Stolypin brought about many reforms, and the Revolution of 1917 would not have had to happen if there had not been a leftist party,[4] and if it had not been for the catastrophic situation in the capital.

General Alexeyev tries to locate the revolutionary forces:

After the liberal actions of some of the members of the government, which made it possible to institute military discipline, almost the entire thing collapsed. There were incidents of soldiers taking away their officers' weapons and forming committees in order to decide certain things themselves. There was unrest as a result of unemployment, inflation, and food shortages. It was impossible for agriculture and industry to keep up with the demands of the war. At that point, the war was lost, as far as the Russians were concerned.

Students at the universities had various opinions, but even for them the change came too suddenly. About fifty percent of them were prerevolutionary, another fifty percent were anti. In spite of this, they did help in attempting to restore order. They got weapons from the police and patrolled the streets on a twenty-four-hour basis. They went to sleep almost in full uniform, with their weapons at the ready.

Yekaterina Volkonskaya:

At the beginning of the war, I had just finished school. After that, I went to an accelerated course in order to become a nurse. At first, I worked in Petersburg, then in a train that took wounded soldiers from Warsaw to Petersburg. When there were no more beds available in Petersburg, they were taken to other provinces. There were a lot of wounded soldiers. In those days, I happened to be working in Petersburg. When the shooting began on the streets, I had to stay in the hospital for several days, because it was too dangerous to walk home.

On the day that the czarist regime was finally to be toppled by the revolutionaries in Petrograd and the Duma established for the first time a council (Soviet) of Workers and Soldiers Deputies,[5] Vasily Vitalyevich Shulgin, a liberal member of the Duma, woke up to a sample of what 12 March (27 February) was to bring:

It was nine o'clock in the morning. The telephone was ringing and ringing.
"Hello?"
"Is that you, Vasily Vitalyevich?" It was Shingaryev.
"It's time to go to the Duma. It has begun."
"What are you talking about?"
"It's begun. There's been an order to disarm the Duma. The city is in an uproar. Hurry! They're taking over the bridges. We may not be

able to get through. A car has been sent for me. Come at once to my house, we'll drive together."

"I'm coming."

That was the morning of the 27 February 1917. In the last few days, we had truly been living on the edge of a volcano. Petrograd was without bread, transportation had collapsed—among other things because, in addition to everything else, there had been unusually strong snowfalls, ice —and then everything that had to do with the war. There were battles on the streets. They were directed in general against the government. One could hardly find anyone on the streets who was in favor of the government. But as if that weren't enough, the government itself wasn't on its own side. There was not a single minister who believed in himself or in what he was doing. There was no one who could really slam his fist down on the table. Toward the end, the ministers simply stopped even coming to the Duma.

"That is the answer," said Shingaryev, as we were driving to the Duma. We had gotten to Kamenostrovsky Boulevard. In spite of the time, which was relatively early for Petrograd's standards, the streets were full of people. One had the impression that the factories were revolting, because on the Vyborg side of the Neva, in the workers' part of town, the workers were jammed together in massive street meetings. But even our side, the area on the right bank of the Neva, where all the palaces and government buildings, as well as banks and businesses, was full of masses of people who were walking slowly to the Duma. Amid them, as if to spite them, came a burial procession with the coffin of Duma member Alexeyenko. Our car was only able to get through the crowded streets because we were recognized as members of the Duma by policemen fighting desperately for order, and also by some members of the crowd.

Before we managed with great exertion to get to the Duma building, Shingaryev said, "Right up to the last moment I was hoping that they[6] would see the light and agree to make concessions. But no; they even disolved the Duma. That was their last chance: to make an agreement with the Duma—any kind of agreement, in order to prevent a revolution. It was the last chance."

"Do you think this is the beginning of a revolution?"

"It looks like it."

"Then it's the end."

"Perhaps the end. Perhaps the beginning."

"No, I can't believe that. If this is a revolution, then it's the end."

"You may be right. Unless we start believing in miracles—which can

also happen. At any rate, the Duma was what stood between the government and a revolution. If the Duma is swept away, then we will stand
face to face with the crowds on the street. If only we could last out for
another two months."

"Until the offensive?"

"Exactly. If the offensive goes badly, we'll have a revolution anyway.
But if it succeeds. . . ."

"Then everything would be forgotten."[7]

The French correspondent from *Le Temps*, Loudovic Naudeau, was
also a witness to the climax of the unrest in February, on that day when
the mass of demonstrators marched toward the Russian parliament in
the Taurian Palace:

> A stream of people drunk with joy, some of them soldiers, some
> workers, students, and women with children took over the Palace of
> Justice, the prison, the arsenal and the Peter-Paul Fortress. They were
> all greatly enthusiastic on this unfortunate Monday. All the police stations
> went up in flames. All the prisons were opened. Entire companies of
> soldiers were happy and friendly, because they did not have to fight any
> more. They distributed their weapons and ammunition among the people.
> Thousands of weapons disappeared in this way. They were carefully kept
> by the factory workers, and later they formed the first provisions for the
> Red Guard.

This depiction is filled with a romantic picture of the revolution.
The Palace of Justice, like the telegraph office and the Peter Paul
Fortress, were all in fact taken by a well-planned action of the Soldiers'
Council of the Provisional Government.

Vladimir Zenzinov gives a picture of the Duma, where—despite the
order to disband—an emergency session was being held, with petitions
from workers' and soldiers' delegations:

> It is almost impossible to describe the way the building looked during
> those days. That was where the heart of the revolution was beating. The
> first revolutionary government began there. Groups of soldiers and sailors
> who had gone over to the side of the people were streaming constantly to
> the building, encircling it with huge crowds on all sides. On the inside,
> there was intensive activity. Here, the crowd came to a halt, and this was
> where the revolutionary organizations and the Provisional Government,

which had now been called into being, held their sessions in various rooms. Rifles were strewn around on the ground as were cases of ammunition, dynamite, and hand grenades.

It was not just petitions which were carried in by the revolutionaries. Ministers were dragged in too. Kerensky proudly claims in his memoirs to have saved Suchomlinov, the former Minister of War, from lynching by an angry mob on that night in the Duma:

> I was the only person still standing between him and his attackers. I yelled at them, saying that I would not allow them to kill him, thus besmirching the name of the revolution. I explained that they would only be able to get to him over my dead body. For a moment, they were undecided, but then I won the game.

At midnight on 27 February (12 March), the Executive Committee of the Imperial Duma was formed. Among its members were Rodsyanko, Kerensky, Cheidse, Shulgin, Milyukov, and others. Prince Lvov became the prime minister. The Petersburg Workers and Soldiers Council was officially called into being, and made an appeal to the population of Petrograd for the condemnation of the old government. The Military Commission of the Provisional Committee of the Imperial Duma took over the train station of Zarskoye Syelo, an electric power plant, and other important points in the city.

Alarmed by reports about the unrest, the Czar left the headquarters in Mogilyev for Zarskoye Syelo. He intended to give in to the urgent appeal that had been made to him by his advisers and his own brother Michayl Alexandrovich, who wanted him to form a new government. But by now it was too late. His train was stopped in Pskov. Representatives of the Duma were on their way to him in order to urge him to abdicate.

Later on, Trotsky will summarize those days from the point of view of the historical necessity of class struggle:

> In November, the people's revolution was directed on a day-to-day basis by the party. Its press articles, explanations, and reports give evidence of an outward continuity in the struggle. This was not the case in March. Here the masses were for all intents and purposes without direction from above. The March disturbances were not accompanied by any kind of press. The masses themselves were making history. We will probably

never be able to get a real picture of what was happening on the streets at the time. It is difficult to perceive any kind of continuity or inner logic.

The March Revolution had been initiated from above with the intention of breaking the resistance of revolutionary organizations through concessions. It was the most exploited and suppressed parts of the population that took the initiative—the proletariat, such as the female textile workers, of whom many were without a doubt the wives of soldiers. The lack of bread, which was getting out of hand, served as the decisive stimulus. Almost 90,000 workers, men and women, were on strike on that day (23 February/8 March). Their will to fight was expressed in demonstrations, meetings, and fights with the police. The movement began in the Vyborg District, with its huge industrial facilities. Elsewhere there were no strikes or demonstrations, if one can believe the reports of the secret police.

Red flags appeared in various parts of the city—with slogans for bread and against the autocratic regime and the war. Women's Day went successfully, with enthusiasm and without any casualties. By the end of the day, we were not yet able to see what that day would ultimately bring. On the next day, the masses of people had not grown less; they had doubled. What was significant was that the crowd did yell, "Down with the police!" who were called in against them, but they greeted the cossacks with shouts of "Hurray!" They threw stones, bottles, and blocks of ice at the police, among other things. On the other hand, they were friendly to the soldiers. This meant a new phase of the revolution: brotherhood between the workers and the army. Such a phase is necessary in every revolution.

This is the diary description of a writer, who, like many intellectuals, glorified the revolution at the onset:

Automobiles speed by, splashing dirty water onto the walls of the buildings and spraying the pedestrians who are marching through the streets. Shouting masses of people, soldiers and sailors, a pointed screen of bayonets. Here and there is the report of a rifle. Revolution! The Russian nation is acting as if it has gone crazy, confused by the newborn freedom, which it is trying somehow to touch and feel with its hands.

In Alexander Park, there is a gardener who is all alone immersed in his work. A small build, about fifty. Rather awkward, but patient and peaceful, he is raking in the leaves that had fallen in the autumn of the previous year, clearing paths and flower gardens from the snow which had just fallen. He is not paying the slightest attention to the loud activity and shouting around him, and he is deaf to the trampling, cries, and singing of the hordes, as well as to the shots. He does not even see the red flags that are being carried past him. I look at him to see if he might look up after all and see the masses going by him or the trucks filled with shining bayonets. But he continues to bend over his work, as intent on what he is doing as a mole. And perhaps he is just as blind as a mole, too.

In the meantime, the rapidly formed Executive Committee took its first steps. Kerensky had the ministers arrest the Czar and take him to the Peter-Paul Fortress, with its rich history of political prisoners. Zarskoye Syelo, where the Czarina had been waiting with her five children for the arrival of the Czar, was put under guard on Kerensky's order by the soldiers of the Petrograd Soviet. The capital itself was divided into military districts, each headed by a commander. Bridges and important buildings, such as the telegraph office and the National Bank, were occupied.

A delegation of representatives of the Provisional Committee of the Imperial Duma, chaired by A.I. Guchkov and W.W. Schulgin met on 2 (15) March in Pskov. The Czar had already heard of the events in Petrograd, informed by a flood of telegrams from the capital and from High Commander General Alexeyev in headquarters. Rodsyanko, Grand Duke Michayl Alexandrovich, and Alexeyev had appealed to him in their notes for concessions, the convocation of a legislative assembly, and the appointment of a responsible cabinet. But the directive to form a new cabinet came too late. Now the three men believed the Czar's abdication to be necessary for—as they formulated it—"the salvation of the country and of the dynasty."

At first, Generals Danilov and Russky (commander of the northern front) spoke to the Czar, who received them in the parlor wagon of his train. Russky:

I handed him the strip of paper covered with telegraphic characters. He took it and read it through carefully. In it was a report from Danilov to Alexeyev about the situation in the city, the behavior of disloyal troops and their desire to fight on to a victorious end to the war, but also including their desire to force the Czar to abdicate. Then he stood up, walked to the window, and looked out thoughtfully. I too had risen. After a couple of difficult moments of silence, the emperor turned to me and began in a relatively calm voice to go over the situation as it had arisen, mentioning several factors which prevented him from accommodating the wish that had been expressed to him.

In the meantime, telegrams from the high commander as well as from General Bryusilov on the southwest front, General Evert on the western front, and Grand Duke Nicholas Nikolayevich on the Caucasus front arrived. They, too, were in agreement with the idea already expressed by General Alexeyev, urging the Czar to abdicate in favor of his son. According to other reports, however, telegrams which came in urging the Czar to stand tough were kept secret from him.

The Czar decided to give in to the pressure of all these appeals. However, after he had consulted with his doctor and apparently had come to the conclusion that his son Alexey would always be in a state of dangerous health, since there was still no cure for chronic hemophilia, he changed his decision. He finally abdicated for his son, too, in favor of his brother, the Grand Duke Michayl Alexandrovich, thus making moot the question about whether Imperial Law even allowed an abdication that included not only the ruler himself but also his son. It was over: The Czar abdicated for both himself and his son in favor of his brother. General Danilov reported further on this historic occasion, to which Guchkov and Shulgin were also witnesses:

> Nicholas was dressed in his simple Caucasian beshmet (soldiers coat), with epaulets from the Plastun Battalion of His Majesty. A silver dagger hung from his black leather belt with a silver buckle. Guchkov, who was about to deliver a lengthy speech, was interrupted by the emperor:
>
> "Today at three o'clock in the afternoon, I had already given voice to my intention to abdicate. My decision will not be taken back. At first, I had decided to relinquish the throne to my son, Alexey, but then, after I had thought about the situation, I changed my decision. I now desire to abdicate not only for myself but also for my son in favor of my brother Michayl. I want to keep my son by my side, and I am certain"—and here his voice began to waver—"that you will be able to understand the feelings that move me in this." After a short silence, the emperor got up and slowly walked out. We, too, had gotten up, and we followed him silently, with respectful glances at the retreating monarch. Finally, the emperor appeared again. In his hand, he held several white pieces of paper covered with typewriting. This was the text of his manifesto. As far as I can remember, it was the same version that had been formulated in head-

quarters, with few changes. After the representatives had read the contents of the manifesto carefully, they asked him to insert several words into the text which they believed to be necessary; the emperor immediately agreed to do this. Then the emperor wrote two commands to the ruling Senate, one with reference to the appointment of Grand Duke Nicholas Nikolay-evich to be high commander, the other to confirm Prince Lvov as the chairman of the Council of Ministers. This last order was in full agreement with the expressed wish of the representatives. After the emperor had spoken for another couple of moments, he said good-bye; he shook all of our hands, and then the door closed behind him. I never saw the emperor again.

According to other reports, when the Czar was confronted with his abdication he is supposed to have taken off his cap in front of his icon and said: "It is God's will. I should have done it long ago."

The declaration of abdication was dated 2 (15) March, but at the bottom it bears the date of signature one day later:

To the Chief of the General Staff,
Headquarters, 2 (15) March 1917

In the days of the great fight against the external enemy, who for three years has been trying to conquer Our fatherland, God has given Russia new and difficult trials. Domestic difficulties now threaten to have a disastrous effect on the ultimate outcome of this merciless war. The fate of Russia, the honor of Our heroic army, the good of the people, and the entire future of Our dear fatherland demand that the war must at all costs be fought to a victorious conclusion. The brutal enemy is now undertaking his last attempts, and We are not far from the moment when Our renowned army, together with Our glorious allies, will finally defeat the enemy.

In these decisive days for the future of Russia, We considered it to be Our conscientious duty to make it easier for Our people to concentrate all of its energies in close cooperation, so that victory might be achieved quickly. For this reason We, in consultation with the Imperial Duma, have decided that the good is best served if We give up the Crown of the Russian Empire and lay down the Highest Rule. As We do not wish to separate Ourselves from Our beloved son, We designate as Our dynastic successor Our brother the Grand Duke Michayl Alexandrovich, to whom We give Our blessing in his rise to the throne of the Russian Empire. We give Our brother the duty of running the government in complete agreement with the representatives of the people in the law-giving bodies, on the basis that will be determined by them, swearing an unbreakable oath to them. In the name of Our dearly-beloved home, We call upon all true sons of the fatherland to fulfill their holy duty with respect to it, obeying the Czar in this difficult moment of national trial, and helping him together with the representatives of the people to lead the Rusian Empire on the path of victory, of honor, and of glory.

May the Lord God save Russia!

Pskov, 3 (16) March 1917, 15:05

(sig.) Nicholas

The Minister of the Imperial Court

Adjutant General (sig.) Count Frederickz

The formulation for the continuation of the war until victory was at this time still a binding slogan even in circles that were not loyal to the dynasty. Soon the patriotism which still supported the war would disappear, torpedoed by agitation. The idea that the evil of war was brought on by God was to be found even in the early Russian chronicles, where, for instance, the rule of the tartars was referred to as a trial given by God. As for the blessing for the brother of the Czar, it must be remembered that the Russian Czar was also formally the spiritual head of his country.

On the day of the signing of this declaration, Czar Nicholas sent a telegram to his brother:

To His Imperial Majesty Michayl

Pskov, 3 (16) March 1917

The events of the last few days have forced me to take this step, from which I cannot turn back. Forgive me if I am burdening you, and forgive me that I was not in a position to prevent this. I will always remain your faithful and devoted brother. I will now go back to Headquarters, hoping that in a few days I will be able to go to Zarskoye Syelo. I fervently pray to God to help you and your country.

Nicky

Vasiliy Oryechov was among those in Petrograd who were waiting for the return of the special train with the representatives of the Imperial Duma from Pskov:

I was standing in the massive crowd of people which was waiting for the delegation in front of the train station. Gushkov and Shulgin came out of the building and walked right by me toward their cars. I can still see Schulgin lifting a piece of paper into the air and calling:

"His Majesty the emperor has abdicated, long live Czar Michayl the Second!"

Beyond that, I cannot remember a thing. I and all the others were devastated. But despite everything the news of the abdication of the Czar in favor of his brother meant that the monarchy would be preserved. There were so many mixed feelings at the time, depression about the situation, war fatigue, and we had to accept any solution.

A young officer:

On that day, when I walked across the Liteyny (Prospect) I saw bois-terous soldiers striking off the coat of arms of the Czar above a gate. I will never forget that.

Kerensky, the revolutionary minister of justice in the Provisional Committee of the Imperial Duma, began increasingly to seize the initiative for the first measures of the new interim government. He was not particularly interested in preserving the dynasty in the form of a constitutional monarchy. Even before the representatives of the Duma, Guchkov and Shulgino, returned from Pskov with the abdicational declaration, he had already been informed via telegram of the contents of the document and put himself into contact with Grand Duke Michayl Alexandrovich. Painting a dramatic picture of a population up in arms against the country's leadership (by which he probably meant the Czar), he left little hope for an improvement in the situation as long as a Romanov continued to sit at the head of the empire even as a figurehead. On the very same day, 3 (16) March, the declaration of the abdication of Grand Duke Michayl Alexandrovich was also published:

A difficult task has been entrusted to me by the will of my brother, who gave me the Imperial throne at a time when the country is troubled by unrest and the confusion of war. Filled with the same idea as the people, that the good of the country goes before everything else, I have decided to take on the highest power only if this is in agreement with the will of all the people. This will should be expressed by the people's representatives in the legislative assembly. Praying to God for his blessing on the citizens of Russia, I call upon all Russians to obey the Provisional Government which has been formed and entrusted with all power by the

Duma, until, within a very short time and on the basis of general, direct, equal, and secret enfranchisement, a constitutional assembly expresses the will of the people and determines the new form of government.

3 (16), March 1917   Michayl

Kerensky was pleased with this decision, as shown by his reply to the Grand Duke, which Kerensky recalls in his memoirs: "Your Royal Highness, you have acted as a noble and true patriot. I promise you my full backing and will defend you from any condemnation."

If one is to believe the report of Princess Paley, the removal of the Romanov Dynasty from power in Russia, which a regency by Grand Duke Michayl Alexandrovich would have prevented, was in fact a cloak-and-dagger affair. Her husband, the Czar's uncle, Grand Duke Paul, had just informed the Czarina of the abdication in favor of Michayl:

> Grand Duke Michayl Alexandrovich fled from the Winter Palace, in front of which aggressive troops had begun gathering, to his friend Putyatin. There he received an unexpected visit from several members of the Duma, who had come to convince him to give up the throne in favor of the people, who would later elect him or someone else. After hesitating a bit, this weak prince gave in, to the joy of the betrayers of their fatherland.

Many observers of this period believed that only a government loyal to the Romanov Dynasty would provide the guidance necessary for the population and the army in this phase of the war. The Duma's representatives, and above all Kerensky, are frequently called "betrayers of the fatherland" by such observers. Their view is confirmed by the initial doubts in military circles about whether it was at all possible to swear an oath to the Provisional Government.

Colonel Dubenzev, like several other eyewitnesses of those days, saw Grand Duke Michayl's abdication as having been responsible for the events that were to follow, since it meant that there was no more identification with a monarchy that held the Russian Empire together. "All he wanted to have was peace of mind," it is said.

Vasily Oryechov, on the other hand, gives another version of events. According to him, the Grand Duke agonized greatly over his decision (which, by the way, did not save him from being murdered by the Bolsheviks):

Though it is true that we were able to see the necessity for the czar's abdication due to political consideration, we were absolutely unable to understand the abdication of Grand Duke Michayl Alexandrovich.

Many years later—around the year 1927 or 1928—I was in Paris, where the widow of the Grand Duke, Princess Brasova, made an interesting remark to me. "You cannot imagine what kind of a situation my husband found himself in. A delegation came from the Imperial Duma. He hesitated. The only person begging the Grand Duke not to abdicate was (Foreign Minister) Milyukov, who later became the leader of the Republicans. He said to him at the time—and I am quoting him literally: 'Your Imperial Highness, without you we will not survive this stormy time.' But all the others, whether monarchists or people who later became Octobrists, insisted on his abdication—that is, the transfer of power to the Provisional Government until the Constitutional Convention." Princess Brasova also told me that her husband had walked like a wounded lion from one room to another and finally gone to the window, from which he could look out over the Angliyskaya Nabyeryeshnaya (English River Bank Street). In doing this, he said, "If I were to see just one single disciplined company down below, I would know what I have to do."

But all he could see through the window were immense crowds of people with red arm bands. So he felt that he was forced to give in.

Among most of us officers, our first thought was to bring the war to a successful conclusion. We believed that our first duty was to fight, and that we would not be able to think about political questions until after the war had ended. That was the general opinion of the officers, at least in the first months of the year 1917. Among the soldiers, of course, the situation was different. Nevertheless, I can report with satisfaction that in my own company and in several others the soldiers had the same thoughts as their officers. But in other companies, the mobilized units were easy prey for the propaganda that had already begun to take root at this time, even before Lenin arrived in Petrograd.

Maria Trubnikova represents the reaction of the unpolitical middle classes, far away from the events in the capital city. At the time, she was a young girl living with her parents in the southern Russian town of Cherson:

On that morning, my mother and some peasant women were sewing padded bandages for wounded soldiers, as they had done ever since the war began. Several days earlier, a peasant who escaped from being a prisoner of war in Austria had come to us. He had not succeeded in getting back to Russia until his third attempt. After his stories, my father had some vodka served up. He also gave the peasant some money.

On this day, I came into my mother's room in order to wish her a good morning. She was holding a telegram in her hands. My younger brother was in her room. When I walked in, she said, "The Czar has abdicated."

I asked her, "What will happen now?"

But she just wrung her hands and muttered that she did not know what would happen. That impressed me and distrubed me at the same time. It was extraordinary for me that my mother, who always knew everything, should suddenly be without a clue.

Back then, there were not yet any disturbances in the provinces, where we lived. That was not to come until later. Those events happened above all in Petrograd and Moscow. Where we lived everything was relatively quiet.

Elisabeth Stenbock-Fermor comes from a family which owned a real estate firm in Odessa at the time. The abdication was met in her family with the following reaction:

In the house where we were living at the time, there was a Greek relative from my grandmother's side. This relative served on the General Staff of the Russian Army in Odessa as an interpreter and code specialist.

Occasionally, he was not terribly sure of his Russian. One day, he suddenly asked, "Do you spell otrecheniye (the Russian word for abdication) with a 'ya' or a 'ye'?" This was the day when news spread that the Czar had abdicated. In school, we learned about it from our teacher. At the time, people were still saying "in favor of his brother." My brother was eighteen at the time and came home on leave three days later. He said, "If the Czar himself had not abdicated, we would fight for him, since we have sworn an oath to him. Probably there would be a civil war then." People had told him that a civil war should not be risked during the middle of the war. The abdication of the Czar, they said, was the only way to prevent this.

Many young people felt this way. They really believed that the Provisional Government and the constitution would solve the country's problems. It was only the older people who could see what was really happening and where it would lead."

On that day, dinner, which usually started right on time at seven o'clock, started very late. We had servants and kitchen help. But they were all sitting down below and crying, because the Czar had deserted them. They had the feeling that something horrible had happened, something which could not be taken back. They didn't have the slightest idea what the Duma, the constitution, or the Constitutional Assembly were, or about any of the things that we knew. Some of them even believed that we were partially to blame for the events, because we had always talked about these things so much.

The housemaids cried at the beginning, too, when everyone was crying. But later, when the new order and the propaganda began to loosen or destroy the old rules of discipline, they were quite enthusiastic, because now they could go out whenever they wanted to. There were no more police—that was the first thing that the committees of the new government got rid of. They replaced the police with the militia. This consisted partly of students who possessed no training of any kind.

Things became so insecure that we did not dare to go out onto the street anymore in the evening, because people were being robbed and attacked. The real revolutionaries and Bolsheviks did not come to us in Odessa until later, at the end of 1917. But personal security was immediately gone. The city was soon flooded with farmers and soldiers who had deserted the front and come to the Black Sea. Many of them wanted to go somewhere completely different, to their homes in the Ural or in the north. But since they were unable to get there, they stayed in the city. Soon the city was in the hands of armed and unorganized soldiers, who robbed, plundered, and murdered at will. They got together in smaller and smaller groups, which then started fighting among each other. Later they sided with the new rulers, and the representatives of the middle class in the old order were systematically terrorized.

At the time, I was attending a higher course for women. In that month, we had final exams. Usually I went to school on foot and picked up my girlfriend on the way. On one of those days, however, she called me up and said that I should not come under any circumstances, because something was happening in the street. By that time, I was already hearing shots from there. Well, one heard that sort of thing from time to time, and if I didn't go to this exam I could not take it again for six months. Since it was not very far, I went, without telling my mother anything about it. I used a different route from my usual one. I passed the test and decided to return home on the usual, quicker path. Beside my girlfriend's house I saw several dark spots in the snow. There were no more bodies there, but I could still see that five human bodies had just been lying there.

Officer Konstantin Kromyadi was a long way from the Russian capital at the time, on the southern front. But the consequences of the soldiers' council that had been formed there, of "Order Number One," and of the czar's abdication complete with the oath of loyalty that was now to be made to the Provisional Government were immediately noticeable even here. Soldiers now had power over officers:

> One day the sergeant of our company came up to me covered with blood. He reported that his soldiers had beaten him up. "That is betrayal," they were saying, "we are supposed to promise again that we will defend the Russian Empire to the last drop of blood, but at the head of this empire there is no more Czar." I immediately start out, going toward the company, but on the way six to seven hundred soldiers come up to me on the open field. One of them approaches and wants to grab my epaulets. Before he can rip them off, I hit him so hard across the head that he falls down. Immediately, I am surrounded by his comrades. In the meantime, several people from my own troop arrive; the artillery commander of the revolutionary committee seems to be reasonable—he holds his people back. I am taken into a nearby building to be interrogated. Fortunately for me, an entire detachment of my men gradually comes up and declares, "Our commander has always been good to us, and we demand that he be let free!" The city commander was surprised. "Be happy that you were not killed—how can you be so crazy and hit a soldier—in the middle of the revolution!"
>
> That was the way things stood. The loyalty of my soldiers moved me to tears. Now I understood more.

Ivan Stenbock was a lieutenant colonel in the Imperial Russian Regiment at the time. He remembers how his regiment had to swear an oath of loyalty to the Provisional Government after the abdication of the Czar:

> It was a big ceremony. Our colonel, von Wahl, carried the flag of the regiment. But there was a red band on the flag of the cavalry guard. The

military band played. Suddenly, an officer got onto his horse—it was not a regiment horse but rather had belonged to a German prisoner, and now belonged to him—and galoped away. He never came back.

Grigory Grabbe, until recently bishop of the Russian Orthodox Church in New York City, remembers the reaction of his father, who was an officer in Her Majesty's (the Czar mother Maria Fyodorovna's) Bodyguard Regiment. He was stationed at the Turkish front:

> After the abdication of the Czar, my father declared that he was not in agreement with the oath of loyalty to the Provisional Government. He did not want to recognize the government and allowed himself to be put into retirement.
>
> Later on, he was thrown in jail by the Bolsheviks. The last thing I know about him is that he did not want to stop praying. As punishment, he was put in solitary confinement. This last news I have of him comes from a Jew who even later was very thankful for the moral support that he had received from my father in prison. One of our bishops met this Jew later on as a taxi driver in Israel. I never learned where my father died.

General Drenteln of the Preobrashensky Bodyguard Regiment, which was later (from April 1917 on) commanded by Colonel A.P. Kutyepov, reports that of their own free will his soldiers wanted to press on to Pskov, in order to assure him of their devotion even after his abdication, and that they were willing to carry out his orders. He names officers who mobilized their soldiers to go to Petrograd in order to fight the unrest, and who apparently did not know that some of their comrades from the regiment had already taken the side of the people there.

One simple soldier who was serving on the southwestern front already had a clearly defined idea that it was assistance "from above"— from the government and members of the military—which made the fall of the regime possible:

> Several officers who were coming back from the capital reported that the situation was tense. That was at the beginning of the February unrest. There were rumors of irregularities in the factories, of demonstrations and difficulties with supply, above all with bread. Later it became known

that these problems had all been caused artifically—by people with revolutionary ideas, by socialists, and by all those who wanted to provoke unrest and weaken the army. Why? In order to prevent the continuation of the war. German secret agents were everywhere, even in the factories, and they knew how to win over the working classes to their cause. These agents did everything they could to poison the morale of the army, especially in the replacement battalions which were stationed in Petrograd—and they were successful.

Two weeks before the Czar's abdication, major revolts had been expected in the capital. We heard rumors that our guard division was being prepared for a possible assignment in Petrograd, where it was to restore order at the command of the Czar to his chief of staff. But instead of the order that we had expected to go back to Petrograd, all the young officers in the cavalry guard received the order to inspect roads in the western territories—roads that we had only just won back from the Austrians. This order was absolutely idiotic, of course, because the roads were almost impassable anyway. Many were covered with snow, and the rivers could not be crossed. It was obvious that this order from headquarters had been made in order to keep our guard division with its four regiments out of commission. In the events that were to follow, it would no longer have been possible to bring back the young officers fast enough from their duties.

I was traveling through the forests, and at noon I took the food that the Red Cross nurses gave us. I still remember quite clearly that we were connected to the outside world by means of a radio receiver. On this day, we heard through this machine that the Czar had abdicated. When I told my superior this, he broke out in tears. There was also an old gray-haired army colonel sitting at our table. When he heard the tragic news, he began to sob and said, "Now that the Czar has deserted us, I will go and serve the Turkish sultan." This old colonel had lived all his life in the belief that it was his duty to serve one lord and master, and this lord and master was the Czar, who had his power through the grace of God, consecrated to his position in a Moscow church during a solemn ceremony. For this colonel, the Czar's word was the word of God, because the Czar ruled everything and commanded by the grace of God. And now the old colonel was bereft of this highest thing, which he loved and honored. So nothing more was left for him but to declare, sobbing, that he would go over to the Turks, the archenemy of Russia, and serve the sultan. One really has to understand the psychology of such an old, faithful officer in order to know what his words meant.

Count Xaver Schaffgotsch, at that time an Austrian prisoner of the Russians, reports that by then loyal troops by no means controlled the situation at the front:

> After the so-called March [February] Revolution, the entire camp started falling apart, and the Russian guards made friends with us, threw down their weapons, drank tea and smoked with us.

What was the situation in the schools? It became evident that the teachers and principals are in sympathy with the change of government. Vladimir Semyonovich Averino came from a liberal Moscow lawyer's family, but the family's loyalty to the Czar was never open to question:

> I was thirteen years old at the time, and of course I knew nothing about politics. We never talked about it at school. On 3 March 1917, when our principal Olga Nikolayevna Yakovleva called together all 150 students and informed us of the abdication of our lord the Czar, and of the revolution and the new government, the news came like a bolt from a clear blue sky. When she had finished, she asked everyone to start cheering; I don't remember how loud our cheers were, or whether I cheered with them. I can't remember anything but the words, "There is no more czar," and how she said that the pictures of the Czar would be taken down from the walls. Many people were simply horrified.
>
> On that same day, we had to go to the clothing department, where our school tailors sewed red-rimmed buttons onto our uniform jackets. It is only a measure of our political ignorance that, for instance, I, who was so terribly worried about the departure of our leader, nevertheless allowed them to sew a red button onto my jacket.
>
> Toward evening of the same day, I got together with some friends from a higher grade—I was in one of the middle grades—and we decided to stand guard on the steps that night in front of the portrait of the Czar, in order to prevent the principal from taking it down.
>
> Of course, our guard duty—there were five or six of us—was complete nonsense, and no one prevented us from doing it. Not all of us managed to stay all night. But on the next day or the day after that, someone from the administrative office came and took the pictures away while we weren't there.

In the meantime, the ex-Czar Nicholas II went from Pskov back to headquarters in Mogilyev. General N.M. Tichmeyev remembers the Czar's last days at the General Staff:

As if it were happening today, I can still see him in front of me in his gray Kuban Cherkesse.[8] The white Cross of St. George glistened brightly on it. I can still see his left hand, with which he was holding his cossack's dagger and clutching his cap of lamb's wool. His right hand was hanging loosely at his side, but it was trembling. This trembling only stopped once, when he brushed his hand over his mustache mechanically, which was a habit of his. I can still clearly remember his face, which was pale and had grown narrow, sunken in, tired, and expressionless. His eyes— these amber eyes that then turned gray again, which had used to shine so brightly—seemed sad this time. Above all, I can still remember the smile with which he tried to reassure us when the crowd broke out in tears. He was suffering greatly. And yet, he was in every way His Imperial Majesty, the man we had in front of us, the Czar of all the Russians. He was suffering not just for himself, but for all of us, for the army and for Russia. It was not for nothing that he had pressed those who were urging him to abdicate: "Will they be able to get along with the people?" How right he was to have his doubts! They did not get along with the people. He may well have been one of the only people in those days who truly understood how dangerous Russia's situation really was.

One of the ruler's few days at the General Staff was a holiday. The ruler came into the staff church and went up to his place in front, to the left of the priest. The church was packed. During the service came the moment of the "Great Passage," which the priest himself begins from the altar with the words, "The most pious, mightiest, the great ruler, our Czar."

We did not hear these words this time. They had become illegal because of the abdication. Instead we heard others, which had not been foreseen by any kind of canonical rules, and which our staff priest, Father Vladimir, thought up on the spur of the moment. He mentioned the ruler in his prayers in unusual words that we had never heard before. But he mentioned him, nevertheless. "I was not allowed to include him as usual in the prayer," explained Father Vladimir later, "because he was no longer the sole ruler or even the ruler. But I simply couldn't include another prayer [Author's note: for the Provisional Government], because this would have insulted him. And I couldn't just leave him out, since he was standing there next to the altar, where I had grown used to seeing him at every service during the one and a half years that he had spent as commander in chief at the General Staff."

In those times, what this man did was a great risk. But he was not afraid to take that risk.

On the evening of 7 (20) March came a coded telegram from the Ministry for Transportation in Petrograd. In it, we were told that early in the morning of the next day, four members of the Imperial Duma would arrive to take the ruler back to Petrograd. The departure from Mogilyev was set for nine o'clock in the morning. We were forbidden to say anything about it to anyone. We were ordered to prepare the locomotive for the emperor's departure. The point of this shameless secrecy order was evidently to prevent the ruler from having time to prepare for his departure and say good-bye to us. It is unclear to me exactly what they were worried about in Petrograd. What could the rulers in Petrograd have to fear from a man who had just sacrificed himself for his country?

The telegram had not been addressed to me. I learned about it accidentally and insisted that the chief of staff should be notified of it immediately. Otherwise, I said, I would do it myself. My demands were met, and in this way the ruler was informed. The messengers from Petrograd, on the other hand, were delayed because of countless propaganda speeches on the way.

At 10:30 on the morning of 8 (21) March, I learned that the ruler wished to say good-bye to the rank and file of his staff, and that the chief of staff requested us to assemble in as large numbers as possible at 11:00 in the quarters of the general on duty. This was precisely the farewell ceremony that people in Petrograd were evidently trying to prevent.

Right on time at 11:00, the ruler appeared in the door. After he had greeted the chief of staff, he turned to the soldiers and cossacks—they were from His Majesty's Bodyguard, and also from the Regiments of His Majesty and the Georgyevsky Battalion—and greeted them with a quiet voice, as he was always wont to do in enclosed spaces. "We wish Your Imperial Majesty health and happiness," was the response that came as one voice from the lower ranks.

Later on, I was forced to read in the newspapers that the "soldiers of the revolutionary army, conscious of their revolutionary pride, reacted with disdainful silence to the greeting made to them by Nicholas Romanov." All of that is mean-spirited nonsense written by the lackeys of the revolution.

After he had heard the answer from the lower ranks, the ruler quickly walked to the middle of the room and stopped several steps away from me, with his face turned toward us. I could see his face clearly right up to the tiniest details, just as I described it before. Outwardly he was quite calm, and it was only the trembling of his right hand that betrayed his apprehension.

When he stopped, he was silent for a few moments before he began to speak—clearly and comprehensively, as usual. His excitement was evident because occasionally he stopped unexpectedly in the middle of a sentence. I can still remember the first words of his speech exactly: "Today I am seeing you all for the last time. That is the will of God and the result of my decision."

Furthermore, he said that he believed his abdication would be useful for Russia, and that it gave hope for a victorious end to the war. He thanked us for our faithful service to him and the fatherland and asked us to serve the Provisional Government faithfully, conscientiously, and fervently, fighting at all costs to the very end against the "cruel, devious enemy."

The ruler had come to the end. His right hand was no longer trembling. In the room, there was the silence of the grave. No one was coughing; everyone stared without moving at the ruler. Never in my life have I experienced such a total, oppressive deathly silence in a room where, after all, several hundred men were gathered together.

After a quick bow, the ruler went back to the chief of staff. From there, he began a review of all of those present, giving the oldest generals his hand and nodding to the others. When he had again gotten to within a few paces of me, the tension in the room had finally broken. Behind the ruler, someone sobbed loudly. This noise was enough, and now tears and wailing broke out all over the room in various places. People had simply been holding it in before.

Tears were running silently down people's cheeks. Besides sobbing and sniffing, I could also hear whispers: "Quiet, otherwise you will disturb the ruler!" But that was not enough to put an end to this outbreak of feeling and devastation. The ruler turned to the left and to the right and to the people who were sobbing. He tried to smile. But his smile did not succeed, it simply distorted his face. There were tears in his eyes. Nevertheless, he continued with his review.

When he arrived at me, the ruler stopped and asked me with a nod to my subordinates: "Are those your men?"

I, too, was very excited, and I noticed that to the right of me General Yegoreyev was evidently no longer in control of himself; I pushed him forward, holding him around the waist, and replied: "These are my men and this is the chief commissariat officer."[9] The ruler shook his hand and became pensive. Then he looked me directly in the eyes and said, "Remember what I said, Tichmeyev: Do everything in your power to get hold of what the army needs.[10] Now this is more important than ever before. I repeat; I will not be able to rest at night if I know that the army does not have what it needs."

The ruler gave me and Yegoreyev his hand and then continued. When he got to the officers of the Georgyevsky Battalion,[11] which had just gotten back from duty in Petrograd, he gave each of them his hand. The crying in the room got worse and worse. The officers of the Georgyevskiy Battalion, most of whom had been wounded several times and had not yet recovered from their wounds, could not go on anymore. Two of them fainted. At the same moment, a strong bearded Kuban cossack who was standing directly opposite me at the other end of the hall collapsed.

The ruler, who had been looking around everywhere with tears in his eyes during this entire scene, could stand it no longer. He interrupted his review and walked quickly to the door. Everyone rushed after him. In the crush, I could not hear the words of the chief of staff, which he directed to the ruler. All I heard were the last words of General Alexeyev, which he said in a trembling voice: "And now, Your Majesty, allow me to wish you a pleasant journey and, as for the rest, a happy life, inasmuch as that is possible."

The ruler briefly embraced General Alexeyev, kissed him twice, and walked out quickly. I never saw him again.

The situation in Petrograd calmed down for a while. The ambassadors of foreign countries, above all the Allies, were reassured and sent cables back to their countries. This one was sent by the British ambassador Sir Buchanan on 6 (19) March 1917:

Today I had a conversation with Mr. Milyukov (the foreign minister). He expressed satisfaction with the current situation. He admitted that the army was quiet, but that there were still major differences of opinion among the soldiers about whether or not to recognize the new government. The government, he added, would send emissaries to clear up the situation. As far as the post of commander in chief was concerned, he said that Grand Duke Nicholas Nikolayevich, who still had this position, had said himself that he would be forced to resign. I asked about the Constitutional Assembly, and His Excellency Milyukov replied that a call to convene it would be made at the earliest possible opportunity, but he did not say when. About Finland, he said that the project for a decree about Finnish independence would be declared, but that no decisions could be made before the meeting of the Constitutional Assembly.

As far as Poland was concerned, he declared himself firmly against independence and an independent army. He believes that Poland must be autonomous and should have territorial militia that would have to be part of the Russian Army.

According to the reports that I have been receiving, the extreme left wing has lost ground, and I hope that it will never gain political significance. Its goal is to control the land completely and carry on the war independently of the Duma. It is thus anomalous that the Duma, which made a demand for a responsible cabinet, nevertheless has given in to the revolution and will now not have the right to control the government.

Mr. Milyukov, who has just left me, came to the following conclusion about the current situation. The revolution, he says, has cost lives only in Moscow, and now there is complete order there. He believes that the election of the new emperor will stabilize the situation for good. The only candidate who he believes has a chance is Grand Duke Michayl. His Majesty Nicholas II enjoys great popularity after the publication of his manifesto.

Aside from the outdated idea that it would be possible to preserve the dynasty by means of the Czar's brother, the February Revolution certainly did cost human lives in Petrograd, even if the official statistics were smaller than the ones people actually suspect: In Petrograd, 1,443 people died, among them 809 soldiers and 60 officers.

Most important for the Allies, however, was Foreign Minister Milyukov's assurance that the war would be carried on to the end, and his reconfirmation of the "London Protocols" signed in 1914 between Russia, England, and France to the effect that Russia would not engage in a separate peace.

The American ambassador Francis had already suggested to the secretary of state of the United States that the extension of recognition by the United States to the new regime would provide moral support for the government and set an example for other countries to do likewise.

As early as 9 (22) March, the American ambassador in Petrograd read the declaration of recognition:

Mr. Prime Minister! I have the honor as American ambassador and accredited representative of the government of the United States in Russia, in accordance with the directives that have been given to me, to confirm that the government of the United States extends its recognition to the new government of Russia, and that I as ambassador of the United States am happy to continue the connection with Russia under the new government. May the warm relations that exist between our two countries continue, and may they lead to mutual satisfaction and respect.

The Allies' trust proved to be too optimistic. Thanks to increasing concessions by the Provisional Government to the revolutionary wing, such as the one that freed soldiers to a large extent from the requirement of absolute obedience to their superiors, discipline in the army and above all at the front—and this is where it is most important in a war—began to collapse. The government was no longer able to assert its authority, because the gap between the bourgeois committee of the Imperial Duma, in which Kerensky was the only member of the left wing, and the deputies of the Petersburg Workers and Soldiers Soviet was too large.

On 22 May 1917, the Provisional Government relieved the loyal chief of staff Michayl W. Alexeyev of his duties as commander in chief of Russia's armies. He had been one of the last leadership personalities in Russia to remain true to the dynasty. Within half a year, on 27 December 1917, after the October coup had swept away the government, he was to call into being a volunteer army consisting of cadets, cossacks, and landed lords. This army would resist the "Red Army" under the name "White Army." But in the meantime, Alexeyev said good-bye to what remained of the once proud Russian Army, which was now deep in the process of decay. In doing this, he bade farewell to the old Russia:

> For almost three years, we have been walking along the thorny path of the Russian Army together. I have walked with you through the joys of our glorious victories. I have suffered in the depths of my soul in the difficult days of our defeats. But my belief in God's providence has always been unshakable. God leads the Russian people and extends his blessing to the Russian warrior. Even now, when the principles of a military power have begun to grow shaky, I stand firm in this belief. Without it, life would be meaningless.
>
> I bow deeply before you, my comrades in arms. I bow to all of those who have carried out their duty honestly. I bow to those in whom the heart of love to Russia beats. Above all, I bow to those who, in the days

of unrest, maintained their determination to save the fatherland from destruction.

Give honor to your old soldier and former commander in chief.

Remember me fondly!

General Alexeyev.

NOTES

1. The policy of pan-Russianism, which tried to exclude national representatives as much as possible from participation in the government, was to continue in the post-Russian era in every way, right down to the policy of Russification.

2. From March of 1917 on, Kerensky was the minister of justice and thus a member of the Provisional Government. After the resignation of Prime Minister Lvov, he became chairman of the Council of Ministers, which he remained until the Bolsheviks' coup on 25 October 1917, when he fled Petrograd.

3. Stolypin had also been called to Saratov as a result of the peasant unrest.

4. Evidently, Sacharova identifies "leftist" with radical and terrorist groups.

5. The soldiers' councils were later to be the first things that Trotsky got rid of when he was forced to restore order to the army.

6. The chief ministers are evidently being referred to here.

7. Representative Shingaryev, who is being quoted here, was later to be assassinated in a carefully planned action by the Bolsheviks, who were trying to prevent moderate leftists from achieving majority decisions.

8. Soldier's coat of the Kuban cossacks.

9. The commander of a field unit in the rear.

10. General Tichmeyev was responsible for the train transportation of supplies and soldiers in the army.

11. The Geozgyevsky Battalion was a special troop that had been formed during the war from soldiers and officers bearing the Cross of St. George in order to protect headquarters.

General Sacharov, the Czar's general adjutant. He was shot by the revolutionary
Senko.

Concern over the attacks of anarchists (36 died in this attack).

Zensiert
Paul Hoffmann & Co.
Berlin-Schöneberg.

734.

Besuch Kerenski's (X) an der russischen Front.

Kerensky, the war and navy secretary, on the Russian front.

In the streets of Petrograd during the revolution of February 1917.

rge Russian family on their patio.

mily scene in the garden.

The estate of the Kvyatovskaya family, east of Moscow.

View of a typical Russian country house.

ding across the lake on a Sunday.

pical country scene.

Ставка

Начальнику Штаба.

Въ дни великой борьбы съ внѣшнимъ врагомъ,стремящимся почти три года поработить нашу родину,Господу Богу угодно было ниспослать Россіи новое тяжкое испытаніе.Начавшіяся внутреннія народныя волненія грозятъ бѣдственно отразиться на дальнѣйшемъ веденіи упорной войны.Судьба Россіи,честь геройской нашей арміи,благо народа,все будущее дорогого нашего Отечества требуютъ доведенія войны во что бы то ни стало до побѣднаго конца.Жестокій врагъ напрягаетъ послѣднія силы и уже близокъ часъ,когда доблестная армія наша совмѣстно со славными нашими союзниками сможетъ окончательно сломить врага.Въ эти рѣшительные дни въ жизни Россіи, почли МЫ долгомъ совѣсти облегчить народу НАШЕМУ тѣсное единеніе и сплоченіе всѣхъ силъ народныхъ для скорѣйшаго достиженія побѣды и,въ согласіи съ Государственною Думою признали МЫ за благо отречься отъ Престола Государства Россійскаго и сложить съ СЕБЯ Верховную власть.Не желая разстаться съ любимымъ Сыномъ НАШИМЪ,МЫ передаемъ наслѣдіе НАШЕ Брату НАШЕМУ Великому Князю МИХАИЛУ АЛЕКСАНДРОВИЧУ и благословляемъ Его на вступленіе на Престолъ Государства Россійскаго.Заповѣдуемъ Брату НАШЕМУ править дѣлами государственными въ полномъ и ненарушимомъ единеніи съ представителями народа въ законодательныхъ учрежденіяхъ,на тѣхъ началахъ,кои будутъ ими установлены,принеся въ томъ ненарушимую присягу.Во имя горячо любимой родины призываемъ всѣхъ вѣрныхъ сыновъ Отечества къ исполненію своего святого долга передъ Нимъ,повиновеніемъ Царю въ тяжелую минуту всенародныхъ испытаній и помочь ЕМУ,вмѣстѣ съ представителями народа,вывести Государство Россійское на путь побѣды, благоденствія и славы.Да поможетъ Господь Богъ Россіи.

Г.Псковъ.
2 Марта 15 час. 5 мин.1917 г.

Министръ Императорскаго Двора
Генералъ Адъютантъ Графъ Фредериксъ

Николай

Czar Nicholas II's abdication document, dated March 2, 1917.

ar Nicholas II on one of his rare visits to Moscow, (on the extreme left, General
charov).

landlord on his way to church.

General Sacharov (center) with one French and several Russian officers.

e wife of General Sacharov; she died
ring the famine period.

Staff Captains Oryechov and Tchernav-
skiy on the Crimea.

ypical Russian peasant on his way to
scow.

Scenes of the past: Peasants going to
church.

Farewell from yesterday: children playing on an estate.

Vladimir Avyerino as a child on Volga river, around 1917.

"All the News That's Fit to Print."

The New York Times.

THE WEATHER

VOL. LXVI...NO. 21,608. ....   NEW YORK, SATURDAY, MARCH 17, 1917.—TWENTY PAGES.

THE ROMANOFF DYNASTY ENDED IN RUSSIA;
CZAR'S ABDICATION FOLLOWED BY MICHAEL'S;
CONSTITUTIONAL ASSEMBLY TO BE CONVOKED

WIDE REFORMS PLANNED

Universal Suffrage and Full Political Amnesty Are the Bases.

CROWDS CHEER PROMISE

Duma Committee and Workingmen Busy Planning for a Constituent Assembly.

FOOD PRICES FALL RAPIDLY

Calm Restored in Petrograd, but Partisans of Old Régime Are Still Being Arrested.

LONDON, Saturday, March 17.—Universal suffrage in elections to be held for members of a new constituent Assembly and full political amnesty will be features of the new régime in Russia, according to dispatches from Petrograd. In fact, Deputy Kerenski, the new Minister of Justice, who is a Socialist, accepted the portfolio on the stipulations that there should be absolute freedom of speech and of the press, and full political amnesty, and that the Assembly should be convoked.

Addressing an assemblage of thousands of soldiers and civilians from the gallery of the lobby of the Duma, M. Kerenski, says a Reuter dispatch from Petrograd, dated yesterday, announced that the Provisional Government took office by virtue of an agreement with workingmen's and soldiers' delegates. The council of these delegates approved the agreement by several hundred votes to 15. The first act of the new Government, M. Kerenski stated, was the immediate publication of a decree of full amnesty. Continuing, the Minister said:

"Our comrades of the second and fourth Dumas, who were banished illegally to the tundras of Siberia, will be released forthwith. In my jurisdiction are all the Premiers and Ministers of the old régime. They will answer before the law for all crimes against the people."

"Show them no mercy," many voices in the crowd exclaimed.

"Comrades," M. Kerenski replied, "regenerated Russia will not have recourse to the shameful methods utilized by the old régime. Without trial none will be condemned. All prisoners will be tried in open court.

"Comrades, soldiers, citizens, all measures taken by the new Government will be published. Soldiers, I ask you to co-operate. Free Russia is now born, and none will succeed in wresting liberty from the hands of the people. Do not listen to the promptings of the agents of the old régime. Listen to your officers. Long live free Russia!"

The speech was greeted by a storm of cheering.

The labor leader, Cnkveidse, addressing the officers and soldiers, paid a glowing tribute to the soldiers and workingmen who had participated in accomplishing the revolution. He recounted the recent provocative efforts by the secret police in publishing proclamations regarding the murders of officers by soldiers. He exhorted the soldiers to regard their officers as citizens who had helped raise the revolutionary flag and as brothers in the great cause of Russian liberty.

Subsequently officers, soldiers, and workingmen carried M. Chkveidse on their shoulders through a cheering throng of soldiers and civilians.

Apparently the new Provisional Government is proceeding promptly to organize itself on a stable basis, to reconstitute the Governmental departments, and prepare steps for the vigorous carrying on of the war. There is no sign of serious hindrance to the completion of the work of this extraordinarily swift and successful revolution.

Former Premiers Golitsine and Goremykin have been placed in the Fortress of St. Peter and St. Paul, as have Generals Soukhomlinoff and Bellaeff, former Ministers of War; A. B. Protopopoff, former Minister of the Interior; J. G. Chtcheglovitoff and M. Makaroff, former Ministers of Justice, and M. Malakoff and General Kurloff, former Chiefs of Police. Other prominent persons under arrest are being detained temporarily in the Duma Building.

It is announced that there will be no further trials for political offenses, and that the Government has opened the bar to Jewish lawyers, who have been excluded heretofore.

At a conference of the members of the Duma Executive Committee and delegates representing the workmen, which lasted until 5 o'clock this morning, says a dispatch from Petrograd, an agreement was reached concerning the transitional period before the election of a constituent assembly. The executives insisted on the interests of the war on the necessity of order being re-established before holding the elections.

Search Houses for Sharpshooters.

Calm has been quickly restored in Petrograd, although numerous partisans of the old régime have been firing from roofs and garrets upon the troops and inhabitants. By order of the Executive Committee soldiers have entered the houses where firing is taking place and removed suspected persons.

Thousands of the police have been imprisoned. All the police stations have been destroyed or sacked, and all suspected houses are being searched for ammunition and arms.

According to a dispatch sent from Petrograd yesterday afternoon, the State Bank and all the private banks reopened during the day.

Stringent orders have been issued for the rearrest of a number of criminals who escaped during the liberation of political prisoners. Some of them, disguised as soldiers, have been pillaging private houses and threatening their occupants. Official orders have been issued that the criminals are to be shot at sight if they offer resistance to arrest. Genuine patrols and search parties are wearing distinguishing signs and also carry written authorizations.

Among the latest persons arrested is the Countess Klein-Michael, who is well known in Court circles and for a long time has been conspicuous on an intriguer and a tool for the dissemination of pro-German propaganda. Hitherto she had enjoyed immunity because of influential connections. The Countess was taken under guard to the Duma Building.

The factories have formed a police service for patrolling the factory districts, enrolling one out of every ten of their workmen.

The question of naming officers to replace those who were disarmed by their own troops is one which will be decided promptly.

In the present spirit of the officers and the men in the ranks there is no reason to apprehend disciplinary troubles, as the officers rejoice equally with the men in the overthrow of the autocracy. The officers have issued a proclamation to their men, in which they refer to the "accursed old régime."

There will be a great parade of troops in Petrograd today before the new Ministers.

In the meantime the Provisional Government is doing its utmost to straighten out the numerous tangles. The Duma and the Zemstvo Council are working hand in hand, although issuing separate proclamations.

Despite the non-appearance of newspapers the public is better informed of what is going on than ever before. A special squadron of motor cars has been commandeered by the Executive Committee, and these cars go about the city distributing printed bulletins free to everybody. Thus the most authentic news gains speedy circulation.

Through this "in service President Rodzianko has . . .lied earnestly to the people not to in.. a Government buildings, telegraphs, the water supply equipment, factories, &c., and also to continue the public services and avoid bloodshed.

In the meanwhile he is energetically tackling the food problem, and the public is confident that the combined efforts of the Duma and the Zemstvo will soon assure an adequate supply. Large stores of flour have been uncovered in various parts of the city. The prices of food are falling rapidly in the city.

A minor instance of the popular feeling was shown when the appearance of a few intoxicated persons on the streets caused such indignation that the culprits were promptly imprisoned.

GAVE UP SON'S RIGHTS, TOO

Czar Yielded at Midnight Thursday; Grand Duke Michael Yesterday.

DUMA IS NOW IN CONTROL

Executive Committee Acting with Cabinet It Chose After the Revolution.

NATION BACK OF CHANGE

New Ministers Assume Their Duties and Are Starting Preparations to Push the War.

PETROGRAD, Friday, March 16, 5 P. M., (via London, Saturday, March 17.)—Emperor Nicholas abdicated at midnight last night on behalf of himself and the heir apparent, Grand Duke Alexis, in favor of Grand Duke Michael Alexanderovitch.

Trains Are Rushing Food to Hungry Russian Cities

LONDON, March 16.—"Train service has continued throughout the revolution," says Reuter's Petrograd correspondent in a dispatch dated this afternoon. "Hundreds of previously idle cars are now rushing supplies to the populous centres, which actually faced starvation. Grain stores everywhere may be requisitioned at fair prices, and estates of over 125 acres may be taken over temporarily by the Local Committee.

"The Government has appealed to the conscience and sense of duty to humanity of the peasants to bring forward all the grain possible, saying that the nation is placed on its honor to do everything to relieve the food situation."

At 2:30 o'clock this afternoon Grand Duke Michael himself abdicated, thus bringing the Romanoff dynasty to an end.

The Government, pending a meeting of the Constitutional Assembly, is vested in the Executive Committee of the Duma and the newly-chosen Council of Ministers.

A manifesto to this effect was issued by the Duma Committee today and it will be telegraphed to the General Army Headquarters this evening.

Unless improbable events occur, Russia has today become a republic.

The outcome depends on how the manifesto of the new Government is received by the 6,000,000 soldiers at the front.

Except for the unqualified rejection of the throne by the Czar Nicholas II.'s only brother, the Grand Duke Michael, the Romanoff-Holstein dynasty might be preserved by any number of Czar Nicholas's kinsmen. But the title of Autocrat, since the days of the first Michael Romanoff, in 1613, may only be conferred by a Romanoff. As the Czar chooses no successor after the Grand Duke Michael, and the Grand Duke names no successor at all, the dynasty ends as a reigning house unless a new Government places it upon the throne. Even so, the Romanoffs might decline to recognize the authority of such a Government, as they assert that their right to reign and rule is entirely independent of the will of the people.

The house of Romanoff is descended from Andrei Romanoff, who is said to have gone to Moscow from Prussia in the fourteenth century. Michael Feodorovitch Romanoff was the first of the family to ascend the throne. This was in 1613, when he was 17 years old. He died in 1645. The direct male line of the Romanoffs terminated in 1730 and the female line in 1762, when the Holstein-Gottorp branch came into power and has since ruled.

Chapter Four

——————//——————

The Red Wheel

Lenin's departure from Zürich in the "sealed train" and the impact of revolutionary agitation at the front.

Petrograd, spring of 1917. Even after the abdication of Czar Nicholas II under the pressure of the revolutionary wave and at the urging of his own ministers, the situation in the capital city failed to calm down. All over there were uprisings, which even spread to Moscow. In addition to cries from the population for bread, there were now mutinies involving demoralized soldiers and deserters from the front, who made common cause with the revolutionary factory workers.

The time had come for Lenin in Zurich to manipulate the situation in the direction he desired, so that he could fulfill his revolutionary objective.

Via his intermediary Ganetzky, Lenin made contact with the Central Committee in Petrograd, which telegraphed a reply: "Ulyanov should come immediately."[1]

The signal for Lenin's long-planned departure from Zurich had come.

German financing of the Russian revolutionaries extends further back than 1917, because the Germans' need for peace on their Eastern front existed even earlier than that. Hence the Germans already had contact with the Russian revolutionaries, whose seizure of power meant for the Germans the possibility of a peace treaty. To recapitulate.[2]

Alexander Helphand-Parvus, Jewish Russian revolutionary in exile, former participant in the Revolution of 1905 and later a cofounder, with

Trotsky, of the Petrograd Soviet, spent the beginning of the war in Constantinople, where he was involved in dubious financial transactions with the Turkish government.

Then came Turkey's entry into the war on the side of Germany and Austria-Hungary. Immediately after that, on 9 January 1915, the German ambassador in Constantinople suggested to his superior, State Secretary Zimmermann of the Foreign Office in Berlin, that he meet with Parvus. Reason: to assist Russian revolutionary organizations that carried out subversive (with respect to the Russians) and pacifist propaganda.

On 13 January 1915, Parvus, who before that point had been ordered out of Germany several times, was received in the Imperial headquarters by a civil servant (who was later to become an adviser to Count Mirbach, the first German ambassador to Soviet Russia in Moscow in 1918).

On 9 March 1915, the German Ministry of Foreign Affairs received a long memorandum, signed by a certain "Doctor Helphand," which contained a detailed and extensive plan for the organization of a "political mass uprising" in the center of Petrograd—which, among other things, would cause a complete paralysis of the rail routes leading to the front. Parvus went on to explain tactics for the seizure of power by means of a propagandistically inspired general strike and the creation of "revolutionary committees." Among the tactics taken into consideration were: the involvement of national separatists from the Ukraine and the Caucasus, as well as Turkish and other minorities, in order to help the revolution; support for propagandistic agitation; the creation of coalitions between appropriate groups in Odessa and Bucharest and between sailors in the Baltic fleet and others in Antwerp; the construction of figureheads in Italy, Copenhagen, and Stockholm, etc. Lenin was already shown by the memo to be the leader of the Bolshevik faction of the Russian Social Democratic Party that was now to receive German support.

Parvus demanded two million gold marks as initial financing. He received them immediately.

On 26 March, the German middleman Fröhlich wrote to von Bergen, the ambassador-level diplomat who was dealing with Parvus:

Re: Doctor Alexander Helphand-Parvus.
  The German Bank has transferred 500,000 marks to me, which I enclose here. I would like to point out that the sums given to Parvus do

not take into account losses resulting from conversion and exchange of funds in Copenhagen, Bucharest, and Zurich.

On 6 January 1915, the German foreign minister wrote to the German treasury requesting five million marks for the support of revolutionary propaganda in Russia in accordance with paragraph six on "extraordinary budget items."

With the help of such funds, it was not difficult for Parvus to set up an appropriate central headquarters in Copenhagen with the false cover name "Institute for International Economic Research." It served as a contact office with Berlin on the one hand and with Petrograd on the other—both before and after Lenin's arrival. Eventually, even more money flowed into strengthening the Bolshevik Party in Russia, bringing it to power—and keeping it there.[3]

Reports from the German ambassador in Bern, Freiherr von Romberg, to his home office in Berlin, described the reaction of the revolutionaries who had been assisted in this way, as well as Lenin's plans in the event of a revolution. Von Romberg wrote, not without a trace of humor, that Bucharin was so excited about the action that he was unable to sleep for an entire night and simply could not comprehend that even his book *War and the Working Class* had been financed with the help of this German money.

At the behest of the government in Berlin, the German embassy in Bern took care to organize plans for the transit of the revolutionaries not only through Swiss and German territory but also through other countries as well. The German Kaiser himself was concerned that the transit go as smoothly as possible. On 12 April 1917, the representative of the German foreign office at general headquarters transmitted the following message:

> During breakfast today His Majesty the Kaiser saw to it that, in the event of a Swedish refusal to allow transit for the revolutionaries, the High Command itself should be prepared to transport them over the front and into Russian territory.

Thus, nothing more stood in the way.

Swiss socialist Fritz Platten,[4] party secretary in Zurich, was the middleman between the Russian revolutionaries who wanted to return and the representatives of the German embassy in Bern. The group of about thirty revolutionaries, including the Austrian Karl Radek, who was pretending to be a Russian for the time being, was to ride in a train which they were forbidden to leave until they were out of Germany. The part of the car that was filled with Russians was to be declared foreign territory and would be separated symbolically from its guards—German officers—by a chalk mark. In the end, Fritz Platten tells what happened:

> The ninth of April [for Russia, 27 March] had already been set as the departure date by the German authorities. By 9 April at eleven o'clock all necessary measures had been taken, and the train station administration in Zurich had been informed of our departure.
>
> The fellow travelers gathered together in the Zähringer Hof Restaurant for a predeparture lunch. But the continuous going and coming and the swarm of people around Lenin and Zinoviev, who were both being stormed with thousands of questions, looked a lot more like a disturbed ant colony than anything else. At 2:30, the group of emigrants began moving in truly Russian fashion, loaded down with pillows, blankets, and what have you, walking from the Zähringer Hof to the Zurich train station. The train left punctually at 3:10 P.M.

The red wheel was beginning to move.

The red wheel—as Alexander Solzhenitsen has entitled the events of the Russian Revolution—began rolling out of Zurich with Lenin's train.

Angelika Rohr was a medical student in Zurich at the time and remembers that spring day in April 1917:

> In the morning, I heard from my neighbor that Lenin would be leaving for Russia today. Lenin was well known in our city, but not as a Russian emigrant with revolutionary ideas. He had also set up a student cafeteria where we could go to eat for free. True, it was always the same old soup day in and day out, but even so that was quite something in those war years when we were all so poor and hungry.
>
> I was electrified. Lenin was leaving? "If you hurry up, you might still be able to catch him in time!" I got dressed in a jiffy and rushed off. At that time, I lived high up on the Zurich Mountain, and the paths to the train station were winding and difficult. So I took a shortcut and hurried so much that I sometimes slipped and fell on the inclines.
>
> It was about noon when I reached the train station. There were only

a few people there. No one prevented me from going to the train platforms. I ran through the immense, badly lit main hall to the train tracks.

There was only one track with a train on it. There were Russians standing around the train. Among the people waiting there with the people who were about to leave were some students whom I knew—in fact, practically the only people there were students. It occurred to me that no one had a suitcase. They had boxes and packages but no suitcases. One woman student had put on a Katzeveyka—a sleeveless fur jacket. The middle of the spring at the Zurich train station, and a Katzeveyka! I walked along the side of the train and saw up ahead a car in front of which a crowd of people had gathered. About fifty people in all. This crowd was swarming around a man who stood in the open window of the car: Lenin.

The window was not big, and Lenin was a rather voluminous man. He completely filled it. He was leaning out of the window and gesticulating with his hands. At first, I just watched for a while, but then I went up closer, and it became clear to me that everyone standing in that crowd had a question to ask him and he was answering them. In German. And I was just getting there when he said, "We will open up the prisons!" Of course, I liked that. I was standing at the edge, since I had arrived late, but gradually I began to work my way through the crowd. I got pretty close to Lenin, and then I decided to take a very close look at him. I liked the fact that he had so many tiny lines on his face all around his eyes, so many striking tiny lines.

Suddenly, the bell rang to signal the departure of the train. There was confusion, and a crush of people, since everyone wanted to shake Lenin's hand one last time. People tried to reach out their hands to him—they had to stretch pretty high, one hand after the other—and I thought to myself, I should shake his hand too. Then the train started to move. I stuck out my left hand toward Lenin, since the train was moving in that direction, and he held on to it, and I ran along beside the train. It was funny. Hadn't he seen that the train was already moving, and that I had to run? We didn't say a word, there was no time for that. Finally, he let go of my hand. I was standing way up front, far away from the crowd of people, at the very end of the platform. Then I heard the Swiss singing the "International." It was not a pretty song—some of them sang it in French, others in German, and not one of them was particularly gifted musically. I don't know if that is a question of national characteristics or not—but at any rate they were all singing pretty badly. I walked up to them, but when they had finished singing the "International" they all went away, and I saw them later on too, down below in front of the train station. When they got to the square they scattered in all directions.

The so-called sealed train departed. On one vital point, the goal of the German General Staff was the same as the goal of Lenin: to overthrow the current Russian government in order to put an end to the war. For the Germans, the revolution was a means to a goal; for Lenin, the revolution was the goal itself. Thus, the path to the seizure of power was smoothed out.

Lenin's wife Nadyeshda Krupskaya talked about the motivation for this journey, directed solely toward the seizure of power by the Bolsheviks, and made fun of the vigorous protests by some of the Germans:

> The Bolsheviks' journey through Germany caused a great hue and cry among the supporters of the war. Certainly the German government, when it decided to allow our journey, acted on the assumption that a revolution is the worst thing that can happen to any country. They hoped that the return of the internationalist Russian emigrants would strengthen the forces of the revolution. The Bolsheviks in turn saw it as their duty to spread revolutionary propaganda in Russia. The highest goal of their activity was the victory of the proletarian revolution. They were not interested in the considerations of the German bourgeois government— and they also knew that the war-supporters were busy slandering them, but they were certain that the masses would ultimately choose to follow the Bolshevik path.

It is not clear whether Krupskaya knew for sure exactly what Lenin wanted and did not want (for instance, a socialist regime on the basis of democratic multiparty pluralism), or whether she was simply his loyal companion, come what may. By now the two shared a long history of exile together: beginning in 1898 in Siberia, where she had followed him in his exile, and continuing through exile in Prague, Munich, and London, then in Geneva in 1908, in Paris in 1909–1910, and in Krakow from 1911 to 1913. Stalin was also in Krakow:

> Around the middle of February 1913, there was an assembly of the members of the Central Committee. Our delegates went there, and Stalin went too. Ilyich[5] had known Stalin since the conference in Tammerfors. He had met him again at the conferences in Stockholm and London. This

time, Ilyich spoke for a long time with Stalin about the national question. He was happy to meet a man who was seriously interested in the question and knew something about it. Before he had come to Krakow, Stalin had spent two months in Vienna, where he had made a thorough study of the national question. There he also got closer to our comrades Bucharin and Troyanovsky, who were living in Vienna at the time. After the conference, Ilyich wrote to Gorky: "There was an excellent man from Georgia here. He is in the process of writing an article for the journal *Luch Sveta*, for which he has collected material in Austria and elsewhere."

The trip through Germany turned out to be more difficult than originally planned. Fritz Platten, who had given a written guarantee to the German embassy that as the escort of the "political emigrants to Russia" he would take on "full responsibility and personal liability at all times," was the first to violate the strict directive that the "sealed wagon" was to be left by no one. In Frankfurt, when the two officers who were guarding the train left their posts briefly, Platten hurried to a rendezvous that he had planned long before with a female friend of his. Radek remembers:

The isolation had been broken, and German soldiers ran toward us. They had heard about the transit of Russian revolutionaries who were fighting for peace. Every one of them held a beer stein in his hand. They asked us excitedly when peace would be declared. This mood told us more about the situation there than the German government had wanted us to know.

None of the revolutionaries had any qualms about making fun of their German financiers, whom they essentially despised. Already at this point Lenin's words could be heard quite clearly. In a letter to Alexandra Kolantay, a revolutionary friend of his living in Stockholm,[6] he had said:

Let us never again repeat the mistake of the Second International.[7] At all costs let us have a revolutionary plan and revolutionary tactics. The lessons of the past dictate revolutionary propaganda and the leadership of the masses. They dictate a struggle directed toward an international pro-letarian revolution and toward the seizure of power by the soviets of the workers delegates. By no means will this power be shared with the con-stitutional democrats and their lackeys.

During the period of exile, Lenin had still spoken about working together with the councils—the soviets—as the elected representatives of the workers and soldiers, who constituted his target audience. But during the journey through Germany—apparently after a secret meeting with the representatives of the German General Staff in the Berlin train yards—Lenin abruptly changed his style. The first to take notice of this change were the people who came to greet him on his arrival at the Petrograd train station, still thinking that he was their ally.

Here stood the delegation of the Social Revolutionaries, led by Nikolai Cheidse, the leader of the Menshevik faction of the Social Democratic Party of the Third and Fourth Duma periods, and accompanied by Suchanov and Skoblev. Again, as on his departure from Zurich, Lenin got to listen to the Marseillaise on his arrival in Petrograd. Paradoxically, Lenin was officially greeted in the Imperial waiting room. Shlyapnikov, the master of ceremonies, divided the mass of workers and soldiers waiting in the room in order to clear a path for the guest who was about to be greeted. The leftist journalist Suchanov remembers the scene:

> Lenin appeared with a rigid face, his round cap on his head. Cheidse began speaking in a solemn manner:
>
> "Comrade Lenin, in the name of the Petersburg Soviet and of the Revolution itself, we welcome you to Russia! We believe that it is now our chief task to safeguard the Revolution from aggressive forces from within and without, and to protect it from destructive dangers in the spirit of revolutionary democracy. What we need now is not disagreement but the mutual work of all democratic forces gathered together. We hope that you will follow these goals together with us!"
>
> Cheidse paused in his almost prayerlike manner.
>
> Lenin stood there with his scornful face, as if the whole thing had nothing to do with him at all. He looked around at the people, stared at the ceiling of the Imperial room, then contemplated the bouquet of flowers in his hand, which was completely in conflict with the rest of his appearance, and he turned his back on the speaker and on the entire delegation in order to seize the floor himself:
>
> "Comrades, soldiers, sailors, workers! I am happy to greet in you the victorious Russian Revolution, the avant-garde of the international proletarian army! The hour is near when the peoples of the world will raise up their weapons against the exploiters, the capitalists. The Russian Rev-

olution, carried out by you, has ushered in a new era. Long live the socialist world revolution!"

The delegation was more than just dumbfounded about the rudeness of Lenin. Already at this moment, there were signs of basic differences of opinion—among other things, for instance, in the question of the seizure of property, which was by no means one of the goals of the Social Revolutionaries, since they believed it would lead to great difficulties in feeding and clothing the population. These differences of opinion necessarily led later on to a schism within the Social Revolutionary Party, which the original revolutionary goal had envisioned as unified. Nevertheless, Lenin worked for the schism, while the Social Revolutionaries fought against it.

As early as the following day, Lenin drew a line between himself and the Social Democrats at an official forum, when he made a speech at the first Bolshevik Party Conference. The first thing he wanted was to change the name of the Bolshevik Party to the Communist Party, in order to separate it clearly from the Mensheviks in the Social Democratic Party. The Mensheviks, despite their domestic political struggles for democratic conditions, were in favor of continuing the defense of the fatherland "until the imminent victory," which was precisely what Lenin and his German financiers did not want. The Mensheviks also wanted to work together with the Soviets—something which no longer seemed desirable to Lenin. Such cooperation ran the danger of achieving precisely the longed-for multiparty coalition compromise that would leave the Bolsheviks' demand for total power unsatisfied, jeopardizing the achievement of their goals.

In the vast reaches of peasant Russia, Lenin was still practically unknown at this time. The British diplomat Bruce Lockhart, then consul general in Russia, tries in the following passage to describe Lenin's personality objectively, contrasting Lenin the political man and his peasant simplicity with the ideological, argumentative intellectual Trotsky, the organizer of the Revolution:

Small and somewhat squat, with a short, strong neck, broad shoulders, a round red face, a high intelligent brow, a protruding nose, a brown moustache, and a short and stubbly beard, he seemed at first glance more like a greengrocer than like a leader of men. But there was something in his steely eyes that got my attention. In this scornful, half-smiling, half-supercilious look, there was something that expressed limitless self-confidence and an unshakable feeling of superiority.

During the period that followed, I was to have ample opportunity to be amazed at his intellectual powers. But at this particular moment, I was more impressed by his terrible will to power—this decisiveness without any scruples, and the absolute lack of any emotion.

Because of all this he stood in stark contrast to Trotsky, who, unusually silent, was also present at our meeting. Trotsky was full of emotions, an individualist and an actor. With his vanity, he even laid himself open to attack from me. Lenin was impersonal, even inhuman. His vanity was far removed from any flattery. The only approach one had to him was to appeal to his extremely well-developed sense of humor, even though his humor was of the nervous kind.

In the following months, I was besieged by a great many inquiries from London. I was supposed to check out whether the rumors of serious disagreements between Lenin and Trotsky were true, because this information was of importance for our government. After this first meeting, I was able to give an answer. Trotsky was a great organizer and a man of undoubted physical presence. But psychologically he was as incapable of resisting Lenin as a fly is of resisting an elephant. In the Council of Commissars, there was no one for whom Trotsky was anything but their kind of man. But Lenin was a demigod for all his followers. His decisions were accepted—without question or comment.

Supported by the brilliant speaker and strategist Trotsky, the Bolsheviks now began aiming slogans and appeals at the masses, calling among other things for the end of the war and the violent appropriation of property in the cities and in the country with the slogan "Grab nagrablennoye" (Steal what was stolen). Thus the revolutionaries managed to fill the vacuum of helplessness that had descended on the suffering population while the divided government was unable to act. Who by now could remember the appeal of War and Navy Minister Guchkov, who, with a very clear picture of what was going on, had called on the population of Petrograd to display moderation:

To the population and the army! Citizens and soldiers! In view of the imminent danger, the Provisional Government is again turning to you. Watch out! The Germans are still strong, and they are now quickly marshaling their forces on the northern front in order to attack Petrograd, for they are waiting to hear word of a revolutionary collapse in Russia.

Free citizens will then become German lackeys. A Prussian sergeant will then be the one to impose order on us and to rule over us, again establishing the power of an emperor above us.

Russians! The eyes of all Russia are turned toward you. Obey your superiors, because an army without discipline is not feared by the enemy. Do not listen to pernicious speeches. Many German spies, disguising themselves under gray soldiers' coats, are fomenting disorder and rebellion among you. Continue to have confidence in your officers, as before.

Signed: War and Navy Minister A. Guchkov.

The propagandists promised just about the opposite. "Order No. 1," a concession made by the Provisional Government immediately after the establishment of the Council of Workers and Soldiers Deputies, promised soldiers more civil rights, while limiting the power and authority of officers. Thus, for instance, officers were no longer allowed to call their men by their first names. Moreover, the order made the validity of military commands dependent on their agreement with the guidelines of the Workers and Soldiers Soviets, thus practically inviting soldiers to show disobedience to authority. It is no wonder, then, that many soldiers took the slogan "Steal what was stolen" all too literally.

Antoinette Berthoud, a French woman employed at the time as a maid in Petrograd, remembers one particular episode:

I remember a true Bachic orgy that spread lightning-fast over all of Petrograd like an epidemic. The revolutionaries had opened up wine cellars filled with the best reserves of wines and other spirits owned by the rich. News of this caused a veritable orgy of drinking. At least if one didn't have bread, one had wine! Men, women, and children set out like lunatics for the aristocratic neighborhoods, where they took everything they could get their hands on. Instead of pulling out corks, they simply broke the necks of the bottles. Half of the contents flowed out of the bottle and onto the floor in this way, but there was still plenty left! There was a general drunken revelry such as I had never experienced before, so absurd, unruly, and disgusting. Strong men arrived to take away entire kegs, but even they did not get very far, because after the first ecstasies they could not stand up straight anymore. Soldiers sent out to restore order made friends with the mob. Many of them remained lying in the red puddles, and the soldiers were not ashamed to perform bodily functions in them as well. Later on, the houses of the owners were set on fire, and the sky above Petrograd glowed red. . . .

This is precisely the episode—among others—that Xenia
Alexandrovna Giovanni née Drushinikova remembers. In 1917, she was
twenty-one years old. Here she describes several moments between the
spring and autumn revolutions, typical for the atmosphere of raging
unrest and enmity:

> There were always shots to be heard on the street. All of Petrograd
> was flooded with soldiers coming back from the front with leave or without
> it. They no longer obeyed their commanding officers. They walked along
> in a pitiful condition, with torn epaulets and buttons, shabby, dirty, and
> hungry. They had taken up the slogans of the revolutionaries and hoped
> for freedom and a piece of land after their return—everything that the
> propagandists had promised them. And then there was the main slogan:
> "Steal what was stolen"—an invitation to steal from the "bourgeoisie."
> My family was not as hard hit as the others, because we belonged to the
> modest middle class, and our money at that time was just enough to pay
> for what we really needed. In order to survive, we rented out half of the
> house in Novgorod, the city of my birth, which we still owned. But others
> were hard hit in those times, and many simply starved.
>
> When we heard that something had happened in Grochovaya Street,
> we ran there. Already on the Moyka Canal at the end of the street we
> could smell the strong odor of wine. Two houses further on was the place
> where soldiers in the wine cellar had simply broken open the barrels. The
> soldiers weren't even drinking anymore; they were simply destroying. It
> was terrible.
>
> We ran on. On a balcony on Senate Square (Senatskaya Plochchad)
> we saw Kerensky giving a speech. The mob of people wanted to hear
> more and more all the time. He cried: "Liberty, equality, fraternity!"
> From time to time, he drew back, because he was already quite tired. But
> the mob kept calling him out again. He was a very good speaker, that is
> well known, and he was a famous lawyer. Among his listeners were mostly
> students and young people. All of them expected him to make major
> innovations. Again and again, we saw trucks like sardine cans go by packed
> full of people, mostly former courtiers or gendarmes, policemen, or gen-
> erals with their service markings torn off. Proponents of the old regime.
> Most of them were being taken to the Peter and Paul Fortress. Elsewhere,
> we saw fire. In Offizyerskaya Street, the police headquarters was burning.
> It was arson. What a sight that was! Papers, masses of documents, and
> notes. The wind blew everything into the air. It was terrible to see so
> much destruction.

Hard times were beginning. There was no more bread to be had. One had to stand in long lines for everything. After the revolution, all the groceries completely disappeared from the stores. Some merchants hid away their goods in order to save them away for later. But most of the businesses simply did not exist anymore because they could not get replacements or shipments anymore. The roads had been monopolized for military supplies. One could hardly buy anything anymore. There was unimaginable hunger.

My mother took me to Novgorod. It was a little better there, but even there one had to be careful not to get in the way of a stray bullet.

Tatyana Botkina, daughter of the court physician Dr. Botkin, who was later executed along with the Czar's family, describes here the often simple mechanisms of unrest—different from the intentionally caused or motivated unrest described earlier:

At first it was said: Now we have nothing more to fear, because the Czar has called in the Duma, and then there was the Provisional Government working together with the Soviet. But it was so easy for agitators to give simple people or a few thugs three rubles and say: Break in a window there and buy yourself a vodka. But that doesn't mean that the revolution came from the simple man. It came from above.

Petrograd, 19 March 1917, in the diary of a writer:

Soldiers with steel helmets, who have just gotten back from the front, are surrounding the Peter-Paul Fortress. They walk around casually, dragging machine guns behind them or resting their rifles sloppily on their shoulders. Sometimes, one of them can be heard calling out cheerfully to passersby: "Hey you! Hurry up! There will be a shoot-out soon!"

The city's inhabitants are wandering around so that they will be able to get a glimpse of the battle that is expected. They come closer by using the surrounding parks, continually hiding under the protection of trees here and there, and craning their necks to see.

Despite the winter, there are already flowers growing in some of the gardens near the fortress. The gardener is working on precisely this patch. His smock is strikingly clean, and he has a shovel in his hands. Walking up and down his little patch of garden, he yells angrily at soldiers and spectators as if they were sheep that he is somehow unable to drive in the right direction: "Where are you all going? Is this garden here for you to be trampling around on it? Isn't there enough room for you on the sidewalks?"

A bearded soldier in uniform responds with his rifle under his arm: "Old man, watch out for yourself rather than for other people, or else we'll blow you away."

"Oh will you now? Just try it! A beautiful shot, you."

"Can't you get it through your head that this is war? And there will be a battle here soon."

"Oh really? Well then you just go on with your battle, and I'll go on with my work." And, taking some more cutting tools out of his pocket, he adds angrily: "Please be so good as to tramp out of here again. You don't belong here."

"This is war."

"What does that have to do with me? Whoever gets the urge can go out and fight whenever he wants to, and you certainly have enough people to help you at it. But I'm all alone with my work. You'd be doing something more worthwhile if you cleaned your rifles—they all look a bit rusty."

Then there is a whistle, and the soldier, who, during the entire conversation, has been trying in vain to light up a cigarette, puts it back into his pocket and runs away through the trees.

The gardener spits after him disdainfully and shouts in anger: "Why the devil do you have to run over my grass? Aren't there enough other places to run?"

From the point of view of former soldiers, the situation looked different—depending on where one happened to be standing. Ordinary soldiers at the front rarely knew what exactly was going on in the capital city. Rumors and visiting representatives of the Provisional Government determined the level of their knowledge and the general mood.

Vasily V. Orychov was an officer. Like many of his comrades, he, too, had believed that a constitutional monarchy could be preserved in Russia if past mistakes could be avoided and above all if Prince Michayl Alexandrovich were to take over the regency. But the military did not concern itself with politics at the time:

The fact was that most of the officers I knew were concerned first and foremost with bringing the war to a successful conclusion. We thought that until we had fulfilled our responsibilities and done our duty we would not be able to turn to the work of solving political problems. At least in the first months of 1917, when our situation was not yet so bad, that was the general opinion. The great mass of soldiers probably thought a bit differently. In my unit, they all thought like I did, but in general the enlisted men were an easy target for the propaganda that had already begun well before Lenin's arrival in Petrograd, and which then was strengthened even further. It was said that we had to end the war, because it was not serving any useful purpose—that it was a capitalist war going on even after the removal of the Czar, because we only had bourgeois ministers in the government. For instance, Milyukov had declared that the war must be continued until its victorious conclusion: the taking of Constantinople and the Dardanells. What the devil did we need to do that for? Let it be, brothers! We will easily be able to sit down at the negotiating table with the Germans, because they too are tired. Let us end the war!

Then came the delegates of various factions in the Provisional Government calling on us to carry out our patriotic duty and rejoicing that now we had a government elected by the people, who would now take their fate into their own hands. Even Kerensky came—an extraordinarily good speaker who filled me, too, with excitement. But he was unable to make the idea of defense credible and solid again, for the soldiers had lost confidence in it.

In the year 1917, Colonel Boris F. Dubenzev was stationed with His Majesty's Cossack Bodyguard in Rovna. He reports an incident which points to the strategic laxity of the decision makers and commanders of essentially loyal regiments:

It was the early summer of 1917. I was supposed to go out and buy horses with two of my colleagues. We arrived at the train station in Rovna—at that time there was still no unrest in the province—and were told by the stationmaster that our regiment had been ordered to Petrograd, because there were uprisings there. The trains were already waiting. As it turned out, we knew nothing about it because General Alexyev in the headquarters of the General Staff had decided to postpone our involvement. Why he did that—one would have to ask the man himself, I suppose. But when we came back three days later after buying the horses, we already saw mutinous soldiers standing around at the train station. One part of our regiment had already been sitting in the train when the order came down to keep us back. If we had gone to Petrograd, there would not have been any revolution. Each one of us was prepared to sacrifice his life for the fatherland.

By this time, Lenin has been planning and preparing for his systematic seizure of power for a long time, but despite all the signs of anarchy he still did not believe that his real chance had come yet. One witness to this was the farmer who took Lenin in when he was forced to take refuge from his own angry followers (when they learned of his German support) and from the police force of a government that was now alarmed and had ordered the arrest of revolutionaries suspected of subversive activities and propaganda. By now, the Ministry of Justice[8] was receiving more and more convincing proofs that Lenin had received German financing and was thus a foreign agent.

At that time, Alexander Nikolayevich Yemelyanov had hidden Lenin in one of his haystacks to the north of Petrograd toward Wyborg and had given Lenin food and materials to write with. His father before him had belonged to the Bolshevik Party, smuggling weapons for revolts by water from Finland to Petersburg and later to Petrograd. He himself was only a little boy when Lenin took advantage of the hospitality and loyalty of his family:[9]

> My father had warned me that I had to watch out for my six brothers, and that we couldn't make a sound. My father picked up the comrades at the train station in Sestroryezk. They arrived on the train from Petrograd at three o'clock in the morning. I lay down on the floor of the loft and was able to watch the comrades coming across the yard. When they said hello to each other, Lenin warned my mother that she should not say anything to anyone. She reacted almost with hurt pride: She knew the rules of conspiracy. Then she cut Lenin's and Zinoviev's hair. With Lenin that was an easy task, but Zinoviev had such a full head of hair! My father said we would turn the two into perfect Finnish peasants. The border was only six kilometers away, and back then lots of seasonal workers always came over from Finland for the harvesting of the hay. My brother, a genuine anarchist, wanted at all costs to talk to Lenin. He climbed up to the loft, where Lenin and Zinoviev had already gone to bed, and asked them accusingly why they still hadn't seized power yet. Then Lenin answered, "Seizing power is easy. Keeping it is hard. Without a revolutionary atmosphere on the part of the masses an armed uprising is impossible." When my brother left the loft a half hour later, he had become a fervent Bolshevik.

According to Yemelyanov's story, it was Zinoviev rather than Lenin who was greatly upset about the rumors that Lenin was a spy for the

Germans and had taken their money. What bothered Zinoviev was not so much that the bourgeoisie was angry—he was even proud of that—as that there were questions raised about him even by the workers. In the face of this pressure, Zinoviev tended to make a lot of excuses and paint himself lily white. Lenin had no time for this. His job was to keep himself as up-to-date as possible on the situation in Petrograd.

Later, the Yemelyanovs gave Lenin a cottage in a birch forest behind their house. In order to get to it, one had to paddle a boat over a pond, and then hike for a while. This was a tiresome task for those who supplied Lenin daily with food and information.

Whenever I arrived, Lenin was sitting there and writing. He was working on *State and Revolution*, but living there was very unhealthy for him. At night, damp fog rose from the meadows and reeds. We had to find a way to get him to Finland. Finally, he got dressed up as a stoker and traveled across the Finnish border. But before that, I was witness to a discussion that determined my worldview from then on.

Back then, Lenin had asked my father: "What do you think, should we seize power now?"

"Of course, Vladimir Ilyich!"

"And why is the mood of the masses auspicious at this moment?"

"Because the Provisional Government has not solved the problems of the workers, the peasants still have no land, and there's still no peace."

"If the Milyukovs, Guchkovs, and Co. were to solve these problems, we would have to surrender our party books to them. That means that we will have to seize power now."

The Yemelyanovs disappeared later on. Feeling that the ideals of the revolution championed by Lenin had been betrayed when they were put into reality, they were sent for decades to concentration camps. The one surviving son cited above was rehabilitated in the milder political climate of the anti-Stalinist 1960s, and he is now allowed to show the historical farmhouse to anyone who is interested in seeing it.

While Lenin was preparing for *State and Revolution* not only theoretically but practically, his intermediary in Stockholm sent him German money, and he received news about the course of events in Petrograd. Things were progressing well for his plans. And yet Lenin knew that he could not use the most recent events for the seizure of power, because the discovery of his naturally controversial contact with the Germans and his acceptance of financing from them had discredited the Bolshevik Party too strongly for it to be able to come to power and keep it. But at that time he—and with him Sverdlov—was the only one who realized this, and thus none of his comrades could understand why he did not then seize power. Moreover, by now the forces of law and order had sounded the alarm.

In the following account, Princess Lydiya Vazilchikova remembers the year 1917 before the October coup:

> Toward the end of August, the situation began to get tenser and tenser, and army units started showing up in areas where there was a danger of unrest. But the number of agitators kept growing, and the propaganda increased. One morning, an angry crowd of people gathered in front of the gates of Lotarevo. My brother and his wife were surrounded and brought to the village school that my father had built. There Boris was subjected to an interrogation in front of the very icon that the peasants had given him as a token of their gratitude a short while before. The employees in the house and on the farm were too scared to defend him. The local peasants watched impassively. Boris was then taken to the next train station under military guard. The officer on duty wanted to let Boris go when they got to the train station, but the scoundrel did not want it to happen this way. As fate willed it, there were mutinous soldiers walking through the train station at that moment. Egged on by this man, they threw themselves upon my brother and tore him to pieces.

Brutality and cruelty coming from bitterness grown into hatred: In the following period, Lenin proved himself well able to incite these pent-up aggressions, making good use of the despair widespread in a country that had little to eat and of the demoralization that had resulted from inadequate preparations for enemy attacks on the front. Thus, slowly but inexorably, the powder keg was moving toward revolution.

NOTES

1. Ulyanov—the real last name of Vladimir Ilyich Lenin.

2. For a long time, the German documents pertaining to these secret actions were kept under lock and key. Hitler commanded that the documents be destroyed shortly before the German capitulation, but his command could not be carried out. Thus, the documents came into English hands, were stored at Oxford, and have only recently been returned to the German Foreign Office.

3. Michael Pearson estimates that the sum total given out by the Germans, for these purposes was about forty million marks—today equivalent to several hundred million DM (in *The Sealed Train*, Berlin, 1977).

4. Later on Fritz Platten—like other people who knew the story—was liquidated along with his family in the Soviet Union.

5. Krupskaya tended to call Lenin "Ilyich" (from Vladimir Ilyich).

6. Already back then, Stockholm was a place of refuge for leftist political refugees. Lenin's go-betweens, who at first had supplied him with news and information from Petrograd during the time of his exile in Switzerland, and who later sent on to him secret information from Germany and the money of the German General Staff while he was in Petrograd, were also in Stockholm. With this money, Lenin was able to finance the propaganda for his revolution.

7. It is possible that Lenin was here playing on the division of the Social Revolutionaries into Bolsheviks and the less radical Mensheviks that had come to light at the conferences in Brussels and London. After all, Lenin was in no way interested in cooperation with another group.

8. Lenin was warned by a colleague in the ministry and was thus able to escape.

9. Ulrich Schiller interviewed Alexander Yemelyanov.

Chapter Five

———— // ————

Blood on the Snow

The sequence of events preceeding the storming of the Winter Palace and the day after.

> The moment people find out how Lenin got to Russia and who helped him get here, he will be so discredited that he will no longer pose any danger!

This was the way Foreign Minister Milyukov reacted in the spring of 1917 to the confidential warning of his British colleague that Lenin and other revolutionaries, financed by Germany, were on their way to Petrograd in a sealed train car with the avowed goal of overthrowing the Provisional Government.

When these facts were revealed in the summer of 1917, the sailors and workers whom Lenin had been able to win for his following indeed reacted with outrage.[1] Nevertheless, the times, the circumstances, and well-planned propaganda had long since been playing into the hands of the revolutionaries. Liberalization had been carried to extremes by cabinet members in a government fighting to retain its bourgeois seats in parliament. This liberalization allowed the revolutionaries to work without interference. There were now concessions such as the already-mentioned "Order Number One," which at the very least put the authority of commanders and officers into question, if it did not positively get rid of them. Political prisoners—even including terrorists—were given a general amnesty. Censorship of revolutionary and anarchist publications was eradicated. All of this meant that the revolutionaries were now able to argue quite openly in favor of bringing the war to an end and refusing to obey commands at the front and in the garrisons. Though Lenin, because of the suspicions against him, was forced to go into hiding, the machinery of his party continued to work for him.

Konstantin Kromyadi was at the front at the time and remembers the delegations sent by the Provisional Government—sometimes headed by Kerensky, who had in the meantime advanced to minister of war— in order to stave off the moral (and physical) disintegration of the army by making speeches to the soldiers:

The Germans had sent commandos to us Russians during breaks in the fighting, in order to provoke us. They tried to convince us that we should make friends with each other. When they spoke like that among themselves, they were shot to death. The Germans pushed their people into demoralizing us. The minister of war had once tried to convince our Czar that he ought to try to provoke a revolution in Austria-Hungary in order to overthrow the emperor and bring about a peace treaty. But Czar Nicholas had turned this down: As Czar, he would never try to overthrow another emperor. Then all of them started coming, first Milyukov and Guchkov and other representatives of the Duma. They told us that we had to go on fighting. Soon we would be able to take our own fate into our hands. We must not give back what we had gained, and we must remain strong.

Vasiliy Oryechov on the same topic:

The delegations were always solemnly greeted by the officers—in the hope that they would succeed in strengthening the fighting spirit. The soldiers couldn't have cared less. I can still remember well Representative Dyemodov, a cadet. He was well educated and gave a patriotic speech. He talked about a Constitutional Assembly in the near future, with more rights and no oppression by the government. Then another delegation came: a certain Kotenyev, and with him Posner, a Social Revolutionary, with the Bolshevik Virsha. I still remember that day. An assembly of 1,500 soldiers was arranged. Suddenly, a completely different picture was presented to us: The war was the decline of Russia and of the people. All it was good for was in helping to achieve the goals of the imperialists. "We plead for brotherhood among the peoples and promise you that we will distribute land to the peasants fairly. We will take everything away from the capitalists, even the factories. Workers' committees will be set up, and they will control industry, and as soon as the war is over there will be a just peace. Germany is already tired, and there are similar problems there, too. We will make friends with the German people, and there will no longer be any armies." Applause and cheers. Several officers left the field in protest. But by this time the commanders had already lost much of their authority. Commissar Stankyevich was quite disturbed. He made a written protest, but it was far too late for this.

That was in early summer. For a long time, Lenin's ideas, along with his calls to refuse to obey authority, had been making their way through the front. And in the garrisons of Petrograd, a city which was fighting for its daily bread, it was not difficult to win over soldiers with sweet-sounding promises.

Commander in Chief General Alexeyev sent a concerned telegram to War and Navy Minister Guchkov. On 13 May 1917, Guchkov resigned.[2] Kerensky added this position to his others. Ten days later, General Alexeyev, too, was relieved by the Provisional Government of his position as commander in chief.

Kerensky tried to stop the radicalization inside the government (caused by the extremist attitudes of the Bolsheviks) by making concessions. He would not, however, compromise on the Bolsheviks' program of making peace with the Germans. He also started holding democratic conferences in preparation for the Constitutional Assembly. Moreover, as minister of war he now decided on dates of attack in order to strengthen the troops' self-confidence. The offensive of 6 (19) July, however, was catastrophic for the Russian side. Many of the commanders had not been installed until a couple of days earlier by Kerensky. The soldier used the privileges that had been given to them by the Soldiers' Soviet,[3] debating into the early hours of the morning about the plan of attack—which they then failed to carry out, with the exception of Bryusilov's Division. Commanders of the 10th and 11th armies sent telegraphic reports of desertions and refusals to obey commands. The German enemy was now able to break through the Russian front almost without resistance. In the meantime, the Bolshevik wing of the revolutionaries used the catastrophic situation—which had been reinforced by its own intelligence giving to the enemy—for its own agitational purposes in Petrograd.

Pierre Pascal, a second lieutenant in the reserve stationed at the time in the French military mission, gives a picture of the situation in the capital in this diary entry:

16 June, midnight:
Cossacks are going along the main street. Perfect quiet, not a sound, the crowd is walking by. The soldiers with their machine guns are chewing on sunflower seeds. The Pavlovsky Regiment at the front had refused to obey the order to march. There are supposed to be demonstrations against the government. The Page Corps is refusing to participate. In the darkness, I can see only soldiers on horseback. I can hear the speeches at the Offizyerskaya. Whistles. A single shot sounds through the night along the canal.

17 July:
One of the reasons for the mutiny: to steal a march on the propaganda demonstrations that have been set for the 17th, 18th, and 19th. At 2:30, the Nevsky and the Liteyny were closed off. The maid reports: sixteen ships from Kronstadt have arrived and are lying at anchor near the Nikolayevsky Bridge. The sailors—we don't know if it is 3,000 or 40,000 of them—are roaming the streets. Sometimes they fire off shots. People are saying: Things are going to get hot again. On the Moyka, people stop a tank truck. The men from the Preobrashensky Regiment killed the driver. The crowd in front of the Taurian Palace has been dispersed. Military Commander Polovzov has declared a state of siege in Petrograd. He is planning a purge.

Toward evening, shooting begins close by. Then there is peace again. The soldiers are walking along in a relaxed way, making jokes. Almost all the regiments have gone out. The offensive at the front was weakening. Kalich was lost. General Bryusilov says that the army will not last out the winter because of the total lack of organization in the rear and the many desertions.

18 July:
The mass media are making reports about an intelligence action that proves Lenin to be a traitor. He is said to be receiving money from the Germans via a certain Furstenberg in Stockholm. The money is evidently transferred through the Via Bank and the Siberian Bank, according to Justice Minister Pyerevyersev.

From the front, Kerensky has given a telegraphic order to arrest Lenin and his friends Kamenyev, etc. The *Pravda* office is supposed to be closed. Lenin himself has disappeared, though. Durnovo, the stronghold of the anarchists, has fallen, and Kamenyev, Sinoviev, and Simenson have been arrested. An accordion is playing below my window. The Bolshevik Regiment of the grenadiers reports ten dead and twenty-five wounded from yesterday.

Polovzov took action. He called in all the forces of law and order to pacify the people. Sailors from Kronstadt had gotten off their ships and were marching through the city. People knew that they were even more combative than their comrades in Petrograd. At the Taurian Palace, there was a shoot-out. Sixty cossacks died, and in the morning dead horses were found. The square in front of the palace was protected by a "real" army: infantry, guards, military cadets, and cossacks. The invasion that was expected by the sailors in Kronstadt, who were considered to be extreme enemies of a bourgeois government, put the keepers of law and order into a near state of panic. Meanwhile, soldiers returned home from the failed offensive. Pierre Pascal wrote on 21 July:

This was the most depressing day for a long time. The front line has been broken through. The defenders retreated, and the Germans pushed on without resistance. 1,000 canons lost. In the evening, there is a rumor that 85,000 men surrendered. The German Navy is on its way toward Petrograd. Reval is in a state of revolutionary uproar. Unrest in Charkov. Nishny is in the hands of the rebels.

Since yesterday evening, there have been gunfights here again. At the Nikolayevsky train station, anarchists planted bombs and attacked troops returning home from the front. During the day, I had already heard shots coming from the summer garden. In the evening, then, from 11:30 until shortly before midnight, there was the terrible clatter of machine guns: a response from the Peter-Paul Fortress. Evidently, everything happened at the Palace Bridge and in front of the stock exchange. One regiment had been on its way from Palace Square to the House of the People in order to take up a position there. They were shot at by machine guns that had been placed on the roof of the stock exchange. The Bolsheviks had announced that at 9:00 P.M. "something" would happen. Polovzov had announced appropriate precautions. At the post office and the telegraph office, defenses had been erected.

Even Petrograd's Workers and Soldiers Council was uneasy in the face of this militant attack by the Bolsheviks. It distanced itself from the

anarchist actions obviously intended to overthrow the government.
Though it criticized Kerensky, the council sided with the Provisional
Government and agreed to a ban on further demonstrations. The time
for the final seizure of power had not yet come. The government,
alarmed, quickly regrouped. All bourgeois and right-wing ministers left.
The "Constitutional" Assembly, long promised, was put off again—but
as a result of the "Democratic Conference" Russia was nevertheless
officially called a "Council Republic"—in Russian, a "Soviet Republic."
The country's councils were given more autonomy. Because of the
generally chaotic and discouraging situation, it was impossible to put an
end to the decay of law and order. The forces of order had been
replaced by a soldiers' militia, which was susceptible to propagandistic
manipulation.

All of this was happening at the same time that the enemy was
standing in front of Russia's gates. In the south, Tarnopol had fallen,
large parts of Galicia and Bukovina had also been lost. In the north, the
port city of Riga, on the road to Petrograd, was threatened by an
invasion of the Germans.

Once again, Kerensky attempted to reverse the demoralization of
the population and the army. Again, a last attack was planned at the
front. In order to strengthen the troops' morale, patriotic volunteers and
women's brigades were recruited to serve as shock troops at the front.
Vasiliy Oryechov was there:

A whole series of storm troops was formed, and I volunteered for the
Fifteenth Storm Troop. Almost all of us were volunteers, both the officers
and the men. My brigade consisted of three companies, with about six
hundred men. Half of them were career soldiers, the others were wet
behind the ears—university and high school students.

We went into position on the western front near Smorgony. The attack
began simultaneously on the southwestern and western fronts on the
Kovno toward Vilna. The women's battalion under Commander Boch-
karyeva took up a position on our right flank. The women fought very
well; their discipline was extraordinary.

We attacked on 17 September. Almost no regular troops participated.
The day before, Kerensky had been here and given one of his typical
speeches. But we could already see that he was a broken man. Compared
to earlier—exciting, cheerful, infectious—the man who now spoke was
worn out. He no longer called on people to carry out their duty, but made
disparaging remarks. Instead, he talked about cowardice, meanness, and

betrayal of the fatherland, and about the holy cause of the revolution. Some of the troops stood there with dark looks; others cheered. Then there were meetings of the soldiers' committees, where the soldiers unanimously decided to carry out our "revolutionary" duty.

The next day at the "H" hour—i.e., at seven o'clock in the morning —the signal was given to attack. But the women's battalion was almost the only one to go to battle. We prepared the artillery fire. At first, everything went very well, but then suddenly everything stopped. We sent a messenger there to tell us what was going on, and it turned out that our batteries had been seized by soldiers of our own infantry, who had taken away the cannons! We went into a crazy situation. The worst of it was that our own soldiers stabbed us in the back—not the ones from our battalions, but rather the ones from the infantry units that were supposed to attack. The attack was called off, though where we were it did not end in as much disgrace as on the southwestern front. By the way, the Germans did not follow the retreating soldiers—we don't know why. But the southwestern front fell apart completely. Our soldiers fled in panic. Fighting broke off altogether. We were sent into the reserve at Minsk—or more accurately at Kosyryevo. A new formation was announced. At the front everything was quiet.

Later, the military leadership was changed due to the influence of the Bolsheviks. A noncommissioned officer named Mesnyakov became commander of the western front. He belonged to the extreme leftist Bolshevik faction. They demanded the removal of officers' epaulets and decided that orders should only be carried out after a vote by the soldiers' council. We decided not to go along with these rules and tried to join with other units that had not yet been corrupted by the Bolshevik attack on rank. The Polish units that had been formed under Polish officers after the February Revolution were a great help in this. Their excellent discipline provided a good role model. Like us, they were interested in continuing to defend the fatherland, since their areas were occupied by the Germans and could only be won back through unified efforts with us.

Because of desertion by infantrymen from the peasantry, Riga has fallen into German hands—despite excellent conditions for its defense. The military situation now became critical for Petrograd as well, because of the threat of the approaching Germans. Kerensky assured himself of the support of the military in defending the city. The moment seemed to have come for two things at once: the protection of the capital city against the German Army and the prevention of a

seizure of power by the Bolsheviks. Kerensky ordered General
Kornilov, the Siberian general who had succeeded in restoring a certain
amount of military discipline by enacting the death penalty for deserters
(he was greeted by many Russians as the "only possible savior of
Russia"), to march on Petrograd.

But at the last moment—the troops were already on their way with
loyal front units and cossacks from General Alexander Kreymov's elite
Third Cavalry Corps—Kerensky became uncertain. He was afraid of
giving up power to a possible military government and was certain of
losing the support of the Social Revolutionaries. These risks did not
seem to justify the action for him. Leftists were calling up images of
counterrevolution. Afraid of losing power, Kerensky changed his mind.
He stopped the troops on their way to Petrograd and had Kornilov
arrested as a "traitor." The prisoners wound up in the Peter-Paul
Fortress. The seven hours following midnight on this 27 August were
the decisive and irreversible moments when Kerensky himself allowed
Russia to fall prey to the Bolsheviks.

Vladimir Bulgakov was a soldier among the defense troops that
were supposed to form the core of the defense of Petrograd:

> We were members of the reserve and belonged to the unit on the
> northwestern front that was withdrawn again without ever having a chance
> to fight. When we get to Luga, the Tversky Column is given the order
> to call off the maneuver, on the grounds that Kerensky wants to prevent
> further bloodshed. General Krymov was said to have shot himself to death.
> This not only shocked us, it surprised us, since General Krymov had
> been a happy, well-loved, and handsome man, and was never depressed.
> In reality, this was simply a piece of disinformation intended to demoralize
> the troops. Krymov had been ordered to go to Kerensky, who said that
> he would not harm a hair on his head if he collaborated with him. Krymov
> hesitated—he had a lot of confidence, if for no other reason than that
> Kerensky was said to be a freemason, and one freemason does nothing to
> harm another, and so he decided to go to the requested meeting after all.
> With the messenger Yeremeyev as an escort, he appeared in the palace.
>
> In Kerensky's foyer sat a second lieutenant of the navy in a white
> uniform. The moment Krymov walked in, the lieutenant pulled out a
> revolver and shot him dead. The messenger rushed to the second lieutenant
> and grabbed him by the collar. Kerensky then walked into the room and
> shouted; "Don't move from that spot! Let him free at once, or you too
> will be dealt with!" Yeremeyev was momentarily shocked and let go of

the man. But this shock was to plague him from then on. He could never forgive himself for his pettiness. Perhaps freemasons put pressure on him, too—at any rate, he went back home and killed himself. That was Yeremeyev of the Ninth Don Regiment, General Krymov's messenger and a large, broad-shouldered man—a brave soldier for his fatherland.

There were all sorts of rumors about the "Kornilov Affair." According to some, it was Kornilov who had lied and planned a coup; according to others, it was Kerensky. The Putilov factory was in flames. As a weapons factory, it was a symbol of the unwanted war. Counterrevolutionaries and rebels were constantly being arrested. Telephone connections were frequently interrupted. Posters called for vigilance against the threat of a military coup. The large print on the various appeals all looked the same from a distance: "Do not believe those who . . . !" Whom to believe, then?

The rumor circulated that Kornilov had been murdered. Then again that he was in prison. Then again that he would retain command of the army until the arrival in the general staff of the reactivated General Alexeyev. Reports were circulated and invented about clashes—with and without the loss of blood—between troops loyal to Kornilov and supporters of the Provisional Government or of the Workers and Soldiers Soviets. The atmosphere had grown tense again.

The unsuccessful fall offensive and the supposed military coup that had gone awry, added fuel to an atmosphere that further helped to support Bolshevik slogans. From his hiding place in Finland, Lenin made inflammatory appeals to his comrades[4] and the Central Committee in Petrograd. His earlier appeals for "All Power to the Soviets!" had now given way to screamed warnings about the "counterrevolution," the military as a "danger from the right," and reports of the approach of German troops to Petrograd. In a letter of September 1917, Lenin agitated for the Central Committee and the Petrograd and Moscow Councils of Workers and Soldiers Deputies (which had existed since the end of August) to seize power:

> Now that the Bolsheviki have achieved a majority in both of the Workers and Soldiers Councils of the capital cities, they can and must take the power of the state into their own hands. They can do this, because the active majority of the revolutionary elements within the population of both cities is sufficient to pull the population along with them and overcome the resistance of the enemy.

"All the News That's Fit to Print."

The New York Times.

THE WEATHER
Fair and warmer today; Tuesday, continued warmer; southwest winds.

VOL. LXVII...NO. 22,069 ....   NEW YORK, MONDAY, JUNE 17, 1918.—TWENTY-TWO PAGES.   TWO CENTS In New York | THREE CENTS

AUSTRIANS CROSS THE PIAVE AT TWO POINTS; CLAIM 16,000 PRISONERS, BUT ALLIES GET 3,000; AMERICANS DEFEAT THE GERMANS WITH GAS

ITALIAN ARMY STRIKES BACK

Checks Massed Attacks by Austrians by Strong Counterattacks.

RECOVERS TWO MOUNTAINS

Enemy Detachments That Succeeded in Crossing Piave River Are Being Pressed Hard.

VIENNA CLAIMS WIDE GAINS

British Eject Invaders from Positions They Stormed at Beginning of the Drive.

ROME, June 16.—A battle of great violence, in which large masses of infantry are being used by the Austrians in an attempt to break through the Italian lines, particularly in the eastern sector of the Asiago Plateau, in the Brenta Valley, and on Monte Grappa, and during which they succeeded in crossing the Piave River at two places, is described in the official report from Italian Headquarters to-day.

Unofficial advices from the front say the objective of the drive across the Piave was Treviso, but that the enemy was pressed back.

The enemy's attacks in the mountains, which were met in the advanced defensive area, at first carried some of the Italian positions there, but later the line was re-established at most points.

The Italian forces are firmly holding the Asiago front. The War Office announcement says they have completely reoccupied their original positions on Asolone and Monte Solarola and are closely pressing the enemy who crossed the Piave.

During their wide offensive the Austrians, after a violent bombardment, attacked the French positions, (between Osteria di Monfenera and Maranzine,) but the very efficacious fire of the French broke down the thrusts. The enemy casualties were heavy, and in addition he left numerous prisoners in the hands of the French.

The battle is in progress along the whole of the front.

Official Version of the Battle.

The text of the official statement reads:

A great battle has been in progress on our front since yesterday.

After artillery preparation, which was exceptionally intense on account of the violence of the fire and the number of guns employed, the enemy has begun his expected offensive by launching large masses of infantry to attack our positions in the eastern sector of Asiago Plateau, at the end of the Brenta Valley and on Monte Grappa, by attempting at several points to force the Piave, and by carrying out heavy local demonstrative action on the remainder of the front.

Our infantry and that of the allied contingents fearlessly bore the tempest of the destructive fire, and, supported by a barrage of their own artillery, which had already prudently anticipated the enemy's preparation with a timely and deadly counter-preparation bombardment, bravely sustained the enemy's onslaught in the advanced defensive area.

On the 150-kilometre front more intensely attacked the powerful storming columns of the enemy occupied in their initial rush forward only a few front line positions in the Monte Di Val Bella region, in the Asolone area, and at the head of the Monte Solarola salient.

Some troops succeeded in passing to the right bank of the Piave River in the Nervesa area and in the Fagare-Musile region.

During the day our troops initiated along all the front, attacked energetic counterattacks, which succeeded in holding back the powerful pressure of the enemy and in regaining a good portion of the positions temporarily yielded, on some of which, however,

isolated detachments had with great valor continued to remain at all costs.

The struggle did not diminish in violence during the night, and is continuing fiercely. But our troops are firmly holding the front along the Asiago Plateau, have completely reoccupied their original positions on Asolone and at the Monte Solarola salient, and are very closely pressing the enemy infantry which has passed to the right bank of the Piave.

The number of prisoners so far counted is more than 3,000, including 89 officers.

Our own and the allied airmen are taking a strong part in the battle by bombarding the crossing points on the Piave and by attacking the enemy's massed troops with machine gun fire. Thirty-one enemy airplanes have been brought down.

British Retake Lost Positions.

LONDON, June 16.—The Austrian troops who penetrated the line held by the British on the Italian front have been driven back and the British line has been completely re-established.

This announcement is made tonight in the official statement issued by the War Office on the operations in Italy, the text of which follows:

The pocket in the British front, mentioned in the communiqué of last night, has been cleared of the enemy during the night and the early hours this morning and we are now again established on our original front line. (Four Austrian divisions attacked the British line on Saturday, and on the left penetrated the front to a depth of

a thousand yards along an extent of 2,500 yards. There the enemy was held.)

Over 350 prisoners have been counted and we have, in addition, captured two mountain guns and a considerable number of machine guns.

In the early hours of yesterday, when the hostile attack was first launched, invaluable assistance both in infantry and artillery was immediately provided by the Italians on our left, and this assistance was largely responsible for bringing the Austrian infiltration to an immediate halt.

Heavy fighting is continuing in many places along the Piave, on the eastern end of Montebello Heights, and astride the Brenta Valley.

Three additional enemy airplanes were destroyed in air fighting yesterday, seven having previously been reported. The clouds remained low and distant reconnoissances were impossible. The energy of our air service has been mainly confined to attacks on bridges for troops, which the enemy was attempting to throw across the Piave. In these attacks the aviators have been very successful.

CLAIM 16,000 PRISONERS.

Austrians Admit All Gains in the Mountains Were Not Held.

LONDON, June 16, (British Admiralty, per Wireless Press.) — The Austrian official communication received here by wireless tonight says:

Yesterday morning our armies, after artillery fire lasting several hours,

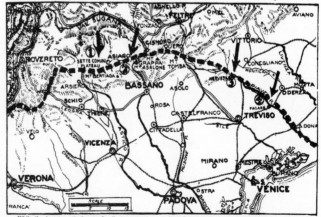

Scene of the Great Drive in Italy

While the Austrian attack extends all along the front, indicated on the map by the broken black line, their principal efforts in the mountains were directed at the Sette Comuni plateau, (1,) and eastern end of the Brenta, from the river to the regions of Monte Asolone and Monte Grappa, (2.) On both of these sectors the attack at first made some progress, but by fierce counterattacks the line was re-established. Along the Piave River the Austrians succeeded in crossing in the vicinity of Nervesa, (3,) and in the Fagara-Musile area, (4,) but the detachments which reached the west bank are being closely pressed, according to the Italian official report.

Cadets of the Alexandrinian military academy in Moscow, with their command
Konstantin Konstantinovich.

Pioneer camp of the Alexandrinian military camp.

e 3rd company of the Petersburg military academy.

lets of the Alexandrinian military academy gather for a prayer.

Lenin during a speech to the All-Russian congress of Soviets in 1917.

October revolution, Moscow, 1917.

. Stolypin and the deputy secretary of the interior and governor of Petersburg,
rlov (right).

Lenin's arrival in Petrograd, April 1917.

Lenin around 1917.

The route of Lenin's "sealed train," from Zurich to Petrograd.

…dek, Karl: revolutionary, agitator and author.

Revolutionary navymen controlling I.D.'s in Petrograd, 1917.

Lenin, Nadyezhda Krupskaya and A.I. Yelisarova with nephews.

In view of the Democratic Conference, which threatened to take the wind of radicality out of the Bolsheviks' sails by nullifying Bolshevik arguments about broad consensus within the population, Lenin came out firmly against any compromises and demanded sole power:

> The Democratic Conference does not represent the majority of the revolutionary people. Rather, it represents the petit-bourgeois upper classes willing to make compromises. The Democratic Assembly is deceiving the peasants. It gives them neither peace nor land. Only a Bolshevik government will satisfy the peasants. Why is it necessary for the Bolsheviks to seize power right now? Because the imminent takeover of Petrograd by the Germans immeasurably worsens our chances.

Lenin circumvented the argument that the Bolsheviks do not indeed have a nominal majority:

> It would be naive to wait for a formal majority of Bolsheviki. No revolution waits for that. History will never forgive us if we do not seize power now.[5]

These appeals, brought by quiet messengers to the headquarters of what by now had become the Military-Revolutionary Committee in Smolny, the former school for daughters of the aristocracy, became more urgent. Lenin wanted to fend off tendencies toward unification caused by the Pan-Russian Congress of Soviets, set for 25 October. He was also afraid of a threatened separate peace with Germany that would take away his arguments for peace. Lenin had contact with middlemen in Stockholm even while in hiding, and it can be assumed that he was aware of the imminent secret peace negotiations between Kerensky and the Austro-Hungarian foreign minister, as well as of talks aimed at achieving a separate peace between the Germans and the English (allies of the Russians). This would have pulled the rug out from under Bolshevik propaganda based on promises of achieving peace. On 10 (23) October, Lenin returned to Petrograd in disguise. With great force, he called upon his indecisive comrades in arms Karmenyev[6] and Sinoviev to work for a coup d'etat. He did not want to run the risk of waiting for the results of the election for the Constitutional Assembly set for the 11th (24th). In the morning hours, after a long night of heated discussion, he managed to get the upper hand over his skeptical comrades.

The leader of the Bolsheviki recognizes Trotsky, Sinoviev,

Kamenyev, Stalin, Sverdlov, Uritzky, Dzherzhinsky, Kolontay, Bubnov, Sokolnikov, and Lomov to be motivated organizers and determined planners of a coup d'etat. The Military-Revolutionary Committee's chief instrument was the Red Guard, which consisted of armed workers and sailors. These were mostly men of Baltic (Latvian) origin, who were glad to cooperate with the Bolsheviks if for no other reason than that they were enemies of Germany. The Red Guard also consisted of soldiers interested chiefly in getting rid of a government that continued to fight the war. The Red Guard officially designated itself as the "organization of the armed might of the proletariat in the struggle against counterrevolution and in defense of the achievements of the revolution."

Both sides—the Provisional Government as well as the Military-Revolutionary Committee of the Bolsheviks—called upon the population to maintain discipline. In appeals that followed one after the other, they warned the Petrograd garrisons of the danger of losing the revolution— each meaning something quite different by this. "Revolution" varied according to who was talking about it. The Bolsheviks appointed commissars who worked to assure the support of the armories and the postal and telegraph services. Meanwhile, the government's attempts to protect administrative and government centers were purely defensive, if that.

The journalist Suchanov (Nicholas Nikolayevich Himmer) remembers one of the last days before the October coup:

> At 11:00 in the evening, I was sitting in the editor's office and rushing to finish my lead article. It was the same subject that I had discussed an hour earlier in the editorial meeting. The change of mood, which strengthened the Bolshevik Party, was a dangerous thing. The situation could only be mastered and the revolution brought into an orderly path if the leading members of the Menshevik Social Revolutionaries changed their behavior. When I read my article to my editors Avilov[8] and Basarov, they objected to my formulation, "The Bolsheviks are preparing for a coup d'etat." This seemed to them a doubtful and tactless assertion. I became very angry. Basarov supported me, but Avilov stuck to his guns. Basarov yelled at Avilov, Avilov yelled back, both of them yelled at me, and I yelled at both of them. Finally, I threw the article into the waste basket, but it was needed, so we got it out again and went to the door still yelling at each other. Avilov and Basarov went home, and I ran to the printer's to publish the article.

After all, Trotsky himself had responded the day before to questions about an imminent uprising—intended to put down a counterrevolution and save the achievements of the revolution: "Yes, an uprising is about to take place, and the Bolsheviks will take power into their hands as the majority in the Congress. The necessary steps have already been taken by our Military-Revolutionary Committee." Wasn't that clear enough?

It was not just Trotsky who had made such announcements. But the day, hour, and method of this coup d'etat remained unknown. Hence, no one took these assertions seriously.

Suchanov speculated about Kerensky's reaction to this danger— inasmuch as anyone inside the government recognized it to be a danger:

> What could he do? It was clear that it was high time for action. The Peter-Paul Fortress had been taken and was in the hands of the Bolsheviks, the arsenal had been seized, and the government's order to remove Bolshevik commissars had been disobeyed.
>
> Reliable units had been called up. If they did not obey commands, nothing could be done. Special units had been called in to guard the Winter Palace, and guard divisions had been formed. There were loyal forces inside the city—perhaps even entire divisions. Several thousand men could be recruited from among the military cadets, the landed gentry, and members of other loyal units. But a decision to act and to seize the initiative had to be taken.

On the morning of 24 October (6 November), the Kerensky government held a crisis meeting (as it had done for days and nights before), which was supposed simultaneously to set guidelines for the approaching preparliamentary assembly for the Congress of Soviets. The minister spoke about dangers "from the left and the right." Alarmed about the activities of the Military-Revolutionary Council, he ordered cadets from the military academies to storm the Bolshevik printing presses. Trotsky ordered in a unit of his Red Guard, consisting of soldiers from the Lithuanian Regiment. In the afternoon, another unit of cadets attempted to storm the Bolshevik headquarters, but it was overwhelmed by Red Guards and imprisoned in the Peter-Paul Fortress.

Kerensky's request to arrest all the members of the Military-Revolutionary Committee was turned down by Justice Minister Malyantovich.

In the meantime, battle-ready torpedo boats were arriving from

Helsinki. The Smolnyi headquarters of the Bolsheviks looked like a fortress. At the same time, rebels had taken up positions at all strategic points—in front of the Winter Palace and at bridges. Officially and in their appeals to the population and the barracks, the Bolsheviks said they were only working for "protection against the imminent threat of counterrevolution." Colonel Polkovnikov, commander of the Petrograd military district, called on his units to stay inside their barracks and disobey "orders" from anyone else, but his appeals achieved little. The bridges on the Neva had been raised to allow free passage for ships. For this evening, at any rate, the population did not expect any special events. Yelena Sacharovna remembers:

> We had been invited to a wedding by some friends. Everything was quite peaceful. It wasn't until late in the evening, when we went away, that we saw people running toward the Nevskiy and heard shots.

According to the Russian calendar, the evening of 25 October had arrived. The way the revolutionaries saw it, the course of events surrounding the storming of the Winter Palace looked about the way Alexander Belyshev described. He was a commissar on the battleship *Aurora*, which had placed itself under the command of the Military-Revolutionary Committee and was lying at anchor near the entrance to the city:

> The Revolutionary Committee in the Smolny summoned represent-atives from the *Aurora*. The ship's mechanic and I went. We went to the third floor, in the left wing of the building. There we entered the office of the commissar. A man with a pince-nez wearing a black jacket was sitting at a desk.[9] Spread out in front of him was a large map of Petrograd. He told us that the Revolutionary Committee had named me commander of the battleship *Aurora*. I replied, "The decision of the Revolutionary Committee is an order for me."
>
> We decided to lead the battleship up the Neva and anchor it at the Nikolayevsky Bridge. I went to our high commander and told him that the order had been given to let down the bridge. He replied that because of the situation it was not good to weigh anchor in front of the Winter Palace. But a little further on the ice covering would be strong enough and would allow access without gangways, if this should prove to be necessary. At 3:30 in the morning on 25 October, then, the battleship was lying at anchor by the Nikolayevsky Bridge. When the men who

were guarding the bridge saw our armed battleship and the spotlights
directed to the bridge, it became clear to them that they had better obey
our orders to let down the bridge after our passage. Thus, the armed units
were able to cross over from Vasilyevsky Island and begin the encirclement
of the Winter Palace.

The sailor Lipatov remembers the moment when the signal was
given to attack:

In the early morning, I could hear as if from a distance shots coming
from the direction of the encircled Winter Palace. Our battleship was
lying at anchor by the Nikolayevsky Bridge. Suddenly, a little sloop with
a report from the Revolutionary Committee came and gave us the order:
At nine o'clock in the evening, the deadline would run out for the Provisional Government to surrender. If it refused, a red rocket would be
shot up from the Peter-Paul Fortress. This in turn would be the signal
for the *Aurora* to give off a warning shot that would usher in the storming
of the Winter Palace. The deadline drew closer. There was absolute silence
on board. Everyone was staying at their posts and looking toward the
Peter-Paul Fortress. The hands on the clock showed that the deadline had
already passed. Another ten minutes, another fifteen minutes. Finally the
shout: "The signal, the signal!" Out of the darkness rose the rocket.

Almost none of the attackers owned a watch. Hence the rocket flare
and the warning shot were of elementary practical importance for the
attack. Shots were made with three and six inch cannons from both the
Peter-Paul Fortress and the *Aurora*. When the attackers were pushed
back by machine gun fire from the defenders of the Winter Palace, they
resorted to artillery fire of which they possessed four pieces.

Sergey Smirnov is a member of one of the units that had taken up
position on the banks of the Neva opposite the Winter Palace and were
waiting for the signal to begin:

The attack began from four sides at once. The general attack began
right after the warning shot from the *Aurora*, planned for 9:45 in the
evening. At this time, our unit was standing at the corner of house number
four, the home of the former police commander of Petrograd. From here,
we began the storming of the Winter Palace, which was on the other side.
We had been given the mission of taking the Saltykov Gate and fighting

through to the interior of the palace. Our troops consisted of 140 men. We ran quickly to this entrance, the ceremonial gate. The doors were chained shut; it was a huge, heavy metal gate with cast iron fittings. We had to break it open with heavy battering rams, and thus we made it inside. Once we had gotten into the place, we ran right up to the second floor, and our troops immediately took control of several glittering rooms. We fought through to the throne room. There we met a large mass of people—Red Guards, sailors, soldiers. Antonov Ovseyenko, the leader of the attack, stopped in front of a door behind which the government was probably meeting. He knocked on the door. Finally, he ordered us to open it by force. For the Provisional Government, that moment meant—as Mayakovsky put it later: "Your time is up!"

From the perspective of the Winter Palace, though, people were obviously in the defensive. For many days now, the rooms in the upper story had been occupied by cadets, and they looked like huge bedrooms full of weapons. Now the cadets set out to defend the Winter Palace, although they were aware neither of the massiveness of the attack that was planned nor of the high battle morale of the revolutionary troops.

The ministers of the Provisional Government were holding a crisis session, and their meeting room was specially guarded. The then justice minister P.N. Malyantovich describes the scene, which looked a good deal less heroic from his perspective:

> We were conferring among ourselves, practically paralyzed in our passivity, waiting defensively. Suddenly, we heard noises down below. The noises gradually got louder and closer. When we heard this multiplicity of individual noises, which finally grew and grew into one single mighty sound, we sensed that some decisive, final moment had come. Suddenly, it became clear that the end was at hand. The noise grew and grew, and it overwhelmed us like an immense wave. Our intimidated minds were filled with a painful certainty like a gust of air. It was clear: This was a slaughter, we were in the process of being taken by storm. Resistance was pointless—sacrifice would be senseless.
>
> The door was swung open, and a cadet rushed in, saluted, and gasped excitedly but with determination: "What are the orders of the Provisional Government? Should we defend ourselves to the last man? We are prepared to carry out every order of the Provisional Government."
>
> "No, that will not be necessary! It is pointless! The situation has been decided! We do not want a bloodbath! We must surrender!" everyone

shouted in a chorus, without any kind of discussion, and without looking at each other. We knew already that the decision was in everyone's eyes.

One of us—I believe it was Kishkin—got up and said, "If they are here, that means that the palace has already been taken."

"It has been taken. All the entrances have been blocked off. Everyone has surrendered. This is the only room that is still protected by our guards. What is the command of the Provisional Government?"

"Tell them that we don't want a bloodbath. We give in to force, we surrender," replied Kishkin.

There was a sudden noise behind the door. It broke open. Like a plank of wood being flung away in a high arc from its plane, a little man flew into the meeting room, catapulted in by an advancing mob of people, which streamed after him like a flood of water and began to flow into every corner of the room until it had filled it up entirely. The little man was wearing a loose, open coat, an immense felt hat had been drawn down low over his head with its red hair, coming down in front all the way to his glasses. He had a short mustache and a little goatee. His narrow upper lip curved up to his nose when he spoke. His eyes were colorless, and his face betrayed tiredness.

But when he rushed in, he immediately cried out in a piercing, high but determined voice: "Where are the members of the Provisional Government?"

"The Provisional Government is here," replied Konovalov,[10] maintaining his seat. "What do you want?"

"I inform you that all the members of the Provisional Government are under arrest. I am Antonov, Chairman of the Military-Revolutionary Committee."

"The members of the Provisional Government give in to force and surrender, in order to prevent a bloodbath," declared Konovalov.

"To prevent a bloodbath! And how much blood have you spilled?" came from one of the corners behind the guard. Many voices are raised in agreement. With a generous gesture, Antonov puts an end to the scene.

"Enough, comrades! It is enough! That will all come later! Now we have to write a protocol. I will write that in a moment. Now I will ask. . . But first I demand that you give up all the weapons in you possession."

Members of the military give up their weapons, and the rest declare that they don't have any.

The room was packed with soldiers, sailors, and Red Guards, some of whom are carrying several weapons at once: one rifle, two revolvers, a sword, two machine gun belts.

When it became known that Kerensky had fled, we could hear the most vulgar kinds of curses from the mass of people. Some of the men screamed, "Kill them! Or else they'll run away too! Why waste time with them?"

The next moment, the ministers were taken away to the Peter-Paul Fortress. The man just quoted was indeed able to get away, because in the middle of the Neva Bridge shots were suddenly fired from the fortress at the crowd of people rushing toward it. The guards fled, along with the minister. In the midst of this chaos, and during the methodically carried-out revenge on the remnants of bourgeois Russia, others had less luck.

M. Philips Price, the *Manchester Guardian*'s correspondent in Petersburg, was keeping a watch on the Smolny headquarters of the revolutionaries:

At the same time, there was a meeting at the Smolny Institute, where the delegates to the Second Soviet Congress from the Petrograd Soviet were supposed to be elected. Trotsky was the chairman, and on the stage stood the same small, bald-headed little man whom I had seen six months earlier as the leader of the tiny Bolshevik group at the first Council Assembly. It was Lenin,[11] without his mustache, which he had shaved off in order to change his appearance during the period of hiding, which was now to come to an end.

The Petrograd Soviet was a unified phalanx of Bolshevik deputies, and continuous applause thundered through the hall as Lenin spoke of the beginning Soviet Congress as the sole organ which was capable of carrying out the revolutionary program of the Russian workers, soldiers, and peasants.

Beside me someone whispered that news had just arrived that the Military-Revolutionary Committee, assisted by Red Guards from the factories and some of the garrisons, had occupied the Winter Palace and arrested all of the ministers but Kerensky, who had escaped in a car.

I went one floor below to the Bolshevik Party office. Here I found a sort of improvised spiritual revolutionary general staff. It was sending out messengers with instructions to all parts of the city who were to return as soon as possible with news and information. In the other offices, and in the old Menshevik and Social Revolutionary People's Committee quarters, there was a deathly silence. A couple of secretaries were busy organizing papers, and Rosanov, the publisher of *Izvestia*,[12] was trying to maintain his composure.

The Second Soviet Congress, which was called into session late in the evening on 25 October (7 November), was indeed faced with the *fait accompli* of the Bolshevik seizure of power. The Red Guard was in control not only of the Winter Palace but also of the building where the Congress was meeting. One speaker after another rose to protest the coup d'etat in the noisy hall, but the Bolshevik leaders simply made fun of them. Trotsky's response to the betrayed and bitter Social Revolutionaries, who had thought themselves to be fighting for the same cause, was to go down in history: "Why don't you go off to where you belong: on the junk heap of history!"[13]

What was it like for the city's inhabitants, who found themselves more or less by coincidence in the center of action? Arkady Petrovich Stolypin was still living with his mother and his siblings in a side wing of the Winter Palace, in the official apartment of his father, Minister Pyotr Stolypin, who had been murdered in 1911. He remembers:

My mother and I were on foot in the city and walked past the Winter Palace. At first, there was no evidence of anything going on of the sort that Eisenstein and other filmmakers showed. Nothing like that happened. Barricades had been set up in front of the palace using wooden planks. Behind them, cadets and the women's battalion were looking out—the "Death Legion," as it called itself. Cadets were standing in front of the palace, but no one was in command of them. I was a little boy and lived in one wing of the Winter Palace. I knew all the various entryways, and I could have gotten into any wing. The real events did not happen until late in the evening, when everyone pressed in. There was no real storming necessary, because there was no resistance; all that was left there by the time we went by were the remnants of the cossack troops—in the place where the Atlases support the decorative pillars. Further on, I saw a troop of the Red Guard posted near the bridge, but no one was really fighting; everyone was just looking at each other. There were no orders or directions. Finally, Kerensky fled, and the cadets and cossacks dispersed in all directions.

Kerensky himself undermined discipline in the army. He had already imprisoned Danilov and other generals, and I do not understand how he could have thought that the army would support him under these circumstances. There was no one in the Winter Palace who could really have given orders. The few cadets and volunteers quickly left, and several of the troops of workers and part of the garrison remained neutral. Thus the troops of the Red Guard were able to force their way into the Winter Palace and arrest the Provisional Government. If there had really been any kind of organized resistance, the Reds probably would not have succeeded in overthrowing the government. But everyone despised Kerensky, and above all no one had the slightest idea what the Bolsheviks really were! Many people—even people from the aristocracy and from wealthy families—were happy that the Provisional Government had come to an end and that Kerensky had run away. They thought that nothing could be worse than what he had done or not done. The army had dissolved, the Germans were approaching, there was no more discipline, supply transports were disorganized, and no one comprehended who the Bolsheviks really were and what they were going to do.

Nina Alexeyevna Krivosheyna was twenty-one years old. On the evening when events came to a dramatic head, she was at the theater with her aunt:

> On the evening of 25 October (7 November), I was in Petrograd and went with my aunt, Natalya Sergeyevna Polevaya, to the "Narodny Dom" to hear Shalyapin. They were doing Verdi's *Don Carlos*, and although I had already heard Shalyapin and been at some of his concerts, I had never seen him as King Philip. By the way, I only saw that opera once in my life—on that one historic evening. Of course, the house was packed. I remember nothing of the performance itself—except for Shalyapin. His voice has been preserved on records. But words cannot do justice to his acting. Only those who have seen him can understand it. The performance was routine—except that whenever Shalyapin appeared there was applause and shouting, and many people got up from their seats and called to him.
>
> After the first act, everyone was waiting for the curtain to go up again. There was excited silence. Suddenly, the lights went out, and it was completely dark. The audience was deathly still. A sudden murmur of voices—and then silence again. There was not even any glimmer of light from the stage. There was a rumbling from behind the curtains. Silence again. A wave of whispering in the uncertain audience. And silence again.
>
> Gradually, it became unbearable. But no one got up from their seats. And there was no panic. Tense waiting. Finally, the curtain rustled, and

in the darkness on the stage someone spoke: "We have a little short circuit. Please remain in your seats. The problem will be taken care of right away." There is a whispering in the audience—a fire? Fire? Uneasy sighs and whispers go through the hall. I do not understand why there was no panic. All that happened was this tense expectation within the audience. Another ten minutes went by. Another twenty. Nothing happened.

Finally, I could no longer bear it because of my fear. These sounds behind the curtains—what was that really?

Suddenly, there was light. The performance went on.

After the end of the show, I got my coat and ran out. On the street, I could hear shots and the pattering of machine guns everywhere—finally an explanation for the noises that we had suspected behind the stage! My aunt wanted to hold me back. She said I should spend the night at her place and not go back home alone. But a streetcar was already coming—today there weren't supposed to be any, after all, and so maybe it was the last—and I ran to the stop and jumped on.

The tram was packed full. On the way, a sailor from the Baltic fleet got on and stepped hard on my toes. He excused himself, but an older gentleman who was sitting in the corner murmured, "Still says excuse me, but just wait, we'll show you yet." I didn't understand at the time what he meant by this. Now I noticed that the sailor was carrying rope in his hand and had a machine gun attached to a wide band over his shoulders! The streetcar was going at full speed over the Palace Bridge, and through the window I could see the façade of the Winter Palace. There were masses of people in the darkness there, Cadets were standing together in crowds and warming themselves at little fires—directly in front of the Winter Palace! I could see very clearly that it wasn't just soldiers and military men there. They were mostly cadets. From a long distance, we could hear shots, despite the noise of the streetcar. Stones flew by the window; some of them slammed into something. At the end of the bridge, there was suddenly a lurch—and the streetcar stood still. Evidently, the driver did not want to drive back because of the situation. But then we suddenly went on again. At hellish speed, he turned onto Naberyeshnaya Street.[14] Again, I could see very clearly the faces of the cadets in front of the palace lit up by the fires. Some of them were rubbing their hands together and hitting their arms to stay warm. But the groups were totally motionless; it was like a strangely enchanted picture. On Gagarinskaya the streetcar, which until then had kept on going without stopping, suddenly came to a halt. The driver opened his compartment and shouted, "Last stop, I'm driving to the vehicle park. Everyone out!"

Shocked silence. Like earlier at the theater. The next moment, the streetcar was empty, and the passengers disappeared in all directions.

I walked across the street. Suddenly, I was all alone. Then I heard the hefty shooting of a machine gun. The shots were echoing through the empty street. Was someone shooting from these roofs? Could it be that they were trying to get me? I still had twelve houses to walk by before I got to my own. I didn't want to run, or to show how afraid I was—I walked quickly, as fast as I could. I arrived home breathless with fear. My mother opened the door, pale with worry. "You *know* that today one's not supposed to be out late at night."

"Did you hear this cannon too?" I asked.

"Which cannon? You must have imagined that."

I let it go at that, so as not to disturb her any further.

The next day, there was confusion. Rumors spread through the city. No one knew anything for sure. It wasn't until the evening that it became clear that the Provisional Government had surrendered, Kerensky had fled, and that we had new rulers. But who among us and our friends really knew anything back then about Lenin and the Bolsheviks? We were still afraid of the Social Revolutionaries—and besides, we were not involved in politics.

Later on, I could not understand how our generation could have taken these events so lightly, so ignorantly—just like earlier during the real revolution of 1905 and then in February 1917. And was it possible that the police chief of Petrograd really didn't know that a certain Yugashvili[15] had come to Petrograd from the Caucasus and was living with a worker named Aliluyev? Is it possible that he didn't know what he was doing?

A lot has been written about that day of the October coup. When I think of the bitter sea of lies that has for so many years been spread over this terrible event in all its suddenness and simplicity, words fail me.

In the early morning hours, the following telegram was sent from the Ministry of War in Petrograd to the headquarters of the general staff in Mogilyev:

The situation in Petrograd is as follows: The Nevsky Prospect down to the Moyka is open for traffic, but from the Moyka to the Winter Palace the area is occupied by soldiers and sailors, who are drawing in on the palace from the left and the right in closed ranks. All the other streets are open. The train stations have been taken over by the rebels, who are having guards patrol the city and arrest people who cannot establish their identity satisfactorily. The Smolny Institute, headquarters of the rebels, is surrounded by armored vehicles and tanks with guards. In general, the streets are quiet, and the mass of the population is surprisingly indifferent to the situation. In the city Duma, there is a meeting of the "Committee to Save the Revolution."[16] It consists of members of the Duma and some from the Central Committees of the Soviets who left the Smolny Institute after breaking with the radicals. The rebels, for their part, are maintaining order by keeping the city in check; Till now there have been no excesses or pogroms to speak of.

The rebels' plan was without a doubt worked out in detail earlier and carried out according to plan. The Committee to Save the Revolution now has no reliable forces to turn to, but it is putting its hope in troops coming home from the front.

At the beginning, the rebels had not revealed their goals, and it wasn't until later, when they saw that they were met with almost no resistance. . . .

The sentence is broken off in the middle—perhaps by a question inserted from Mogilyev: "Where are the members of the Provisional Government?"

The answer from the Ministry of War: "An hour ago they were still in the Winter Palace. Now they are under arrest."

As the light of day shed its rays upon the wind, a sea of leaflets fluttered down over the capital and the entire country. The contents of the leaflet was laconic:

TO THE CITIZENS OF RUSSIA!

THE PROVISIONAL GOVERNMENT HAS BEEN OVERTHROWN. STATE POWER IS NOW IN THE HANDS OF THE PETROGRAD COUNCIL OF WORKERS AND SOLDIERS DEPUTIES OF THE MILITARY REVOLUTIONARY COMMITTEE, WHICH STANDS AT THE HEAD OF THE PROLETARIAT AND PETROGRAD'S GARRISON. THE CAUSE FOR WHICH THE PEOPLE HAVE FOUGHT: A DEMOCRATIC PEACE WITHOUT DELAY, ELIMINATION OF PROPERTY RIGHTS FOR LANDOWNERS IN THE COUNTRY, WORKER CONTROL OF PRODUCTION, THE FORMATION OF A SOVIET GOVERNMENT[17]—ALL OF THIS IS CERTAIN.

LONG LIVE THE REVOLUTION OF THE WORKERS, SOLDIERS, AND PEASANTS!

THE MILITARY REVOLUTIONARY COMMITTEE OF THE PETROGRAD
COUNCIL OF WORKERS AND SOLDIERS DEPUTIES.
25 OCTOBER 1917[18], 10:00 IN THE MORNING

The same morning, the British ambassador in Petrograd, Sir George
Buchanan, set off on a tour of the city to look at the results of the
events. He reported on this in his diary:

> In spite of the sharpshooters stationed near the complex of buildings,
> I found to my surprise that there had only been three major hits on the
> front wall of the Winter Palace. But the part facing the city was covered
> with countless shots. The interior of the palace was a picture of devas-
> tation. Evidently, the rebels smashed everything they could get their hands
> on. The same evening, two officers in charge of the women's battalion
> came to my wife and begged her to do something for the women of the
> women's battalion, who had been mistreated by the soldiers in the most
> brutal way. The same evening, the British military attaché General Knox
> went to the Bolsheviks' headquarters and demanded the immediate release
> of the wounded women being kept in the barracks. At first, the Bolsheviks
> wanted to refuse, pointing out that they had resisted to the very end with
> revolvers and guns. But thanks to the firmness and patience of the general,
> a paper was signed to the effect that the badly wounded would be cared
> for.

Evidently, only a few of the defenders of the Winter Palace were
lucky enough for this, as can be seen from the reports of one journalist,
Sorokin, who worked for *Dyelo naroda* (The People's Cause), and was
close to the Social Revolutionaries. Impressed by the course of events—
the leftists' cause had been killed by the Bolsheviks' action—he now
sympathized more with those against whom the original program of his
party had fought:

> The next day, I saw my unfortunate friends in the party. The outlook
> was terrible. Even outwardly the situation looked desolate. On the corner
> of Shamyensky and Baseyny, I ran into a group of soldiers who were
> plundering a wine store. They were drunkenly saying something about
> "Long live the Bolsheviks, death to the capitalist government." Elsewhere,
> it was the same thing. Everywhere there were soldiers, sailors, and work-
> ers. They also stormed the supplies of the Winter Palace. Broken bottles

were spread over all the squares. Some people drowned in the flooded wine cellars.

The ministers were not murdered. Rather, they were imprisoned in the Peter-Paul Fortress for the time being. Some members of the Provisional Government, however, were later killed sadistically. The fate of the women was more horrible than one can imagine. Many had been killed on the spot, and those who managed to escape death were mistreated in such a way that they died in tortured agony. Freedom! Oh the crimes, the unspeakable crimes carried out in your name!

In his newspaper, Sorokin reported on these things—over the protest of leftist editors who toed the party line. But his article was read with such interest by the population that the newspaper had to print it again three times. He did not have much hopeful news to report: the outbreak of total anarchy, rowdiness, plundering, robbing, massacres of loyal cadets in their barracks. The last defenders of the old Russia were falling. Battles in Gachina. Everything in the city was closed—schools, banks, offices. There was hunger, which causes aggression even without ideological barriers.

The bloody battle had only just begun. Its temporary high point would come in half a year. In July 1918, Lenin, together with Sverdlov, would order the murder of the Czar's family, which was being held prisoner in Yekaterinburg. The last living symbols of the old Russia sank into the earth with the blood of Czar Nicholas II, Czarina Alexandra Fydorovna, the Grand Duchesses Olga, Tatyana, Maria, Anastasia, and Crown Prince Alexey, together with their family doctor and several servants.

According to the protocol of the inquiry, this event took place as follows:

After midnight, Yurovsky[19] woke the Czar's family, explaining that there were pressing reasons for it, that they were to be taken somewhere else. Everyone got ready. Alexey, quite sleepy, was carried on his father's arm, Anastasia carried her little dog. Yurovsky led them over the rear garden to the lower floor and into an empty room, sixteen by eighteen feet large, with a double-paned window that was chained off. He let them wait awhile. At Nicholas's request, Yurovsky had chairs brought in. When they arrived, Alexandra sat down next to the window, Nicholas took a second chair and supported Alexey with one arm and his shoulder, and Alexey himself half-sat, half-lay on the third chair. Behind them stood—

as if for a group photograph—the grand duchesses together as well as the family doctor Botkin, the cook, the servant, and the maid, the thin Anna Demidova. She shoved one of the cushions that she had brought under Alexandra's back. She held the others in her hand.

Suddenly, the Cheka Guard tramped in, each with heavy revolvers in his hand. Yurovsky took a step forward into the room and said, "We have to shoot you." Nicholas got up, still holding Alexey. He was just about to say something, and with his free hand he was making a spontaneous gesture of protection in front of his son and wife, when Yurovsky shot him directly in the head. He collapsed immediately. Alexandra was able to cross herself quickly before she, too, died under the bullet. Dr. Botkin was hit while he was trying to help the Czar. Everyone collapsed immediately, except Demidova. The murderers got rifles from the next room and hit her more than thirty times with the butts—she had run back and forth along the wall, screaming, and protected herself from the bullets with the cushions. For one moment, Alexey groaned and made a motion with his hand toward his father. A guard stepped on his head, and Yurovsky fired at him two or three times. Then everything was quiet. Anastasia had only fainted, and when she woke up again she was killed with the bayonetes. A guard smashed the head of her dog with a rifle butt.

NOTES

1. Party friends saw to it that the evidence against Lenin as a German agent sent out by the Interior Ministry was kept from publication. One newspaper did not comply, and the bomb burst. For a while, Lenin believed that the end of his plans had come.

2. This step was also the result of unbridgeable differences with respect to military and peace goals within the government.

3. This is precisely the Soldiers Council—instituted by leftist forces—which Trotsky was later to squash when he became people's commissar and tried at all costs to restore discipline at the front.

4. At this point, they did not yet understand why he was in such a hurry, since the moment did not seem opportune to them. They believed him to be "hysterical and nervous."

5. This appeal by Lenin, which was a call for action, was dated 15 (28) September 1917.

6. Since July (the arrest of Bolshevik leaders, Lenin's escape, and the search through party headquarters) Lenin's party comrades had become cautious. Moreover, after the

protests of members of their own party as a result of the (controversial) suspicions, they could no longer be certain of their support.

7. Among them there were many peasants—especially among the most recently mobilized reserves—who believed the revolutionary propaganda that while they were at the front land was being distributed at home.

8. N.P. Avilov (real name, Glebov) became the Bolshevik people's commissar for post office and telegraph affairs in the first government.

9. Evidently Trotsky.

10. A.I. Konovalov was minister for trade and industry and vice chairman of the Central War Committee in the Provisional Government.

11. Lenin had not come back to the capital until the evening the attack occurred. He arrived disguised and with a mask.

12. At that time *Izvestia* was still the press organ of the moderate Social Democrats, who were in favor of continuing the defensive war in spite of their democratic goals.

13. This quotation is changed from Hegel.

14. Naberyeshnaya: Street along the banks of the Neva on which the Winter Palace is located.

15. Stalin's real name.

16. A group of moderate revolutionaries.

17. "Soviet" is Russian for "council." Thus, "Soviet government" means "council government."

18. Either the leaflet had already been composed on the day of the putsch and then published the morning after, or it was mistakenly dated 25 October.

19. Yurovsky was the commander of the Cheka Guard and had taken over the murder squad. The entire Russian personnel keeping watch over the Czar's family was replaced by Latvians on the night of the murder, in order to prevent loyal behavior in favor of the Czar. Among the supposed Latvians, there were in fact also some Austrian or Hungarian prisoners of war—called Latvians by the Russians because of their poor command of the language.

Chapter Six

———— // ————

Moscow, 1917

The seizure of power by the Bolsheviks in Moscow and the first measures taken by Lenin.

I had played bridge with my friends that evening. When my servant brought breakfast the next morning, he said laconically, "We have a new government."

I was confused. I hadn't heard anything about the coup the night before. I didn't understand what that was supposed to mean. During the revolution in March, it had been clear: A new government has to come. We would not have had to sacrifice the constitutional monarchy for that. But now—what was it supposed to be? I remembered how I had sometimes stood on my balcony and heard Lenin giving speeches:

"All land to the peasants! Workers, drive away your bosses—you yourselves will become bosses of the workshops and factories!"

At any rate, I did not think of that morning's news as the last word.

Yuri Konstantinovich Meyer was twenty years old in 1917. He was a graduate of the Imperial Alexander Lyceum, which had been Pushkin's school. Shortly before the February (or March) Revolution, he had entered the Page Corps to prepare himself for service with a company at the front. Toward summer of that year, when Lenin began to be seen as a threat to the democratic development of the country, this corps had worked out a plan to murder Lenin. For the time being, though, they had not carred it out.

128

Even the bourgeois newspapers underestimated the significance of the Bolshevik coup the day after 25 October (7 November), though their days were now numbered (one of Lenin's first actions would be the elimination of what was now the oppositional press). They refered to the Bolshevik seizure of power as a "short-lived experiment" and called the Bolsheviks "a handful of miserable fools misled by Lenin and Trotsky," whose decrees and appeals "will one day fill up a museum of the historically odd." Indeed, Lenin had not yet solidified his power.

The seizure of power in Moscow was different. There were more merchants and middle-class people here. There was the textile industry. Conservative forces were traditionally in control there, and only a relatively small part of the population was open to agitation by propagandists. The wave of unrest and strikes in the spring had also spread to Moscow. Colonel Ryabzev, the commander of the Moscow garrison, ordered the Kremlin occupied and kept under control by five thousand loyal officers from the military academy. But proletarians in factories and the railroad were in solidarity with their comrades in Petrograd. They organized a supply blockade, while the Red Guard, supported by infantry soldiers who had deserted, and strengthened by help from nearby industrial areas, soon forced Ryabzev to give up. One week after the coup in Petrograd, on 2 (15) November, the red flag was raised on top of the Kremlin. Soon afterward, the seat of government was moved from Petrograd to Moscow—as had oftened happened in times of crisis, when the country was threatened by outside enemies.

Yevgeniya Kvyatkovskaya was in Moscow at the time:

I was with my brother, who was in the hospital with a leg wound. One leg had to be amputated, and a salt solution improved his condition. I spent the night in the hospital in order to help him. Because of the many wounded, the hospitals were full, and the personnel was overworked.

One night, I heard voices below the window. Someone asked a passerby for his papers, his name, etc.—and it all seemed quite strange to me. A short time later, I heard shots—distant cannon shots. Then the sounds of these shots got closer and closer: Our hospital was not far from the Kremlin gate, near the Manege.[1] In the morning, there was an amazingly loud exchange of shots—evidently the gates of the Kremlin were being dynamited! The Bolsheviks had apparently succeeded in getting in: They wanted to storm the weapons storehouse and seize the weapons. At that point, our district was in the hands of the Whites, and we were right in the middle; this "White district" was surrounded by a ring of "Reds," who were gradually coming closer and closer. So the shots were getting closer and closer, and on the streets about all we could see were soldiers and military men. Shots were coming from guns on top of the roofs, where heavy machine guns had been set up.

Several days later, the newly appointed people's commissar for education, Anatoly Lunacharsky, resigned angrily at a party meeting:

> This is barbaric! The destruction of the old Moscow is a scandal! I am not prepared under these conditions to continue as a member of the People's Commissariat.

But he allowed himself to be persuaded, and after the first few years as education commissar he became the first minister of culture in the Soviet state.

Princess Katharina von Sayn-Wittgenstein deplored the destruction of the city in her diary:

> Apparently, St. Basil's Cathedral, the Ivan Veliky bell tower, and other Kremlin buildings have been damaged in Moscow. When the Germans destroyed the cathedral at Reims, we all cried out that it was barbaric, we sent protests to international offices. Now we have destroyed the Kremlin with our own hands, as well as the Uspyensky Cathedral, traditionally the home of the coronation ceremony of all Russian Czars. We have destroyed what used to crown the glory of our fatherland: the beauty of the old traditions, everything that we inherited from our forefathers—respect for culture and art, love of the homeland, belief in God. What will we raise up in its place? In Moscow, the military command has appointed ordinary soldiers to the position of regimental and squadron commanders! What a measure to defend the homeland!

Lydia Vasilchikova:

> For a while, the Red Guards were held in check by the military schools. Some people were stranded at the Hotel Metropol on Theater Square. Later on, they reported that they had to put up with a real state of siege—complete with days of hunger, food supply shortages, the raising of white flags in order to negotiate with the enemy, etc. My husband experienced all this first hand, because as a member of the synod he was

taking part in the election of a new patriarch—the first such election in two hundred years. When it became clear that further resistance was pointless, the cadets laid down their weapons after the patriarch had intervened. But before this happened there were major battles in the streets of Moscow. One cousin of mine, who was standing in the bay window of her house on Povarskaya Street watching the "events," was hit by a stray bullet. Right at that moment, my husband walked into the house. He immediately called Professor Aleximsky, one of Moscow's leading surgeons. On the way to the hospital, the stretcher-bearers had to take cover with their burden in house doors many times before they could run on to the next cover. The whole city was without electricity, and the operation took place by candlelight. But the wound turned out to be fatal, and my cousin died while she was still anaesthetized.

Vladimir Semyonovich Averino also lived in this part of the city:

In Moscow we lived in an aristocratic area near Povarskaya Street. I can only remember one gunfight between young officers of the Cadet Party and the Bolsheviks. The fighters were a long way from each other, so I couldn't see the Bolsheviks. My father went out onto the street and offered the young cadets some wine. I can still remember that well.

Our house was between the Arbat, where there was a czarist military academy, and Gubernatorskaya Square, which was being kept in check by the Bolsheviks. There were shots from both sides. Our villa stood right in the middle, and the windows were full of bullet holes.

But within a few days, the Bolsheviks had seized control of all Moscow. There were simply not enough people resisting them.

In February, everyone had cheered and been triumphant. But in October, when the "real" Revolution—as they call it—broke out, even the "intelligentsia" began to be afraid. Just like the "bourgeoisie," they tried to flee Moscow. I didn't read any newspapers back then—I was just thirteen or fourteen. But my father was glued to the phone all day and spoke to all of Moscow.

One of the reasons the Bolsheviks were able to gain the upper hand in Moscow was that they called on all officers to register themselves. And a great many complied with this registration—whether out of fear, resignation, or other reasons I don't know. There were 900,000 men in the Russian officer corps at the time. About twenty million men were mobilized in total. Only a few of these 900,000 were fighting on the side of the so-called "Whites," though.

Thanks to my father's position as director of railway transportation, we were able to get papers and a seat on a train to the Ukraine. Like many citizens of Moscow, we were trying to get down there because the area had not yet been reached by the Bolsheviks.[2] From there, we went to Kislovodsk in the Caucasus. There, everything looked as it had before—czarist police officials, everything almost unchanged—and we were very happy. Later, I was arrested at a demonstration of monarchists—of which I was one—even though I was only fifteen at the time. But there were no special laws for juveniles at the time; they had all been swept away by the revolution.

I don't think Pasternak gave a correct picture of the revolution in Moscow in *Doctor Zhivago*. He couldn't have: he didn't have any competence in the area. For one thing, he was not on our side—with the "Whites" in the Civil War—and for another he was not even a Russian, and so his feelings were not those of a real Russian. He was a Jew.

Many Muskovites who succeeded in getting a place and papers for the train south thought that the whole thing was a passing phase. But it was clear to my family that we would probably not return to Moscow. The last thing I remember is how my grandmother on my mother's side went with us to the train station. She talked to me for a long time, until the train left. She urged me never to lose my faith in the Russian people, even if it were to look like a rough and violent mass. Her words are the last thing I remember as I left Moscow.

This was to go on later, too. The Germans had occupied the Ukraine as a result of the peace treaty. Now the Ukraine became a place of refuge for many Russians from the north who had relatives there or any kind of possibility for existence—at least inasmuch as they succeed in getting there. Maria Kusnyezowa and Anna Dermota are examples of this:

> In Moscow, we could not see much of a fight. There were street fights between cadets and Bolsheviks, they shot at each other from rooftops and on the streets.
>
> Later, the Bolsheviks went into every house, checked who was living there, arrested a lot of people, and housed a lot of their own people there.
>
> There were many of battle-weary soldiers among the Bolsheviks. They had run away from the front. They had been promised everything under the sun—land, etc. The best troops weren't there anymore, so we only

had unreliable people. It is well known that our elite had died on the Marne, where we had gone to help the French. The second installment came back from the front and took hold of everything they could get their hands on. That was the result of the Bolshevik propaganda.

Meanwhile, Kerensky was not relaxing. Lenin and his revolutionaries were still exhausted from the seizure of power two days earlier when they hear the bad news from their loyal railroad and Navy commanders: Kerensky, accompanied by cossacks led by Krasnov, was standing beneath the gates of Petrograd. He had fled to headquarters, remembered the patriotic elite troops, and assured himself of their help. With appeals as dramatic as ever, he turned to "brave cossacks and good soldiers of the Don, Kuban, from Trans-Baikal, Ussuri, from the Amur and Jenisey, who have remained faithful to their cossack oath", calling upon them "to save the revolution," in order to get them to march against Lenin's Bolsheviks with himself Kerensky at their head. The detachment under General Krasnov stopped in Gachina for the time being. Krasnov was in charge of the same elite troop that not too long ago had set out for Kornilov against Kerensky and the Bolsheviks, and which Kerensky had stopped in front of the city with help from Social Revolutionary forces.

In this critical situation, Lenin remembered his trusty ally, the commissar of the Baltic Fleet, "Central Balt," which was dominated by Bolsheviks. He called up Nicholas Ismaylov, who remembers:

> I will never forget the night of 27 October 1917. There was a telephone call in Central Balt. People said to me, "Come at once, Lenin wants to speak to you urgently!" I must admit that at first I didn't believe it. "Come at once, it's urgent. Kerensky's troops are on their way to Petrograd; they have already taken Tkach and Zarskoye Syelo and are marching on the capital. They want to put an end to the revolution!" I took my service can and drove to the central telephone office, because we had a direct connecting line there. It was nighttime, and I was very excited.
>
> The first question that Lenin asked me was: "How many armored trucks and ships can you send to Petrograd?"
>
> I thought about it briefly and replied firmly, "Besides the ones that are here we can send in additional navy units!"
>
> Lenin's next question came immediately: "Will there also be supply ships to make sure that there is food?"

I replied, "We have enough food on board."

Then came the third question: "How long will it take for the ships to get to Petrograd?"

I replied, "A maximum of seventeen hours, but I can send them out at once."

Lenin replied, "They are to be sent out without delay so that they can block the sealanes as soon as possible." Lenin asked other questions as well, wanting to know about telegraph and telephone connections for the units that were to be sent to Petrograd. He asked about torpedoes and gave directions about how the ships were to be deployed on their arrival in Petrograd in order to defend the Nikolayesky railway line and other important points. Finally, he made certain that I would set the ships in motion immediately. After that, Lenin said good-bye. I did the same and went to carry out his orders.

The "Committee to Save the Revolution" and the "Committee to Save the Fatherland" were in solidarity with Kerensky's action. Cadets of all the military schools were immediately posted at all important points, including the Astoria Hotel, where several Bolshevik commissars were meeting.

But Lenin quickly organized an even larger number of factory workers, who were strengthened further by people from Tula.[3] The Red Guard soon drove the cadets from their positions. Ultimately, the workers, in solidarity with sailors and railway workers, offered a free retreat to the cossacks to their homes in the south if they would hand over Kerensky, whose leadership they were not pleased with anyway. In view of this offer, the cossacks surrendered near Gachina. They had changed direction and leadership too many times, and they had to stand in support of this and in support of that: They had long since become confused as to who the real enemy was. But minutes before he was to be siezed, Kerensky was able to escape in a sailor suit.[4] Petrograd remained in the hands of the Bolsheviks.

Lenin's first action was the decree about the appropriation of land and property. From animals on farms to workshops or factories and banks in the city, everything was nationalized and declared to be the "property of the people." It was natural that this representation of the situation was taken literally by the less educated part of the population. Without punishment, people acted according to the slogan handed out (from above!): "Steal what was stolen!" Factory managers and later any representatives of the bourgeois classes at all were arrested or taken away.

I. I. Wachrameyevt took part in the seizure of private banks for the new rulers, in order to nationalize them overnight, as had been planned. This action started in Petrograd:

> One of the most important achievements of the young Soviet state was the seizure of the private banks. The bankers were exploiters. They took too long to pay the workers and supported the counterrevolution. They tried to refuse to give the Soviet state money. So the new Soviet state made the wise decision to nationalize all private banks and turn over all financial affairs into the hands of the state bank.
>
> I remember how I was summoned to the People's Commissariat for Finance on the night of 14 December 1917. When I got there, I stumbled into a meeting chaired by Vladimir Ilyich Lenin. About thirty or forty people were taking part in this assembly. Lenin explained to us in his always clear way that he had called us to talk about carrying out the decree about the nationalization of the banks. He said that this was an important affair of the state, and that we were to carry out our duties responsibly, trying not to use force. I was given the task of organizing a group of sailors and seizing three private banks on the Nevsky Prospect simultaneously. The operation had been planned by Vladimir Ilyich. Usually, the bank workers got there at nine o'clock in the morning. At ten, the bank was opened for customers.
>
> The operation began in this way: We were supposed to be there at 9:30, when the workers were already there, but there were no customers yet, and take control of the bank. The sailors came and stationed themselves at all the entrances and exits. All employees were called on to continue with their work. Then I ran to Lenin and told him that our work had been completed. I was then given three men who had been appointed directors of the newly nationalized banks. The former directors were given the choice of leaving the bank or working as assistents to the new directors. Lenin's directions were followed to the letter by the sailors, without any incidents at all. Valdimir Ilyich had said again and again, "You sailors will be used in the most important moments of the revolution." The sailors justified Lenin's confidence.

Ivan Alexeyevich Krivosheyn was staff chaplain of the horse artillery and the son of the former minister of war, who had been working at a Moscow bank since his resignation. He remembers one scene:

> I was at my father's office. A delegation of workers under the leadership of a Bolshevik commissar appeared and tried to take over everything. They were convinced that the Morosovs[5] had money in this bank. That was naive—perhaps there were some financial papers there, but no money and certainly no gold. My father gave them all the keys. At the same time, he thought about how he himself would manage to escape. He had not yet been recognized as Krivosheyn, but when they did recognize him they would take him immediately and shoot him. So he began walking up and down the corridor, and he went down to the dressing room for certain employees, arranged his hat and tie in front of the mirror, put on his gloves, gave the attendant some money, went through the entrance and was on the street. But there, in the little side street through which these men had come, stood their automobile—so that they could easily see the other end of the street. My father went to the left side of the street and had trouble not falling into a sprint. But he passed by unrecognized.
>
> That day, he didn't come home. He spent the night with friends. Then he drove—two days later—directly to Kiev, where there weren't any Bolsheviks yet, and he sent us news from there. Thus he had for the time being escaped arrest and certain death.

Not all the banks had been nationalized—at least for the time being. One American bank in Petrograd was excepted: the National City Bank office in Petrograd. The reason: The Bolsheviks got money from America through this bank. On 8 December 1917 a telegram from a certain J.P. Morgan to W.B. Thompson at the Hotel Europe arrived in Petrograd:

NEW YORK Y 757/5 24w5 NIL—YOUR CABLE SECOND RECEIVED. WE HAVE PAID NATIONAL CITY BANK ONE MILLION DOLLARS AS INSTRUCTED—MORGAN

The account at this National City Bank office belonged to William B. Thompson. Originally at the head of an American Red Cross mission in Russia from June to November 1917, this millionaire came to the conclusion that the Bolsheviks must be helped in their political struggle. Evidently, Thompson's generous assistance for Lenin's party came in large part from cool economic calculations, with which Thompson had soon managed to convince a whole string of other

American banks and companies on Wall Street. The explanation for this could be found a mere two months later in the *Washington Post* of 2 February 1918:

Gives Bolsheviks a Million

W.B. Thompson, Red Cross benefactor, believes that the Bolsheviks have simply been given a bad press. New York, February 2nd (1918). William B. Thompson, who was in Petrograd last year, contributed $1,000,000 to the Bolsheviks to spread their doctrine in Germany and Austria.

As head of the American Red Cross mission, in which position he was equally generous with his money, Mr. Thompson had the opportunity of studying the situation in Russia. He believes that the Russians are the strongest force working against the growing pro-Germanism in Russia, and that their propaganda led to the undermining of the military regimes of the field marshal empires.

Mr. Thompson rejects American criticism of the Bolsheviks. He believes that they have simply been painted in a bad light by the press and misinterpreted. He made his financial contribution to their cause in the conviction that the money was well placed for the future both of Russia and of the Allies.

Of course, the economic speculations of Thompson and other Wall Street Banks that he was subsequently able to win over to his cause were not just the result of an idealist missionary spirit. The Russian non-Bolshevik newspaper *Ruskoye Slovo* (shortly before its end) saw this quite clearly. In an article about Thompson's agent, Raymond Robins, who took over after Thompson went back to America, it wrote:

He represents the American spirit of work, coupled with American capital, which is running through the hands of the Soviets with the goal of conquering Russian markets.

On his return from Russia by way of England, Thompson found allies—especially Prime Minister David Lloyd George—in a pro-Bolshevik policy that shared with Thompson's calculations not so much political or even ideological interests as the desire to prevent German economic power from getting a hold on Russian industrial and economic markets.

It is perhaps for this reason that the British did not want to compromise themselves in the eyes of the Bolsheviks by following a policy faithful to the dynasty. Despite the blood relationship with the English royal family as well as political commitments as allies, the British refused to grant the former Czar Nicholas and his family refuge in England, thus abandoning him to murder by the Bolsheviks.

At this time, the Bolshevik regime had not yet been officially recognized abroad, and the American initiative was limited to private efforts by economic leaders or their banks. Nevertheless, these institutions and their prognoses for the future, based on thorough examinations of the situation, had an effect on the decisions of the State Department, as they met with officials in a way that prefigures the consultations of today. The American secretary of state, Robert Lansing, even asked for the advice of the American International Corporation about what policies should be followed with respect to the new regime in the Kremlin. At his request, the bank's business director, William Franklin Sands, responded on 16 January 1918:

> To the
> Highly Honored Secretary of State
> of the United States
> Washington D.C.
>
> Sir,
>
> I have the honor of enclosing a memorandum herewith in response to your request for my view on the political situation in Russia. I have broken it into three parts: a historical explanation of the causes of the revolution, inasmuch as that was possible in brief; a further section on suggestions for political behavior; and finally a list of various branches of current American activities in Russia.[6]

As early as January 1918, when the Bolsheviks had lost a great deal of sympathy from within their own population and were forced to take measures to support the regime, Sands predicted in this memorandum an almost total loss of Bolshevik votes in the election scheduled for spring of 1918, and he suggested that American must help "to regain lost ground."

Among the Wall Street firms doing business with the Soviets at the time were—in addition to the American International Corp. of 120 Broadway and the aforementioned National City Bank—Bankers Trust

Co.; New York Stock Exchange; Morgan Building (Corner of Wall and Broad); Federal Reserve Bank of N.Y.; Bankers Club; Simpson, Thatcher and Bartlett; William Boyce; Thompson, Hazen, Whipple and Fuller; Chase National Bank; McCann, Stetson, Jennings and Russell; Guggenheim Exploration, Weinberg and Posner; Soviet Bureau; John MacGregor Grant Co.; Stone and Webster; General Electric Co; Morris Plan of N.Y.; Sinclair Gulf Corp.; Guaranty Securities and Guaranty Trust.

Lenin set about the task of reorganizing the governmental structure of Russia. The ministries were replaced by People's Commissariats. Lenin was chairman of the Council of People's Commissars, Trotsky was commissar for foreign affairs, and Stalin was commissar for national questions. Sverdlov became chairman of the Central Administrative Committee, and V. Bontsch-Bruyevich became business director of the council. Lenin's most drastic measures to gain control of the state were the decrees on the appropriation of land and property as well as any kind of possession or capital; the equal rights of women and men; the subordination of the army and the navy to the new regime; the dissolving of the courts and their replacement by "People's Courts"; the replacement of the police by a militia recruited from among the workers; the monopolization of foreign trade; and the annullment of loans taken out during the czarist period (to the distress of Western European banks). According to *The Wall Street Journal* of 16 July 1986, it was not until sixty-eight years later that a Soviet-British treaty was signed to make good the loans annulled back then. With interest, the sum came to 203 million dollars.

Without a majority, Lenin essentially ruled the country as a dictator, and he was forced to rely on the instruments of repression. After the elimination of intellectual organs of the opposition—such as the non-Bolshevik media—he founded the Cheka—short for Cheryesvychaynaya komissiya (extraordinary commission)—whose job it was to physically prosecute and destroy "enemies of the revolution" and representatives of the bourgeois class whom Lenin expressly declared to be enemies.

The official name for the Cheka, founded as per decree on 7 December 1917 under the leadership of Felix Dzherzhinsky, an engineer of Polish descent, was "Extraordinary Commission for the Battle Against Counterrrevolution and Sabotage." It did not take much to be accused of this. The first publicly announced victims to be shot were cadets and former members of the army. The Cheka organization consisted of an information department, an organization department with subsections, and a death squad. As per an order to all district commissariats, the Cheka immediately spread out all over the country. Brutality was sanctioned a priori, because normal legality had been suspended. After all, Dzherzhinsky's first order had already been to immediately shoot all cadets, policemen, counts, and dukes—and any "representatives of the old regime."

Who became a Chekist?

Dzherzhinsky had recruited the core of his troops from released prisoners, among them criminals. Others were former prisoners of war and deserters, as well as honestly enthusiastic revolutionaries who believed in an end that justified the means. Others may well have been governed by personal hostility to representatives of that other "class" against which they were supposed to fight. Or they became Chekists like Joseph Germek. Here is his story:

I was born in Hungary in 1893. During the First World War, I was a soldier in the Hungarian Army. In 1915–1916, I was taken prisoner and transported to a prisoner of war camp near Petrograd. The prisoners were being used to build a railway line. When the October Revolution broke out, the prisoners escaped. Almost right afterward, I joined the Cheka. I worked for the Cheka under the name Geza Kardas. I spent the next two years working for the Cheka in Minsk, Novgorod, Smolensk, Gomel, and other provincial cities. Around 1919, I had achieved the rank of political commissar of the 29th Cheka Brigade, which was operating on the western front. My highest military superior was the general and later marshal Shukov. During this period, our brigade was sent on retaliation missions to the Baltic.

The only executions I carried out were against priests in western Russia. Around 1919, I led a brigade into a city, where my group was also supposed to kill a young Jew. I took a look at him and decided to prevent this and take S. Zukerman under my wing. He joined the Cheka himself and became an executioner. I married his sister. But a short while later, I wanted to go back to Hungary. Trotsky, whom I knew well, wanted to keep me back and made promises about a "shining future." But I wanted to go back. In Hungary, things were very uncertain after Béla Kun, and so I fled with my wife and brother-in-law out of Hungary to Canada.

Joseph Germek heatedly tries to justify himself when he hears
people say that the professional murderers of the Cheka make the
guards at Auschwitz look like harmless rabbits:

> What do these damn airheads know about the Cheka? They were
> patriots in the highest sense of the word, selfless warriors for freedom.
> They never killed except during battle or in order to execute a counter-
> revolutionary.

Germek does not seem to have known about his highest
commander's definition of freedom. The Social Democratic
representative Grigory Alexinsky relates a dispute with Lenin about this
question:

> Lenin: "Freedom! What freedom?! Where have you read that the peo-
> ple demand freedom?"
> Alexinsky: "But what are they demanding then, your people?"
> Lenin: "Power! The people do not need freedom, because freedom is
> one of the forms of bourgeois dictatorship! There is no freedom in a state
> that is worthy of the name. The people want to exercise power. Freedom!
> What are they supposed to do with that? We have to give the farmers
> land, the soldiers peace, and the workers power. Every action that does
> not start with these three goals is the result of a false interpretation of
> Marxism."

Lenin's most pressing problem was the approaching Constitutional
Assembly, which had long since been demanded by the population, and
which the Provisional Government had promised for fall. Planned date:
28 November (11 December), 1917. Lenin saw this assembly as a
critical confrontation, since the Bolsheviks were in the minority against
the Social Democrats. If elections were held, they would not be able to
maintain power legitimately. He tried to postpone the assembly. But
this was not possible, due to the pressure of the other parties which
were officially still in existence. Hence Lenin ordered several
representatives of bourgeois parties arrested as "enemies of the people."
In preassembly elections, the Bolsheviks got only nine million votes,
compared to twenty-one million votes for the other parties, which
meant 283 out of 715 seats at the assembly. Because of this, the results
of any decisions made legally by the Constitutional Assembly would

have been devastating for the Bolsheviks. As it was, however, the seats
of the "enemy" remained vacant; the assembly refused to confirm the
Bolsheviks' revolutionary measures; and the Bolsheviks left the room
and found another way to torpedo further meetings of the
representatives who had streamed in from all over the country. Sorokin
was one of these representative:

The assembly really opened one day after a day of preparations and
election meetings. There was clear winter weather. Blue sky, white snow,
an optimistic background for the massive election posters which plastered
the city. "Long live the Constitutional Assembly, the master of Russia!"
Masses of people marched through the streets with such banners, greeting
this coming event as the highest authority in their country, the authorized
voice of the people. But when they got to the gates, they found them
closed, guarded on both sides by Bolshevik Latvians[7] armed to the teeth.

Something had to be done immediately. I climbed onto a rung in the
cast iron palace gate and turned to give a speech to the crowd. At the
same time, other representatives continued climbing. They succeeded in
getting the gates open, and the mass of people streamed inside and filled
up the courtyard. Amazed at the courage demonstrated in this action, the
Latvians grew uncertain. We put our hands on the palace itself, the gates
of which were also guarded by Latvian soldiers and officers. Suddenly,
Uritzky and other Bolsheviks showed up behind the gates. I quickly turned
back to the crowd of people and publicly thanked the Latvian soldiers for
their reception of the assembly that was now beginning, and also for the
fact that they had guarded the highest authority in the country and the
freedom promised by them. Afterwards, I quickly embraced the commander of the guard. The entire guard duty was so confused that in the
end they politely opened the gates even wider. We went in, followed by
a lot of the gathered citizens. In the hallway Uritzky,[8] this Jew so repulsive
in his falseness, demanded that we first come into his office and register,
but we shoved him aside scornfully and declared that the Constitutional
Assembly did not need his services. In the hall of the palace, we held our
assembly and called on the Russian nation to defend its Constitutional
Assembly. A resolution was approved stating that the assembly would
come on 18 January, no matter what.

This meant calling off the prevented full assembly but putting it off
to a foreseeable date, about one month later.

mission ceremony at the Smolnyi when it still was an institute for upper
ss daughters.

tersburg cadet corps.

Czar Nicholas II held captive by Red troops.

ober revolution: "The smashing hammer of the proletariat . . ."

Bolsheviks storming the Winter palais on November 7, 1917.

October revolution: street fighting in Petrograd.

on Trotsky.

Lenin during a public speech in Petrograd 1917.

Meeting of Bolshevik Central committee in October 1917.

kady P. Stolypin as a young man.

me minister Pyotr Stolypin, assassi-
ed in 1911.

The sister of Arkadiy P. Stolypin.

The Stolypin family after church on Sunday.

Pyotr Stolypin on his estate.

"All the News That's Fit to Print."

The New York Times.

THE WEATHER
Fair today and tomorrow; moderate northwest to north winds.
Full weather report see Page 21.

VOL. LXVII...NO. 21,839. NEW YORK, FRIDAY, NOVEMBER 9, 1917.—TWENTY-TWO PAGES. ONE CENT In Greater New York. | TWO CENTS Within Commuting Distance. | THREE CENTS Elsewhere.

REVOLUTIONISTS SEIZE PETROGRAD; KERENSKY FLEES; PLEDGE IS GIVEN TO SEEK "AN IMMEDIATE PEACE", ITALIANS AGAIN DRIVEN BACK; LOSE 17,000 MORE MEN

MINISTERS UNDER ARREST

Winter Palace Is Taken After Fierce Defense by Women Soldiers.

FORT'S GUNS TURNED ON IT

Cruiser and Armored Cars Also Brought Into Battle Waged by Searchlight.

TROTZSKY HEADS REVOLT

Giving Land to the Peasants and Calling of Constituent Assembly Promised.

PETROGRAD, Nov. 8.—With the aid of the capital's garrison complete control of Petrograd has been seized by the Maximalists, or Bolsheviki, headed by Nikolai Lenine, the Radical Socialist leader, and Leon Trotzsky, President of the Central Executive Committee of the Petrograd Council of Workmen's and Soldiers' Delegates. Their action has been indorsed by the All-Russia Congress of Workmen's Councils.

A proclamation has been issued declaring that the Revolutionary Government purposes to negotiate an "immediate democratic peace," to turn the land over to the peasantry, and to convoke the Constituent Assembly.

Premier Kerensky has fled. He is variously said to be headed for Moscow and the northern front of the army, and orders for his arrest have been issued. Last night he was reported to be at Luga, eighty-five miles southwest of Petrograd. Several members of his Cabinet have been taken into custody.

The Preliminary Parliament is declared dissolved.

Little serious fighting has attended the revolt so far. The Provisional Government troops holding the bridges over the Neva and various other points yesterday were quickly overpowered, save at the Winter Palace, the chief guardians of which were the Women's Battalion. Here last night a battle royal took place for four hours, during which the Bolsheviki brought up armored cars and the cruiser Aurora and turned the guns of the Fort of St. Peter and St. Paul upon the palace before its defenders would surrender.

Prior to the attack the Workmen's and Soldiers' leaders sent the Provisional Government an ultimatum demanding their surrender and allowing twenty minutes' grace. The Government replied indirectly, refusing to recognize the Military Committee.

Vice President Kameneff of the Workmen's and Soldiers' Delegates told The Associated Press today that the object of taking possession of the posts and telegraphs was to thwart any effort the Government might make to call troops to the capital. The Russkia Volia and the Bourse Gazette have been commandeered.

The city today presented a normal aspect. Even the noonday band accompanying the guard of relief under the previous administration continued its function. There were the customary lines in front of the provision stores and children played in the parks and gardens. There was even a notable lessening of the patrols, only a few armed soldiers and sailors moving about the streets.

How the Revolt Developed.

The Maximalist movement toward seizing authority, rumors of which had been agitating the public mind ever since the formation of the last Coalition Cabinet, culminated Tuesday night, when, without disorder, Maximalist forces took possession of the Telegraph office and the Petrograd Telegraph Agency.

Orders issued by the Government for the opening of the spans of the bridges across the Neva later were overridden by the Military Committee of the Council of Workmen's and Soldiers' Delegates. Communication was restored after several hours of interruption. Nowhere did the Maximalists meet with serious opposition.

An effort by militiamen to disperse crowds gathered in the Nevski and Letainy Prospekts during the evening provoked a fight in which one man is reported to have been killed. Minor disturbances, some of them accompanied by shooting, occurred in various quarters of the city. A number of persons are reported to have been killed or wounded.

Yesterday morning found patrols of soldiers, sailors, and civilians in the streets maintaining order. Further than a continuation of suppressed excitement, the streets of the city presented no unusual aspects. The shops and banks which had opened for business began closing up about noon.

Shortly after noon a Soviet force occupied the telephone exchange, where a small guard had been stationed for weeks. An effort by Government forces to retake the exchange led to a brief fusillade, by which it is believed a number of casualties was caused. The Maximalists remained in possession of the building.

Toward 5 o'clock in the afternoon the Military Revolutionary Committee issued its proclamation stating that Petrograd was in its hands.

The Petrograd Council of Workmen's and Soldiers' Delegates considers this to be the program of the new authority:

First—The offer of an immediate democratic peace.

Second—The immediate handing over of large proprietarial lands to the peasants.

Third—The transmission of all authority to the Council of Workmen's and Soldiers' Delegates.

Fourth—The honest convocation of a Constitutional Assembly.

The national revolutionary army must not permit uncertain military detachments to leave the front for Petrograd. They should use persuasion, but where this fails they must oppose any such action on the part of these detachments by force without mercy.

The actual order must be read immediately to all military detachments in all arms. The suppression of this order from the rank and file by army organizations is equivalent to a great crime against the revolution and will be punished by all the strength of the revolutionary law.

Soldiers! For peace, for bread, for land, and for the power of the people!

Council Welcomes Lenine.

The Petrogad Council of Workmen's and Soldiers' Delegates held a meeting at which M. Trotzky made his declaration that the Government no longer existed; that some of the Ministers had been arrested, and that the preliminary Parliament had been dissolved. He introduced Nikolai Lenine as "an old comrade whom we welcome back."

Lenine, who was received with prolonged cheers, said:

"Now we have a revolution. The peasants and workmen control the Government. This is only a preliminary step toward a similar revolution everywhere."

He outlined the three problems now before the Russian democracy. First, immediate conclusion of the war, for which purpose the new Government must propose an armistice to the belligerents; second, the handing over of the land to the peasant; third, settlement of the economic crisis.

At the close of the sitting a declaration was read from the representatives of the Democratic Minimalist Party of the Workmen's and Soldiers' Delegates, stating that the party disapproved of the coup d'état and withdrew from the Council of Workmens and Soldiers' Delegates.

Later it was announced that the split in the Council had been healed and that a call had been sent out for a delegate from each 25,000 of the population to express the will of the Russian Army.

The official news agency today made public the following statement:

"The Congress of the Councils of Workmen's and Soldiers' Delegates of all Russia, which opened last evening, issued this morning the three following proclamations:

To All Provincial Councils of Workmen's and Soldiers' and Peasants' Delegates.

All power lies in the Workmen's and Soldiers' Delegates. Government commissaries are relieved of their functions. Presidents of the Workmen's and Soldiers' Delegates are to communicate direct with the revolutionary Government. All members of agricultural committees who have been arrested are to be set at liberty immediately and the commissioners who arrested them are in turn to be arrested.

The second proclamation reads as follows:

The death penalty re-established at the front by Premier Kerensky is abolished and complete freedom for political propaganda has been established at the front. All revolutionary soldiers and officers who have been arrested for complicity in so-called political crimes are to be set at liberty immediately.

"The third proclamation says:

Former Ministers Konovaloff, Kishkin, Terestchenko, Malyanovitch, Nikitin, and others have been arrreted by the Revolutionary committee.

Mr. Kerensky has taken flight and all military bodies have been empowered to take all possible measures to arrest Kerensky and bring him back to Petrograd. All complicity with Kerensky will be dealt with as high treason.

Capture of the Winter Palace.

While the All-Russian Congress of Councils had been deliberating the Government forces, including the Women's Battalion, which had been guarding the Winter Palace had been driven inside in the course of a lively machine-gun and rifle battle, during which the cruiser Aurora, that had been moored in the Neva at the Nicolai Bridge, moved up within range, firing shrapnel, and armored cars swung into action. Then the guns of the Fortress of St. Peter and St. Paul, across the river, opened on the structure.

The palace stood out under the glare of the searchlights of the cruiser and offered a good target for the guns. The defenders held out for four hours, replying as best they could with machine guns and rifles, but at 2 o'clock this morning were compelled to surrender.

'RUSSIA OUT' SPURS SPARTANBURG BOYS

Tired Soldiers Speed Up Drill When They Hear That Petrograd Is Moving for Peace.

ANXIOUS FOR THE FRAY

Two More Brigades to be Made of Skeleton Guard Units and Men from Yaphank.

Special to The New York Times.

CAMP WADSWORTH, Spartanburg, S. C., Nov. 8.—Just before sundown a company from the former Second Infantry was wearily going through close order drill out on the parade ground.

The officers, dust from shoes to hats, were hoarse from shouting commands all afternoon and the men, tired of toting their heavy equipment back and forth, were eager for the word to quit. A couple of men from the 102d United States Engineers with nothing to do until mess idly stood by enjoying the grilling of the infantrymen.

Soon a newsboy selling a Spartanburg afternoon paper ambled along and one of the engineers bought a paper. With one last, satisfied grin at the toiling "dough boys," the ex-Twenty-second man languidly glanced at the first page headlines telling the bad news from Petrograd. As they say in the movies, he registered keen and amazed interest, then discipline was forgotten and the engineer shouted at the laboring company:

"Hey, fellows, here's news—Russia is out."

The fagged and dusty company heard the announcement just as they came to a halt. While the Lieutenant drilling the infantrymen indignantly scowled at he excited and offending engineers, there was talking in the ranks. Then the Lieutenant ran the company off into another evolution. He said afterward it was like leading another set of men. The fatigue was gone and until "recall" sounded the company went through the drill freshly and with vim.

Afterward the top Sergeant explained the reason for the change of spirit, thus: "When that guy said that Russia had dropped out, every fellow in the company knew that it was up to the United States to take her place. And, believe me, if you had been doubling over that drill ground for weeks and fairly aching for the welcome word 'Embark,' you'd think any drill was light, too."

A similar sentiment throughout the division was found tonight when the 200 company units were canvassed to find out what the men thought about the news. Everywhere the men were enthusiastic about their chances for quick action. Somewhere in the camp some strategist figured out that if Russia really went out, Germany could throw all the troops now on the Russian front to the Western theatre, and the Allies would have need of reinforcements at once.

This "reliable, inside information" went over the camp like all reports, quickly and thoroughly, and as the newspapermen were assured tonight, the Twenty-seventh being the "best division anywhere," the soldiers became exceedingly optimistic over the outlook.

Lenin giving a speech at a meeting in Petrograd.

ix Dzherzhinsky: Head of the Cheka.

Sverdlov, Yakov: First chairman of the Bolshevik Central Committee who order
the execution of the Czar's family in 1918.

young Yevgeniye Kvyatkovskaya and her brother.

w of the estate of J. Kvyatkovskaya's grandparents.

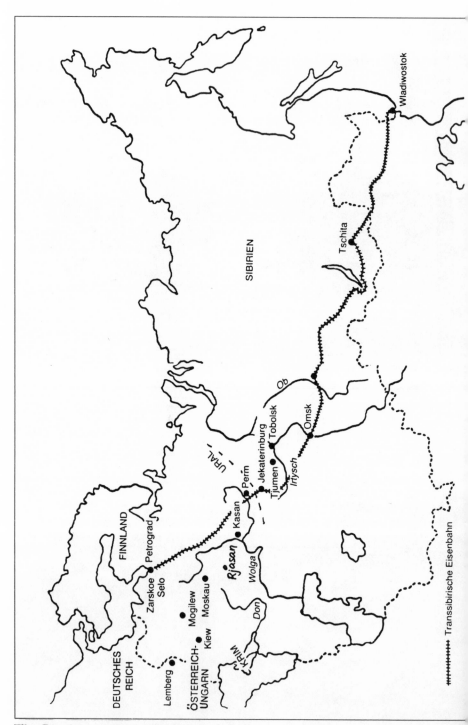

The Russian empire in 1917.

geniya Kvyatkovskaya in a Russian
costume.

Russian policeman on the Red Square in
Moscow before 1917.

sants and workers on J. Kvyatkovskaya's estate.

*Transmitted a: Document No 3
to Despatch No. 1386, dated
July 15, 1919.*

800

*Received at Embassy
11 P.M. Nov. 8/21. 1917*

Monsieur
Ambassadeur des États Unis

Avec la présente j'ai l'honneur de Vous
informer, Monsieur l'Ambassadeur, que le Cong-
res National des Conseils des Députés des
ouv iers et des soldats a établie le 26 du
mois d'octobre a.c. un nouveau gouvernement
de la République Russe sous la forme du Con-
seil des Commissaires du Peuple. Le Président
de ce gouvernement est Mr Vladimir Ilych
Lé n i n e et la direction de la politique
extérieure fut confié à moi, en qualité
du Commissaire du Peuple des affaires ét
rangeres,

En attirant Votre attention au texte
de la proposition de l' armistice et de la
paix démocratique sans annexions ni con-
trubitions, fondée sur le droit des peuple
de disposer d'eux mêmes ,-propositionsap-
prouvés par le Congrés des Conseils des
ouvriers et des soldats,- j' ai l' honneur
de Vous prier, Monsieur l'Ambassadeur, de bien
vouloir regarder le document susmentionné
comme une proposition formelle d'une armistice sans délai sur tous les fronts et de
l'ouverture sans retard des négociations
de paix—une proposition avec laquelle le
gouvernement plénipotentaire de la Répu-
lique Russe s'adresse simultanément à toutes
les nations belligérantes et à leurs gou-
vernements.

Pol. Conde

Letter from Trotsky to the American ambassador in Petrograd for the recogn
of the Bolshevik government, November 1917.

elegation to the Brest-Litovsk peace negotiations, with Trotsky in second
econd from right).

Old Moscow: Lyublyanskaya square.

Kremlin and Savior church.

Louise Patin was a French governess in Russia. She describes the city before this event in January:

It is obvious that these posters, with their huge letters indicating what list to vote for, are intended for an uneducated population. The Bolsheviks' posters are red: "Vote for list 4! You will get bread! Land! Peace!"

The pale blue posters of the cadets are more moderate. The cossacks have white signs with the number 1.[9] On every street corner, in the squares and in the park, one can see Bolshevik soldiers screaming in angry voices and giving pretentious speeches. Men and women of all classes are voting.

But the end of this event was already casting its shadow. Lenin had ordered several representatives of the Social Revolutionary Party, Mensheviks, and cadets, supporters of Constitutional Democracy, arrested as "enemies of the (Bolshevik) revolution." But this was not all, according to their colleague Isgoyev:

I was just leaving my house when I ran into M.I. Ganfaam. He called out to me: "Come quickly—something terrible has happened. A watchman from the Marinskiy hospital has just come and reported that Shingaryev and Kokoshkin were murdered during the night by sailors!" We rushed to the hospital and were told by the nurse that the two men had been sleeping when numerous armed men broke into the hospital and shot them in cold blood. The murder of these two members of the Constitutional Assembly completed the murder of the assembly itself, a fact that could be seen subsequently. A large crowd of people had gathered on the street in front of the hospital.

Official commentary in the Bolshevik newspaper *Izvestiya* came promptly: The tragic occurrence was the work of those who wanted to stain the revolution with blood and discredit it.

Edgar Sisson, since the end of November 1917 President Wilson's special representative, was an American eyewitness to the first and last day of assembly on 5 (18) January 1918:

I saw the demonstrations moving from the Winter Palace over the Nevsky Prospect toward the Taurian Palace, the meeting place. On most of the banners that they carried, I saw the words "All power to the Constitutional Assembly." The men and women marching in an orderly fashion there could easily have been members of the middle class of any other European city or of New York or Chicago. Until they lost their jobs they had worked as teachers, lawyers, civil servants, and business people, as engineers, construction foremen, members of the government, or technicians. Up until that point, they had represented the city's culture, its spirit and individual initiative. Their clothing was clean but somehow poor.

Along the Nevsky stood another line of people who were watching the demonstration with hostility and scorn, occasionally shouting at them but not doing anything more. There were several keepers of order around—not infantrymen or sailors, but rather cossacks from the cavalry. I understood why later.

People wanted to avoid unrest in the city. Sailors had been posted on the Field of Mars and in front of the Taurian Palace. And that's where it happened. The watchers on the Nevsky had formed their own demonstration, and they marched toward the others from the opposite direction. Suddenly, I could hear shots, but it wasn't clear where they were coming from. When I got to the Field of Mars, mounted soldiers ordered us to go back. My peaceful demonstration had been stopped somewhere and chased away. Apparently, this had happened on the corner of Liteyny and Shpalyernaya, where it was only a matter of a right turn to get to the Taurian Palace. Panic broke out among some, and they fled in all directions. Furshtatskaya Street was blocked from both sides. There were trails of blood through the snow. Several demonstrators asserted that they had been shot at from the roofs above. Latvian soldiers appeared from somewhere and formed a blockade along Liteyny Street. They were greeted with cries like "Murderers of the people!" They payed no attention to this and saw to it that the crowd of people was gradually pushed on away from the area around the Taurian Palace.

The meeting place was encircled by a ring of steel. Sisson:

Armed guards were all around us, outside and inside. Sailors with pistols in their belts or rifles hung over their shoulders, soldiers with rifles and ammunition belts were patrolling the building in every hallway and even in every theater box. Even the servants were armed. Lenin himself was there, but somewhere further back under the gallery, as if he were only lending his support. In the course of the coming hours of speeches, he leaned back comfortably in his chair. When political enemies like the few Social Revolutionaries who were there appeared and sharply criticized the Bolsheviks' behavior, calling it a "catastrophe for democracy and the ruination of the country," he smiled in amusement and took notes, and sometimes he even pretended to be asleep. He himself did not speak that evening or night. According to Russian custom, the oldest member was to open the assembly. But the oldest was Shvyezov, a Social Revolutionary. Several Bolsheviks tried to push the old man away from his seat when he stood up, but he was nevertheless able to reach the podium. Before peace had returned to the tumultuous hall, the Bolshevik Uritzky rushed in front of the old men and sounded the bell to call people to order. At this moment, Sverdlov, who had appointed himself provisional chairman, appeared and opened the meeting with the declaration of the rights of the Bolsheviks. Tsereteli's speech for the Social Revolutionaries was the only one that was listened to carefully without interruptions even by his enemies. While he spoke, the sailor in my box kept on pointing his rifle at him, and I wasn't sure whether he was playing with the idea of shooting him by feeling the trigger or whether this was only a gesture. A passing commissar, at any rate, motioned to him with a smile to lower the rifle.

When the non-Bolshevik parties refused to acknowledge the Bolsheviks' decrees about the establishment of Soviet power, the Bolsheviks' left the hall in anger. The Bolsheviks then closed off the building and put it under guard, preventing the continuation of the Constitutional Assembly. The official reason given for this in *Izvestiya* and repeated again by Krupskaya in her memoires was that the Social Revolutionary representatives had been nominated back in the Kerensky era, before the Soviets' seizure of power. Therefore, they were not qualified to represent the population. Thus, the Bolsheviks simply went over the heads of a significant majority of political enemies, but they were forgetting that they still had no legitimate basis for calling themselves and acting as a workers' and peasants' government. Several days earlier, they had used force to break up a peasants' assembly to elect deputies in opposition to the Bolsheviks to the Constitutional Assembly.

On 19 January 1918 at 4:00 in the morning, the gates of democracy were shut for good in Petrograd's Taurian Palace. After all, Lenin had never promised his people democracy. But he had promised them peace. The only chance to preserve his regime was to achieve peace as fast as possible. As early as 26 October (8 November) 1917 he had made a speech on the radio to all nations calling for a cease-fire without territorial annexations or reparations. Two weeks later, Trotsky, now the people's commissar for foreign affairs, had coupled a letter to David R. Francis, the American ambassador in Petrograd, asking for recognition of his regime with an appeal for support of peace initiatives:

The People's Commissar
for Foreign Affairs
Petrograd
7 November 1917
Most Honored Mr. Ambassador of the United States:

I have the honor, most honored Mr. Ambassador, to inform you that on 26 October of this year the National Congress of the Deputies of the Workers and Soldiers Councils formed a new government for the Russian Republic in the form of People's Commissars. The president of this government is Vladimir Ilyich Lenin, and I was entrusted with the supervision of foreign policy in my capacity as people's commissar for foreign affairs.

I would like to call your attention to the suggestion of a cease-fire and a democratic peace without territorial annexations or reparations, founded on each nation's right to decide things for itself[10]—suggestions which have been approved by the Congress of Workers and Soldiers Councils. In doing so, I have the honor, Mr. Ambassador, of requesting you to view the document mentioned as a formal suggestion for an immediate cease-fire on all fronts and the start of peace negotiations. This suggestion is being sent by the authorized government of the Russian Republic simultaneously to all the warring nations and their governments.

I beg you, Mr. Ambassador, to accept my assurance of the great respect and deep honor which the Council Government has for the people of the United States, which, like all the other peoples exhausted by this incomparable slaughter, can only wish fervently for peace.

The People's Commissar for Foreign Affairs
Leon Trotsky
Business Director Bonch-Bruyevich
Secretary N. Gorbunov

As mentioned earlier, the American government continued to hesitate for some time before, spurred on by economic considerations, it finally decided several months later to recognize the Soviet government. But the German government had been waiting for nothing but this offer. On 14 (27) November, it declared itself prepared to enter into negotiations.

For the generation of Russian generals and officers who had been on duty in the first years of the war, a peace treaty at this point meant catastrophe: giving up territory already won and making the real victor accept the dictates of the loser. General Duchonin, high commander of the Russian Army at this time, refused to announce to the allied military representatives the cessation of military action—knowing full well that this behavior would cost him his life.[11] Invoking the "London Protocol" of August 1914, in which Russia had assured the allies that it would not enter into a separate peace or cease military operations on its own, the chiefs of the English, French, Rumanian, Japanese, and Serbian military missions made protests.

Nevertheless, Lenin got his way. On 2 December 1917 there was a cease-fire, on 7 December shooting was stopped along the entire front, and on 9 December peace talks were begun in Brest-Litovsk.

The (Soviet) Russian delegation has been expanded by the symbolic presence of a bearded peasant, a soldier, and a sailor. Moreover, the Ukraine was represented separately. Since March 1917, it had seen itself as an independent Council Republic, and this view was supported by Germany and Austria. The question of the Ukraine, which both sides wanted to claim for their own, subsequently proved to be a sword of Damocles for Trotsky and Czernin (the representative of the Austro-Hungarian government), because both Russia and Austria desperately needed the Ukraine as a source of bread for their starving populations. In the meantime, however, territorial questions were in the forefront of attention when the first German delegation under Von Kuhlmann and the first Russian delegation under Joffe met in November and on 26 December 1917 (8 January 1918) in Brest-Litovsk. At first, Joffe seemed shocked by the territorial demands made by Germany, which amounted to control of former Russian areas: an independent Baltic, Poland, and Ukraine. He was even more shocked when he learned that the Central Committee in Petrograd had little with which to respond to such territorial demands. General von Hoffmann, the man behind these demands, knew well how desperately Lenin needed peace to preserve his revolutionary regime, and he knew that the military forces at the Russian front had become so weak that they would not be able to withstand a German attack. Assistant State Secretary for Foreign Affairs Richard von Kuhlmann reports on the atmosphere in Brest-Litovsk:

The actual meetings took place in the well-kept former officers' casino of the garrison in Brest. There was a large hall in the upper story, which had originally been designed for concert and theater events and was therefore closed off on one side with a curtain.

A large table in the form of a horseshoe had been put into this hall. I sat in the middle of this table with my back to the window, Czernin was to my right, and to my left was the Turkish delegation and members of the German imperial army. Across from me sat the Russian chairman—at first Joffe, who looked out through a monocle as if he were myopic; later it was Trotsky, Lenin's most important adviser, a negotiating partner not to be underestimated; beside him the blond Kamenyev and the historian Pokrovsky. Besides them, on both wings there were Germans and Russians who had been allowed into the meetings.

The Russian delegation was actually larger than mentioned here. It consisted of twenty-eight people and resembled the organization of a chess game without kings. The Soviets were quite concerned to prove outwardly their claim to represent the population and classes mentioned in their self-chosen title. Hence workers, sailors, soldiers were all represented—as well as the the revolutionary woman Bisenko mentioned earlier: She had been the one to shoot General Sacharov while he was reading the letter she had given him. Count Czernin had this to say about her:

> She looks like a beast of prey that has its victim in front of it already and is preparing to pounce on it.

The members of the delegation representing all these classes had almost forgotten the peasants—and this was typical of the Russian mentality: not necessarily to identify with given values but simply to carry them out mechanically. The Russian lieutenant colonel Fokke remembers how one member of the group suddenly thought of this on the way to the train station in Petrograd:

> "We have forgotten someone from the Russian peasantry!" someone called out suddenly in front of us. "We don't have anyone with us who represents the many millions of exploited farmworkers." This was true! But almost at the same moment we spied the figure of a typical peasant with his worn-out coat and backpack. He was just about to turn into a side street up ahead. We drove after him and stopped next to him.

"Where are you going?" asked our Russian peace delegation.

"To the train station, comrades."

"Get in. We'll take you there!"

"Just a minute! That's not my direction, comrades!" protested the peasant, when he saw that we were going in the direction of the Warsaw train station.[12] "I have to go to the Nikolayevsky train station. I'm going to Moscow."

"Which party do you belong to?" asked my colleagues, suddenly concerned that the peasant's loyalties might be for some cause other than the one they represented, thus disqualifying him from the planned action.

"I am a Social Revolutionary, comrades. We all are."

"Left or right wing?" they asked, even more worried.

"Left, comrades, as left as possible, comrades."

"That's good. You're not going back to the country." declared the members, relieved that they had found the right man. They insisted, "You're coming with us to Brest to meet with our enemy. We want to make peace with the Germans."

While this episode is characteristic of the fact that systematic thinking is not one of the typical Russian qualities, it does not negate the fact that Trotsky's strategy was planned well down to every little detail. The course of events and the appearances were like a play organized by a director in the theater, and they offered entertainment for every participant. During the first rounds of negotiations it was still possible for the negotiators to meet with each other outside the bounds of protocol at meals in the parlor on the ground floor. Von Kulmann reports:

A long table was set there. As president, Prince Leopold of Bavaria always sat in the middle. The organization of the table changed every day, and there were always leading members of the various delegations that were represented here sitting to the left and right and across from the prince. At noon people wore street clothes, but in the evening a smoking jacket was required for everyone except military men. Count Czernin tended to decorate his smoking jacket with the Golden Fleece in his buttonhole.

General Hoffmann, the high commander of the German Eastern Army, was also there:

I will never forget the first dinner with the Russians. I was sitting between Joffe and Sokolnikov, who was then commissar for financial affairs. Across from me sat the worker, who was having obvious problems with all the settings and silverware on the table. He tried to do various things with it all, but he used his fork solely for the purpose of cleaning his teeth. Diagonally across from me and next to Prince von Hohenlohe sat the terrorist Ms. Bisenko, and next to her on the other side sat the farmer, a truly Russian apparition with long gray locks and a full beard that resembled a jungle. He made the servants smile a bit when, in response to their question as to whether he wanted red or white wine with his dinner, he answered "The stronger one."

Joffe, Kamenyev, and Sokolnikov made a very intelligent impression. With great enthusiasm they talked about the task that lay before them: to lead the Russian proletariat to heights of prosperity and happiness. Not one of them doubted even for a moment that this would come to pass if the people ruled themselves on the basis of Marxist theory. The vision that floated in front of them, at any rate, was that everyone would be doing well, and some of them would be doing even a little bit better. I suspect that Joffe meant himself here. Of course, the three did not hide the fact that the Russian Revolution was only the first step on the path to happiness for all peoples. Since no communist state could survive if the states around it were ruled by capitalists, the goal they were trying to achieve was world revolution. Besides this, the Russians opened the negotiations immediately with a flood of propaganda speeches and attacks on the "imperialists."

Since the Russian delegation could not simply accept the German demands, it had to consult with the Central Committee. It was impossible to improve the Russian negotiating position by means of military action or even to improve preparedness for such action, since not even propaganda speeches were able to fill the trenches with battle-ready soldiers again. Hence Trotsky invented the slogan "Neither War Nor Peace"—in opposition to Lenin and Stalin and against the suggestion of Bucharin, Kamenyev, and Sinoviev (who plead for a "continuation of the revolutionary war at all costs")—and, at Lenin's request, he returned to the negotiating table in place of Joffe. His determination to end the war without a peace treaty was evident even in his tactics, which determined the atmosphere of the negotiations. Count Czernin noted in his diary:

In the morning, the Russians got here under the leadership of Trotsky. They immediately made it known that they begged to be excused from the meals. We don't see them anywhere else, either, and it seems that the wind is blowing in an entirely different direction from last time.

Kulmann on Trotsky:

The plenary session of the peace delegation took place the next morning. The picture had changed completely. Trotsky was a completely different sort of man from Joffe. His eyes were not very large, but they were sharp and piercing behind his glasses, and he looked at his opponents searchingly and critically. The expression on his face made it very clear that what he really wanted to do was put a definite end to the negotiations that he hated so much by throwing a couple of hand grenades onto the green table—if this could have been made to coincide somehow with his larger political goals. Since I knew that Trotsky prided himself particularly on his dialectics, I was determined to avoid anything that would have given him material for agitation among the German socialists.

Trotsky viewed his opponents with a scorn borne by the pride of his doctrine:

Kulmann was smarter than Czernin, and I think he was also smarter than the other diplomats that I had the opportunity to meet. He had character and intelligence well above average; but he could also become quite angry, not only with us, when he met with resistance, but also with his own allies.

When we started talking about the problem of the occupied territories, Kuhlmann started beating his breast and declared, "Thank God we have no occupied territory in Germany!" At this point, Czernin gave a start, and his face went green: Evidently Kuhlmann had intended this little barb for him. There relationship was not what one could have called a friendship.

General Hoffmann, on the other hand, brought a refreshing note into the conference. He showed no sympathy for the deviousness of diplomacy, and more than once he put his soldier's boots on the negotiating table. We immediately understood that the only really serious reality amid all these useless speeches was the fact of Hoffmann's boots.

Sometimes the general interrupted purely political discussions, but he did this in his own way. Bored by the endless discussions about the right of all peoples to decide for themselves, he produced a briefcase full of Russian newspaper clippings with which he proved that the Bolsheviks had suppressed freedom of the press and the principles of democracy. The articles were by the terrorist Social Revolutionaries and other Russian groups that he evidently approved of. He declared in indignation that our government was based on violence. It was wonderful listening to him. I answered Hoffmann that in a class society every government is based on violence. The only difference was that General Hoffmann used suppression to defend large landowners, while our violent measures had the goal of defending the workers.

On this day Count Czernin noted:

Hoffmann held an unfortunate speech. He worked on it for several days and was very proud of his success.

Hoffmann on Trotsky:

Trotsky had the gift of gab, and he was educated, energetic, and cynical. He gave the impression of being a man who would shrink from nothing to achieve what he wanted. Sometimes I asked myself whether he had really come with the intention of making peace, or whether he was only interested in having a podium from which he could propagate his Bolshevik ideas. But though these ideas stood very much in the foreground, I do believe that he was trying to come to a conclusion, and when Kulmann's equally skilled dialectic drove him into a corner, he came up with the theatrical idea of announcing that, while Russia could not accept the peace conditions of the central powers, he nevertheless herewith declared that the war was over, and that he was thus putting an end to this round of negotiations.

Kulmann on this phase of the negotiations:

Trotsky's decision to abruptly stop all contacts between our delegates made my task as the speaker of our delegation substantially more difficult. Moreover, he had insisted that a stenographer be present to take down all of our negotiations in order that they might subsequently be published. Hence we could not put out preliminary feelers in our speeches and answers. The speakers never got the chance to read through the stenograph and make corrections—as is common in all parliaments. Instead, what they said was immediately telegraphed to the entire world. This was a heavy weight on the climate of negotiations, because we were speaking, after all, for the four allied central powers, and we were equally unable to exchange views with their representatives during the negotiations.

Evidently Trotsky wanted to provoke me to act like a dictator—to make me bang my fist on the table and point to the map of the front line. But I was unable to do him this favor, which would have given him a dangerous weapon: The leftist parties in Germany would have gone for my blood. My room for maneuvering between the demands of the army command for annexation pure and simple and the demands of the Reichstag for peace without annexations and reparations was quite narrow. Hence, my only tactic was to try to trap Trotsky in discussions on the right of all peoples to decide for themselves, leading from there to territorial concessions. I found out how much trouble this gave him when one of his advisers urged me to finally put an end to this "terrible torture" and simply make known German demands.

In view of his skilled negotiating partners, Trotsky became noticeably more excitable and nervous, and also more sarcastic:

> When, in the course of a reply to Hoffmann's usual attacks, I mentioned the German government, the general interrupted me in a voice tense with anger: "I represent not the German government but the high command of the German army!" I replied that I was not qualified to make any judgments about the relationship between the government of the German Empire and its high command, and that I had only been given authority to deal with the government. Gnashing his teeth, Kulmann had to admit that I was right.

The Russians had developed these time-killing tactics partly out of speculations on unrest that has now broken out in Germany, which they expected would increase pressure on the German negotiators. Trotsky skillfully drew this out for weeks, but his tactics did not work. Ludendorff was impatient. He needed peace and quiet on the eastern front in order to defend his western front. Knowing full well the present weakness of the Russian defensive line, he ordered it breached. Lenin saw that he was forced to accept German conditions. On 3 March 1918, the treaty of Brest-Litovsk was signed—by Sokolnikov instead of by Trotsky. Germany occupied White Russia (Byelorussia). The

Ukraine, the Baltic, and Finland were declared independent, but the Ukraine was under German protectorship. Turkey was given the oil-producing center Batumi. Six billion gold marks were paid as reparations.

But the fight was only beginning for the followers of non-Bolshevik parties. On the one hand, they could not accept the occupation of territory that they claimed for themselves. On the other hand, resistance was beginning in areas controlled by the Bolsheviks, and people were trying to keep them out of areas that were not yet under Lenin's control. Frequently, one could hear reactions like those of the officer Vasiliy Oryechov:

> This peace treaty was a slap in the face for those who went off to fight for Russia. In the spring, we still believed that an uprising could be organized within the country, but now, after the brutal murder of General Duchonin in headquarters in Mogilyev and Lenin's declaration on the general peace, it was clear to us that we had to fight on two fronts: against the Germans on the one hand—because this battle was not over for us yet—and also in the volunteer army, which had nothing to do with the Germans, and certainly not with their treaty with the Bolsheviks. Most important for us, of course, was the restoration of order within the country. We were hoping for help from our allies in this. It seemed perfectly clear to us that at such a moment Russia would not be left to random fate, and when we got to the Don River, we were convinced that our allies would arrive at any moment with help in getting weapons, and perhaps even give us support in battle. The fact that Bulgaria had capitulated by this time only strengthened us in our hopes. The allied army on the Macedonian front was moving slowly forward, and our hopes for assistance were not unjustified.

Pierre Pascal, lieutenant at the French military mission in Petrograd:

> There were two points of view among the allies: to go on with the Bolsheviks against the Germans, or to work with the Germans against the Bolsheviks.
>
> The next day, a young lieutenant with lots of medals came to me. During the last period, it frequently happened that soldiers wanted to join the French Army. They were either disappointed by the dissolution of the army or tired of the government's constant changes of course. The handsome lieutenant does not want to fight in the civil war against his

own people, but he does want to continue the fight against the Germans, against whom he had gone to war in the first place.

Princess Sayn-Wittgenstein comments on the news of the peace treaty in this way:

> From today on, everything has changed. Before, it was still possible to cherish a thin ray of hope for something better, but now that has been destroyed forever. We can only say our final prayers over the corpse of this poor Russia which has signed such a peace treaty. Was it possible in all the years from 1914 to 1917 for us to imagine that this war—the "Great War," as we called it—would end so disgracefully? We never thought that it would end in anything but honor and victory. How many sacrifices were made, how much blood shed, how many battles won! For what?
>
> The Germans certainly could not have expected such a glorious victory. They got everything that they could possibly have dreamed of: the complete destruction of Russia as a great power, all possible trade treaties, reparations, the annexation of entire provinces, the separation of the Ukraine. Is it possible for Russia to go on living after this disgraceful peace?

Russia lost one-quarter of its territory, a fruitful quarter of its agricultural land, a quarter of its railroad lines, a third of its textile industry, and three-quarters of its iron ore and coal mines. Meanwhile, the Germans were making use of the fruits of Ukrainian agriculture, and they were in control of the oil in the Caucasus. The cossack Leon Barat was only eight years old at the time, but he still remembers:

> When the conditions for the peace of Brest-Litovsk became known, officers came to my mother and cried about this disgraceful peace which had betrayed Russia. My father had died in 1916 fighting the Austrians. What for?

The officer Kromyadi:

> It is unique in the history of the world that the losers were able to dictate conditions to the winners.

Even Lenin himself was embarrassed by the treaty of Brest-Litovsk, although it must be admitted that if the allies had supported Russia it might have been possible for Russia to achieve better conditions. But the allies were still waiting. They were increasingly half-hearted in their views on allied obligations to the Russians and saw no reason to work together with the Bolsheviks, which would be equivalent to de facto recognition of the new government. At the fourth Pan-Russian Soviet Congress, Lenin had to confess:

> Certainly this defeat is quite painful. All the world can see that we are going through a period of setbacks for the revolution. But this only means that we must work all the harder to do whatever we can to maintain at least part of our position and wait for the rise of the international proletariat, which is having an even harder time than we are in trying to overthrow the well-organized apparatus of autocracy in the countries of Europe.

Three days after the peace treaty, on 6 (19) March 1918, the Social Revolutionaries still remaining in the government resigned for good.

Lenin set about organizing the new regime in Russia. On 25 January (7 February) 1918, the country had been declared a "Council Republic of the Workers, Soldiers and Peasants. Its official name was "Union of Soviet Socialist Republics." Lenin knew that a parliamentary constitutional order of the previous sort would not provide him with any basis on which to rule, since the Bolsheviks did not have a majority. Especially in the southern areas with larger and cheaper plots of land, the peasants would have refused to support him in his policy of expropriation, if they had been asked their opinion.

Among the other decrees in these months were the reform of Russian orthography and the separation of state and church, which was now electing a patriarch again for the first time in two hundred years. Since 1700 (the time of Peter the Great), there had been no one occupying the seat of patriarch. Church property was expropriated, too, and religion classes were banned, but the private practice of religion was not forbidden—at least on paper. In a pastoral letter, Patriarch Tichon called for brotherly love and the end of enmity and the "bestial murder of innocent people." From his appeal, it is clear that the Civil War was already taking place. The patriarch declared "those who are sinning" to be banned from the church in anathema. But he called his brothers "to the spiritual battle for the preservation of the church."

Meanwhile, Lenin explained again and again what Soviet power was in speeches to the population:

What is Soviet power? What is the essence of this new power which people in most other countries cannot or do not want to understand? The essence of this power, and what is winning it so many supporters among the workers of other countries, is this: that previously the state was ruled in this or that way by the rich or by capitalists, and now it is ruled for the first time by the mass of those classes which capitalism used to exploit. Even in the freest and most democratic of republics, the state is ruled by a tiny minority, nine-tenths of whom are capitalists or rich people, as long as the land is in private hands.[13]

In Russia for the first time in world history we have constructed the power of the state in such a way that only workers and working peasants, without the exploiters, are able to form mass organizations—the Soviets (councils)—and these have been given the entire power of the state.[14] This is why the word "soviet" is welcome all over the world and music to the ears of workers, no matter how the representatives of the bourgeoisie in other countries may slander the name of Russia. And that is why the Soviet power is unbreakable and unbendable and will achieve victory throughout the whole world in the near future, no matter how the followers of communism in other countries are persecuted!

The hierarchical committee system had its highest embodiment in the Central Committee, and this organizational structure was immediately carried from Moscow to the cities, districts, and factories of the entire country.

The decrees of this period form the basis for the Soviet constitution approved at the Fifth Pan-Russian Soviet Congress on 28 June 1918 for the "Russian Socialist Federal Soviet Republic," as Russia was now called. Moscow was once again the capital and seat of government. Lenin moved in to the Kremlin.

Russia no longer existed. On 1 (14) February 1918, Russian history had come to an end. The old Julian calendar was replaced by the new Gregorian calendar, as in the west.

The era of the Soviet Union had begun.

NOTES

1. Today called Ploshchad Revolyuzii (Revolution Square).

2. The Ukraine had declared its independence as early as 1917. In analogy to

Russia's council government, it organized a "Rada" government and used this administrative form as a pretext to separate itself from Russia, pointing out the Ukraine's role as the grandfather of the Russian group of states.

3. Tula was a center for the metal industry, known for the production of Russian samovars.

4. Kerensky managed to flee to England. Later he lived in Paris, and finally in the United States, where he died in New York in 1970.

5. Morosov was one of the richest merchants and philanthropists in Moscow.

6. U.S. State Department, Decimal Document No. 861.00/961.

7. Latvians were particularly cooperative with the Bolsheviks at this time and were usually used by them for difficult missions that might have scared Russians off. Russian workers' guards would hardly have driven their own representatives out of the Duma.

8. M.S. Uritzky was part of the radical wing of the Bolsheviks, for which he received a leading role in the Cheka.

9. In Russia, white was the color of the Czar. The cossacks were considered the most reliable Russian patriots, and thus they formed the Czar's bodyguard. Blue was the color of the nobility and red the color of the people.

10. This passage on sovereignty is precisely the one that was used against Trotsky later: General Hoffmann used it to lend legitimacy to German territorial demands.

11. General Duchonin died a patriotic hero. Urged several times by his own people to try to flee, he refused to leave his post and was murdered by the Bolsheviks in front of his wife.

12. Both in Petrograd and in Moscow there are different train stations for different directions. The train stations are named for their directions.

13. In this comment and in his mention of democratic and free conditions, Lenin was making reference to the demands of the Social Revolutionaries whom he had shoved aside, as well as to the Provisional Government which he had overthrown.

14. This is not entirely correct, since Lenin had deprived the councils of their power.

Chapter Seven

——— // ———

White and Red

Establishing the system and the development of fronts of resistance by the so-called voluntary army.

In November 1917, General Alexeyev gave the following speech in Novocherkassk, the cossack center in the South of Russia:

Fellow Soldiers!

In this most difficult hour, we are gathered here together. Never in its entire history has Russia experienced so much suffering, humiliation, and moral decay. Never before has a state in full possession of its moral and physical power—as it seemed—surrendered so unthinkingly all of its cultural heritage, made by our ancestors, grandfathers, and fathers.

The young Rus,[1] still weak and divided, lived through the hard times of the tartar invasion. The blooming cities where life and activity throbbed, the kernels of a young culture, disappeared from the face of the earth; instead the primeval forest rustled in the wind.

The Russian state seemed to have died, but its people lived. Their belief in God, their soul, and their love for the soil of their homeland lived on. And the Russian heart continued to beat. It had not given up the hope that the tartar rule could be thrown off and the country given back its freedom.

Rus lived through these terrible years of confusion. Everything died. The resistance of the people had disappeared. They found no support among their own ruling classes. But even in those difficult days the people did not let their courage fail. The signs of life and of the striving for

159

independence were strong. People were prepared to sacrifice their greatest possession, their greatest good—their lives.

Not so now. Our enemy, through its mercenaries, gathered from among the hordes of Russian traitors, outcasts, and elements for whom a strong, powerful Russia is dangerous and threatening,[2] has made a mockery of that once great and strong soul of the Russian people. It has made use of the people's lack of education, it has killed their belief in God, poisoned their patriotic feeling,[3] and made them forget their love of the homeland. What has remained of our people is human scum.

Russia has died. With it has died the wish to lead an independent, self-sufficient life, to fill that life with ideals and sacrifice oneself for them. What people want most now is merely their personal well-being, their own life—saved in scandalous ways[4]—at all costs.

The idea of the Russian state has fallen apart. Our mighty Russia has transformed itself into a series of republics, each striving for a self-sufficient life, and not understanding that not one of them is capable of living an independent existence, and that in trying to do so they are merely exposing themselves to the danger of being taken and gobbled up by their neighbors.

What could possibly be worse than the decay of the ruling classes and the passivity of the people, who bear this shame and scandal with calmness and humility, while in the meantime it is the officers of the German General Staff who play leading roles in the Bolshevik government and exercise direct control over affairs of state?!

Everyone is tired of fighting, but where is this tiredness more repulsive than in our own army, which is now decayed and infected by the work of the socialists?

The army—where the flower of a people is gathered together—has lost its soul, its sense of honor, and its concept of the fatherland.

This has all died and gone under in a mass which has smothered the spirit of the individual in the thinking of thousands. Mass terror was only possible because of the lack of civil courage among individuals.

But here, in the middle of this stormy sea that is flooding our country with filth and shame and drowning the courage of our people—here an island has formed, here all the heroic courage and honor that live within the soul of man have been saved. The belief in God continues to live on this tiny island, the consciousness of the fatherland, love for it. Here lives the feeling that a life without honor, without ideals, without a willingness to sacrifice oneself and die for them—that such a life is shameful, the life of an animal. In the middle of the collapse and decay of power, people have come forward who put their own personal well-being behind the well-being of their fatherland. For them, the thirst for life—at least for such a shameful life—is less important than the need for heroism in saving the fatherland.

Without forcing itself into the consciousness of the general public, this idea has already taken on life. During the difficult, nightmarish days of Bolshevik brutality, Petrograd and Moscow had already experienced the birth of such heroism among some groups.

This island will grow and become larger. In you I already greet this island, in you, who are the bearers of a great spirit and courage, and of the willingness to sacrifice yourselves.

I thank you for your young and vigilant spirit, which has melded you into a strong fighting body in such a short time. You are thus a mighty foundation for the protection of the highest human values in the middle of that atmosphere of intrigues, mistrust and wantonness in which we live.

I bow down to your bravery, your spirit, and your readiness to put yourselves in the service of your fatherland, regardless of the sacrifices and losses that are inevitable.

We have great ideals—the salvation of our homeland from the deep decay to which it has already been exposed. In our efforts, the source of our courage is the indestructible feeling of honor, for which we are putting our lives and all our strength on the line—in order to reach the desired goal.

Let us dispose of the untimely question as to where we stand politically. Today it is hard to say what style we will give to the building whose ceiling is now about to be destroyed by flames. Let us first save the building—and then let us let the Constitutional Assembly which will then convene decide for itself which architect should give that building form.

Do not believe the pernicious speeches of those who claim that all of this is only black pessimism. Those who are unprepared to serve a great cause are always ready to spit upon the others.

No: to save our once great homeland, which is now dying, and to ressurect it—that is our only goal. It is the star that guides us. The power of circumstances has forced some of us to take upon the burdens of leadership in this cause. Our souls are filled with nothing but the purest, most honorable, and most upright desires.

Believe this.

Then, in common belief and comradely striving, our task will be in strong hands.

Then you will lose nothing.

I call upon you to act. It may be that a heavy burden will come to rest upon your young shoulders, but I live in the deep belief that your pure idealism is the surety for our victory!

In the Civil War that followed, Lenin tried to strengthen the morale of his troops solely with the arguments of class struggle—both in the early period and in the later period of off-and-on success:

Comrades of the Red Army!

The capitalists of England, America, and France are leading a war against Russia. They are taking revenge upon the Soviet Workers and Peasants Republic, because it has toppled the rule of the landowners and capitalists and thus set an example for all the peoples of the earth. The capitalists of England, France, and America are supporting Russia's landowners with money and military assistance.[5] These landowners are leading troops against the Soviet power from Siberia, from the Don, and from the northern Caucasus. They want to reestablish the power of the Czar, the rule of the landowners and the capitalists.

No! That must not happen! The Red Army is strong, it has risen up and driven the troops of the landowners and the officers of the White Guard from the Volga. Only a small effort, only a few more months of battle with the enemy, and victory will be ours. The Red Army is strong in the knowledge and unanimity of the battle for the peasants' soil, for the power of the workers and peasants, for the Soviet power.

The Red Army is invincible, because it combines millions of active peasants and workers who have now learned how to fight. They have learned the discipline of comrades who do not let their spirits fall or allow themselves to be confused by insignificant defeats. They go forth against the enemy with even more spirit and courage because they know that the enemy's complete defeat is drawing near.

Comrades of the Red Army! The bond between the workers and peasants of the Red Army is strong, close, and indestructible. Large landowning and wealthy farmers are trying to organize revolts against the Soviet power, but they find themselves in a disappearing minority. They will no longer succeed in fooling the peasants. The peasants know very well that it is only with the help of the workers that they will be able to achieve victory over the landowners.

The Soviet power will suppress the landowning farmers, the kulaks. It will cleanse the villages of those who treat the small peasants without justice. At all costs, it will form a union between the peasants and the entirety of active agricultural workers—with the poor and those in the middle. This union is growing all over the world. Everywhere, the revolution is at hand. One day, it will also have achieved victory in Hungary. In Hungary, a Soviet power has already been formed, a peasants' government.[6] And all the peoples of the world are striving single-mindedly toward this goal.

Comrades of the Red Army! Stand and be strong, unerring, and unified. Go out against the enemy with courage! Victory will be ours. The rule of the landowners and capitalists, which has been destroyed in Russia, will be defeated all over the world!

The "Red Guard" of the Bolsheviks stood against the "Volunteer Army," which would subsequently go down in the history of the fight against the Soviet regime as the "White Army." White, the symbol of the Russian Czar, was now the symbol of resistance against the revolutionaries by those who want to preserve—or win back—Russia as a unified country with a bourgeois order and a constitution given by a legislative assembly.

Russians faced Russians on fronts in Siberia, the Caucasus, the Ukraine, and the Baltic. In the course of the coming months and years, they were strengthened by English in Murmansk and Archangelsk, by Czech prisoners of war in Siberia who had formed a legion that reached Yekaterinburg shortly after the murder of the Czar's family, by ten thousand Americans, sixty thousand Japanese, and a handfull of Italians as well as French, Greek, and English units in the south of Russia. Meanwhile, units from czarist military academies in the Caucasus ultimately took the field against the allied English, who had occupied part of Persia. They did not want to let the English have all of Persia. Like their allies-become-enemies, however, they were driven back by Kurdish partisans. The picture of the war was rounded off by wars for independence among the Georgians, the Armenians, and the Baltic peoples as well as the Poles, who were trying to win back territory in the Ukraine and White Russia that had been taken away from them.

Amid all this confusion, with allies becoming enemies and Russians their own bitter opponents, the Germans, though they had signed a treaty with the Bolsheviks, suddenly became allies of those anti-Bolshevik Russians who managed to flee to territories under the protection of the Germans from the Ukraine to the Crimea.

On the other hand, the Baltic peoples, who were to be defended

against the Bolsheviks by loyal German troops and Russian White
Guards under the leadership of Yudenich, fought so fiercely against the
Germans for independence that they later became victims of the Red
Guards. Estonians and Latvians proved to be particularly friendly to the
Bolsheviks (the latter formed the hard core of troops in the Cheka and
the guard)—a situation that resulted partly from their dislike of the
Germans. Otto Hellich, who was a German major fighting with the
White Russians under Yudenich in Latvia and Estonia, remembers:

> They were not particularly interested in being saved (by us) from the
> Bolsheviks. I was able to warn several landowners at the last moment
> before the Reds came. But a lot of them didn't want to believe us, no
> matter what. They stayed in their houses and were brutally murdered a
> short time later. Their possessions were destroyed, and everything that
> was not tied down tightly was beaten to smithereens or taken away. Of
> course, the women and girls were raped. The Bolsheviks' battle was pri-
> marily against the landowners. But it was strange that the simple country
> population reacted with positive enmity to our presence. I told my soldiers
> under no circumstances to spend the night in private quarters with the
> peasants. Several of them did it anyway. The next morning, when I called
> the roll, they were missing. They were found with their throats cut.

Despite this, Yudenich was able to control the Baltic for a while,
and he reached Zarskoye Syelo, several kilometers from the old capital
city Petrograd.

The Volunteer Army's ultimate goal was to march on Moscow,
which had again become the capital city. Its more immediate goal was
to keep the Bolsheviks out of southern Russia. The military center for
the army was Novocherkassk. The area around the Don, the Dnyepr,
and the Kuban: hundreds of kilometers of fruitful land, influenced for
centuries by the traditions of the cossacks, faithful to the Czar and
raised in the spirit of military defense of the country. With the
exception of the industrial proletariat in the city of Rostov, it was a
population with little sympathy for the Bolshevik revolution.

Representatives of the former Russian government came through the
front and areas under Bolshevik control, each after different adventures
during the escape: ex-foreign minister Milyukov, ex-president of the
Duma Rodsyanko, ex-high commander of the Russian Armies General
Alexeyev, General Kornilov, freed from revolutionary imprisonment,
and Generals Denikin, Lukomsky, Romanovsky, Martov, and Kaledin.

[7]The resistance army that was now forming consists of sixty percent
cossacks. With respect to men and weapons, the battle was unequal.
But motivation among the Whites was so high that in some battles the
Bolsheviks overestimated their numbers by far. The cossack Leon Barat
from Novocherkassk describes the cossacks, elite soldiers of the Russian
Army:

A Chinese philosopher once said: "The borders of the Russian Empire
are the trimming around the edges of the cossack saddle." There is some
truth in this. The cossack was a warrior, and with his weapons he defended
the Russian Empire, but he is also a farmer and the father of a family. In
all eleven of the cossack regiments in the Russian Empire the worst insult
was to call someone "poor." The cossack was always working and could
not possibly be poor. The traditions and discipline of the cossack are
strong. This is true especially of the pan-Russian and Kuban cossacks,
who were raised according to the rituals of the old beliefs.

A cossack rarely had fewer than four to seven sons. When he was four
years old, he was put onto a horse and led through the city or the village.
He was displayed as the future cossack, who would defend the land some
day. Besides this, his fathers, uncles, grandfathers, and older brothers—
all serving in the border areas near Austria or later on near Germany or
in Siberia or Asia, spread all over the land—told him stories about their
heroic deeds, they sang songs. And almost every cossack song is connected
to a historic event or to the history of the cossacks. In this way, even tiny
cossacks were raised in a patriotic spirit.

The cossack went to church with all of his medals and epaulets. After
he had achieved a certain rank, he stood to the right, and when he was
even higher he stood up front. A cossack rarely came back from his active
military service without the cross of St. George. From his sixteenth year
on, the cossack was prepared for military service, usually with administrative work, but also with messenger service on horseback. People frequently accuse us cossacks of paying no taxes. That is true. But in order
to defend the country we have brought everything ourselves: our own
horses, our own uniforms, weapons. The Kuban and Terek cossacks even
brought their own rifles. Which means that we cost the state far less than
any other army.

The cossacks were not only a symbol of patriotism and defense of the
fatherland; they were also traditionally in the personal guard convoy of
the Czar. They were colorful and decorative. His Imperial Majesty's
convoy consisted of one division of Kuban cossacks and two squadrons

of Terek and Kuban cossacks. There were two cossacks regiments: His Majesty's Don Bodyguard Regiment and the Altaman Bodyguard Regiment of the successor to the throne, the Tsaryevich. The Don, Terek, and Kuban cossacs had their own army regiments.

The cossacks were extremely disciplined. There were never revolts or unrest. It wasn't until front soldiers started coming back after the February Revolution that one could see completely different cossacks. Some of them wore red bands around their jackets—this had never happened before—and their uniforms and behavior were laxer than they ever had been. They had been softened by the propaganda. But these cossacks remained in the minority. There was no unrest among us, there were hardly any Jews on the Don, and in the confusion of the civil war it was the Latvian sailors who carried out searches and executions here. But the largest part of the Volunteer Army consisted of Cossacks.

The young men didn't always go with the volunteers in the White Army, even if they were not followers of the revolutionaries and the "Red Guard." Tatyana Neklyudova remembers this time:

"When Rostov was controlled by the Whites, we returned to Taganrog. It was not calm there by any means; at night we could hear gunfire. In the town itself volunteers were being recruited for the White Army. But the officers of the Transamur Regiment would not enlist in the White Army. So they began recruiting among the school students. The horses which were left by the soldiers of the Transamur Regiment were handed over to them; when a new formation was being established for the Whites near Rostov, these school students also rode along—my cousin was among them. He went along to take care of the horses, and he, like the other boys, did not return.

The worker uprisings in Rostov were increasing—who knows whether this was a result of agitation or not. The Commandant of Kiev's Cadet Academy, Colonel Mastyka, asked the local revolutionary council for free retreat for the Rostov students and guaranteed on his behalf that they would leave the city without fighting. This agreement was signed by Mastyka and the head of the Reds, Starnin. In the morning, the school lined up rank and file in front of the Hotel Evropeyskaya, where they had been billeted. They did not march straight out of town, but first marched left across over Gogol Street, and then made a right turn through the Kusnyetschnaya Street—a dead-end which juts off from Gogol Street. Once the entire school had gone down along this street, the Reds opened fire with machine guns from the roof of the corner house and shot up and down the street on the columns of cadets. Colonel Mastyka was one of the first casualities. A lot of boys immediately fell over dead or were badly injured. The few who were able to save themselves were seized somehow and immediately shot.

Nikitin, an officer fron Pashinsk in the Caucasus, took part in the famous Kuban campaign.[8] But before this he had other experiences:

I was living in Pyatigorsk, and in 1918, when the Bolsheviks took Pyatigorsk, the "ice campaign" was organized in Rostov. A group of three thousand men marched from Rostov into Kuban territory. They were the first White warriors—back then they were not called that yet: it was the Bolsheviks who called us White Guards and themselves the Red Guard. So I was called to the Kuban cossacks—I had just turned seventeen, and was thus fit for duty. I was to register twelve kilometers to the north of Pashinsk, the city where I was born, in the barracks at Krasnogorsk. There I learned that I was being called up immediately. General Shkuro organized the so-called "Wolf's Hundred" in the mountains. That later became a division. My brother and I belonged to it.

I remember that when we were in Kislovodsk and the Bolsheviks came to Pyatigorsk they called all the officers in the area up and ordered them to register. When they arrived, they were arrested, and a hundred men were stabbed, among them General Russky. In Pyatigorsk, they were all thrown into a pit.

Our division was sent to Stavropol. The Bolsheviks had come by way of Astrachan, through Solonchaki. There they had forcibly recruited two thousand peasants under the direction of a commissar. They armed them with rifles and machine guns. They were to take Stavropol. We, the "Wolf's Hundred," had been sent out to chase them away.

And there we were in the middle of the winter marching over the mountain pass; the mountains were not very high there, but there were no roads, and the paths were quite narrow. It was nightime. We rode in a closed chain, each horse following right after the other. It was so cold, so unspeakably cold, that despite the soldiers' coats that covered us and even the horses, we had to stop while coming down from the top of the pass in order to rub our legs warm. Suddenly, three men fell from their horses. They had frozen to death while riding!

From there, we rode on as fast as possible until we got to Stavropol. There we learned that the Bolsheviks were already nearing from Solonchaki, heavily armed. It was ten o'clock in the evening when we got there. We posted lookouts immediately and stayed in a tiny village.

On the other side of the village was a river. That was where the high plain from which the Bolsheviks were to come began.

At four in the morning, we were woken. We got up quietly. And there was this tiny wooden bridge over the river. Only one or two riders had room on it. A volunteer rode in front, with me behind him; we ride together up the incline, behind us the "Hundred," who spread out in various directions. Shots whistle over our heads, machine gunfire breaks out. This volunteer's horse is killed, I gallop quickly ahead, the others gradually catch up with me. The Bolsheviks are scared and pull back. We catch up with them on our horses. Shortly after four o'clock in the morning, we have 105 prisoners.

The sergeant comes to me and says, "Listen, now you will take these 105 prisoners and lead them back, and we will go on to get the others." So I'm all alone, with my cap and my sword⁹ and my Berdan rifle, a cavalry rifle without a bayonet, and with only one or two cartridges—I didn't have any more—and then these 105 men.

I called them forward, and I stood a bit to the side, so that if one of them had rushed me I would have been able to get back. So I had the first empty his pockets—no weapon, then the next—all 105 men. When I had checked them all in this way, we went forward; and they all marched, with me behind them, and I brought all 105 of them into the village completely alone. The next day, still more prisoners were brought. They were all hanged. The sight of it was unbearable. Five gallows were there, so five men were always being hanged at the same time. It was not just terrible for me as a young man to see that—it was also terrible for me as a Christian to see people killed in that way. But nothing could be done. Whenever we fell into their hands they tore off our epaulets first, then the jacket, then the shirt, and then the skin from the body, before they shot us. Whether with a bullet or with a bayonet—they always tortured a man before they killed him.

There are also women traveling with the men who faced the demands of battle in the field every day. Most of the nurses were from noble families and had been serving the wounded since the beginning of the war. Yekaterina Volkonskaya remembers one episode:

I was working in a field hospital. It was in contact with a supply train for the wounded, which had all the necessary items. The wounded could be put up there in special cars designed for that purpose. Besides the director, there was a doctor and six nurses on the staff, as well as an assistant doctor as medic and hospital aide. The wounded soldiers came into the red cars. We, the personnel, slept in the supply cars. Our train started moving north behind the army of the Second Division. At that time, the Volunteer Army was on its way from the south to Kiev and then further north.[10] I belonged to the group that was on its way with horse carts in order to get the wounded and, if possible, treat them there and then. Sometimes, we brought them to the next base, depending on where they were and whether we could get them to the hospital train or not.

We were getting close to Chernigov when we were shot at. We had gotten to a village and had set up an emergency hospital in a school. There the approaching Reds started shooting with artillery. We got our wounded together, laid them on stretchers, and put them onto horse carts. I was sitting next to the driver, a tartar. It was getting on toward evening by the time we drove away—I with two wounded soldiers. The ground was so soft that we never knew whether the cart would make it or break through. The artillery of the Reds begins to shoot at us too.

Suddenly, a ball slams into one of the wheels. I have no idea how we managed to go unharmed—I think the Reds were still being put together out of untrained units at the time, and they didn't know their weapons well. Despite this, we were shocked: The wheel had been hit—but in such a way that it did not break. The driver jumped up and checked out what had happened immediately, trying to see whether we could go on. I saw to my wounded soldiers—they were frightened, but not hurt. Then the tartar said in his broken Russian: "I don't know whether Allah saved us—or your God!"

But there were also nurses who went into the field themselves, sometimes on horseback. Varvara Levitova was one of them. For years, she rode with a division of Kornilov's Regiment on the Don. Several times, she fell into the hands of the enemy and was able to flee; several times she was wounded herself. She thus experienced the changing fate of the various units of volunteers in southern Russia.

I could have gone home at some time, but I would have had to answer to myself for not performing what little help I could. A lot of the "flying nurses" died anyway in the rain of bullets. My parents did not want to let me go—as usual, though I had not even told them that I would not be working in the hospital train, but rather in the field. I did not want to worry them.

My hopes of seeing my friends and the sergeant again when I got to my troop were dashed. All our friends had died in that short time or had been transferred to other regiments. Now further Kornilov Regiments had been formed from volunteers of the reserve. The officers of the first Kornilov Regiment were taken into these regiments as commanders. Our Kornilov shock troop had already fought to the north of Rostov, because the people of the Don themselves were to the north of their capital Novocherkassk. They were defending their city themselves, leaving the rest of the Don area without help, which was understandable. Our army grew even larger when the "people of Drosdov" came to us from around Kiev before the end of our first Kuban campaign. That was what we called the regiment under General M.G. Drosdovsky, which had already grown hard through the battles of this war.

And so, with numerous battles and fights, our regiment, under the command of General Denikin, moved from the coal basin of the Don to the north. My friend Tanya and I were separated from each other, because every nurse traveled with a particular unit, and while I was with the Eleventh Regiment under the command of Chief of Staff Vorobyov, a Kuban cossack, Tanya was in the nearby Twelfth Regiment, commanded by Lieutenant Rumyanzev. Men from the Staff Command helped me to transport wounded soldiers who had been cared for. They were brought to the hospital train and from there to Rostov.

Once, the regiments were put together again, and so Tanya and I marched together. There were fierce battles; our regiments could not maintain their position. They began to pull back. The machine gun posts held the Reds off for the time being, so that they did not attack us during the retreat. While doing this, we had to pass over a tiny bridge over a deep ravine. Tanya and I helped the sharpshooters in taking over their heavy tools and munitions. We had almost reached the other end of the bridge when I was hit by a bullet in the leg. I fell down—the wound was deep. The Bolshevik had shot from a short distance from this side of the ravine. Nevertheless, I was lucky; no bone was destroyed. I was quickly given emergency care and later taken to the hospital and to Rostov. My parents were distraught and amazed at how this was possible in my service [supposedly in the hospital train].

Varvara Levitova, again back in the middle of the battle as "first aid," experiences the expectations and setbacks of her regiment first hand:

In the meantime, my younger sister had followed my example. She was working as a nurse in the sharpshooters' division near Zarizyn,[11] but we didn't see each other again until much later, when she had become a nurse for the Kuban cossacks under General Babayev.

Our battles went successfully, and we were moving forward quickly; large cities were taken—Byelgorod, Charkov, Kursk, and—after even harder battles—Oryol.

Already everyone was beginning to dream of victory over the Red Army and the taking of Moscow. Our commander General Mamontov had succeeded in making a deep break in the Bolshevik front line. We hoped that he would now attack the retreating enemy from the rear, but he, a Don cossack, acted differently. He decided to go back home with his "booty"—that is, to Novocherkassk—and give himself and his cossacks a break.

In one of the battles near Oryol, I was shot for the third time. Fortunately, the bullet hit my belt and did not reach any vital organs. After my recovery, I returned to the regiment—at that tragic moment when our regiment was retreating from Oryol: International Bolshevik regiments had come into our area of battle—above all, Chinese, Jews, and Latvians. The latter were particularly cruel and brutal. That was also the time when Budyonny's cavalry army thrust forward to us. There was nothing left for us but to retreat from Oryol after brutal skirmishes. Kursk followed.

The winter was merciless, we were poorly dressed, our food consisted of bread, and even that was not always available in sufficient quantities. I was riding with the cavalry intelligence of the Second Kornilov Regiment, and we were supposed to spend the night in the village of Spasskoye. Without waiting for our infantry regiment, we rode into the village— Lieutenant Sayzev, his messenger, and I. A wild snowstorm was raging; we couldn't see anything. So we rode directly into a Bolshevik fortress. They had occupied the village before us. Lieutenant Sayzev understood the situation immediately, and with his rifle he pushed us from our horses. It was horrible to realize that we had wandered into the clutches of the enemy. No one had seen us yet—evidently they were still too concerned with getting positions ready for the (White) enemy. My first action was to take the tiny revolver that I always carried with me out of my pocket and throw it into the snow. Ever since I found out about the fate of our nurse Sina, I had always carried a revolver with the last bullet for myself, out of fear of becoming a prisoner of the Bolsheviks. Sina had been taken prisoner near Kursk—as a Red Cross nurse—and had been raped and skewered on bayonets by the Bolsheviks. That was how our regiment found her when they drove away the Reds. So my mind now started working feverishly, thinking about what I should do. I could make use of the snowstorm, since I wasn't seen by them any more than I could see them. This was all happening near a church, and there should be a few peasant houses there. I could see the church wall, so I tried my luck. Thank God, the Reds were completely busy with preparing for their encounter with the enemy, and so I was able to escape their attention. I did manage to get to a cottage, and in the barn I hid myself in a haystack.

All my hopes were now pinned on the battle for the village that was expected. But there was complete quiet. It became clear to me that Kornilov's troops had decided to move on and not take any risks in the unknown nightime situation. I was filled with horror. I saw absolutely no possibility of escape in this deep snow, the bitter cold, and an area that was unknown to me. I saw only one possible way out, and nothing was left for me but to face the risk. So I began at first to take off the insignia of the Kornilov Regiment from my sleeve. They would immediately have shot me for that. I hid this, the hospital bag, and my watch in the straw. I took off the nurse's headband and folded it as a head wrap. But what should I do with the soldier's coat? I had no choice; it was simply too cold without it. So I risked everything: I looked around, reassured myself that no one could see me in front of the barn, and bent over and ran from the haystack to the nearest peasant house, to which the haystack evidently belonged. I simply went in. The peasant looked at me with an amazing lack of concern: Evidently he took me for a member of the Red Army. I bravely told him that I was a "White" and had wandered into Bolshevik territory, and I desperately begged him for some peasant clothing instead of the soldier's coat, and for felt boots instead of my soldier's boots. I waited for his reaction with a beating heart. He might take me to the Bolsheviks immediately out of fear. But he didn't do it; without speaking, he gave me an old coat and felt boots. Then he told me to leave the house, but pointed me in the direction of the parish house, where I might be able to ask for shelter.

I ran in the direction he had pointed. The parish house was guarded by Latvians. Since I looked like a peasant woman, I was allowed to walk in without hindrance. But there, when I admitted to the wife of the priest who I was and gave her my request, she whispered in shock, "For God's sake, go at once, they were just here and almost shot my husband." In complete despair over my situation, I now began to cry. I was desperate. The Bolsheviks could return to their positions at any moment. I could not find refuge anywhere. But then the housewife took pity on me. She hit upon the idea of putting me in the bed and saying I was her sick sister if anyone searched through the house and asked who I was. Who in her position would have done the same thing and risked everything for an unknown girl?

Tatjana Neklyudova reports on the role of the Germans who invaded despite the fact that an official peace treaty had been concluded, and caused the fronts, whose territory had originally been under "White" control, to shift into the hands of the Reds:

"Even the officers, who did not go with the Whites, were not spared by the Reds for this; they were slaughtered like chickens. Now house searches were the rule, even during the day. As the rumor trickled down that the Germans were advancing, the Reds fled in panic, taking everything they could get their hands on with them. Vasya and I climbed up on the roof and watched as beyond the city entire columns of soldiers moving towards us. Everywhere, we could hear people calling: "The Germans! The Germans!" They came then, yesterday still our enemies and now as the liberators of the city. Members of the cavalry were billeted in our house, lancers from Württemberg. They distributed the food.

Suddenly, shots could be heard in the early morning hours. The Reds had taken the city under fire—from the other bank of the bay. Artillery fire could be heard in the city and soon there were the first casualties. The Reds attacked the Germans directly; it turned out that they had unloaded the marine infantry in Polyakovka which had been coming from the sea. They had come with freighters, streamers, and torpedo boats in order to attack Taganrog from there. But the Germans sunk the freighters with their artillery; the infantry was armed only with machine guns. Thus, almost the entire Red front succumbed. Almost no one survived."

More than once that the cities mentioned fell into the hands of the Whites, only to be taken from them again by the Reds. Denikin had already become Kornilov's successor, as Kornilov had died near Yekaterinodar. With Krasnov, Denikin now beat the Bolsheviks away from the Don and the Kuban. But the Red generals Budyonny and Voroshilov were able to fight through to Zarizyn. There, Krasnov took control of the railroad connection between Zarizyn and Moscow, which was important for food and oil shipments from the Caucasus. Stalin ordered czarist officers to be recruited for leadership positions in his proletarian army. He was able to hold Zarizyn—later to be called

Volgograd and Stalingrad. In 1919, Denikin tried to break through the Red line once more. He got to Oryol and was standing just in front of Tula—Moscow seemed within reach. But Budyonny was stronger: Charkov, Kiev, Rostov, and finally Novorossiysk all fell. Officer Konstantin Kromyadi, himself in one of the Denikin units that had been on the way to Moscow, explains how this was possible in spite of the fighting strength of the cossacks:

> The cossacks wanted to found their own independent state. Because of the propaganda, there were also communists among the cossacks. There came a point where unity among the troops no longer existed. They were no longer ready to march on without receiving the promise that they would be guaranteed an independent state. But this demand could not be reconciled with the slogan, "For an unified Russia."

At first, the phenomenon of the White Army's failure seems incomprehensible. But the problem is more complex, as will be seen, and when one looks at the situation in its entirety, the White Army's failure shows itself to be the result of the clever way in which the leaders of the Red Army were able to make use of the weaknesses of the enemy (who were abandoned precisely in these moments of weakness by the allies).

Though the year 1918 proved to be relatively hopeful and successful for the Volunteer Army—in the south, in the Baltic, and in Siberia the armies succeeded in making territorial gains—the end of the Civil War and thereby the consolidation of the Soviet government occurred in a phase of concentrated action on three fronts in the fall of 1919.

Because of previous successes and territorial gains, the army of the Whites had grown significantly, as new patriotic recruits had again seen a clear goal and a good reason for the high risks involved. Young boys, hardly of age, tried to break through to the White front, fully aware of the risks they were running. Two examples were the cadet Georgi Guenichta and Gleb Struve, who came from a liberal family. Georgi Guenichta:

> Two times, I came quite close to being shot. I was only sixteen years old and wanted at all costs to get to the front line near Poltava, in order to fight with them. I was taken prisoner and was supposed to be shot. Then along came a Red commander whom I had known in school in Poltava. Despite our ideological differences, that saved me. Back then

people were shot on the mere suspicion of being on the same side as the Whites. I was cross-examined, because they wanted to find out whether any kind of an organization stood behind my undertaking. Then they took me away in a train with other prisoners. At the Krimenchuk train station we were taken off. We slept on the floor, and I was very hungry. Then someone came through and checked our papers. I was taken to the Cheka immediately and arrested again. This time I was about to be shot. But on the second day, the Whites took Krimenchuk—and that saved me."

Gleb Struve:

I had joined up with the Whites out of my own free will, and I arrived in Novocherkassk. There I was given the assignment of going to Volhynien and getting the weapons of the Volhynians, who had gone over to the side of the Bolsheviks. The weapons were being kept by the cossacks, and I was to get them and take them to Rostov and Novocherkassk. On the way, though, our train was stopped, and we had to leave the car. Some people expected the worst and tried to escape between the tracks. I didn't join them, and with about fifty other comrades I was taken prisoner. When the Whites came, I was freed.

In 1919, the White Army concentrated its movements from three different sides toward what was now the Soviets' center of power, the capital Moscow. High commander of the Russian forces was General Kolchak, who was already entrusted with the leadership of the White movement in Omsk. Lydiya Vasilchikova relates an example of his authority, helped by his prestige even among local rulers during his time as admiral of the Black Sea fleet. The story comes from his last days as admiral, before he got to Siberia:

Things were relatively quite on the Crimean coast for a long time; there were no acts of violence on the part of the populace. The local militia, which consisted of tartars, kept itself out of politics. In Sevastopol, things remained completely quiet even in the Black Sea fleet, thanks to the prestige of its leader, Admiral Kolchak. After the Czar's abdication, several committees had formed in the Black Sea fleet, like everywhere else. The committee assigned to Admiral Kolchak had a short life; he refused to cooperate with it, and declared that he would either give up his command completely or carry it out alone. After a brief consultation, the committee expressed its confidence in him. But later several agitators succeeded in forcing the committee to disarm all the officers of the fleet. Thereupon Admiral Kolchak gathered the sailors onto the deck of his flagship. He declared that such an act was criminal, that it was destroying the fighting spirit and thus the strength of the fleet against the enemy. Moreover, he said he viewed the action as a personal insult and was thus resigning from his command. Before the speechless crew had time to catch its breath, he threw his golden sword of St. George, which had been presented to him because of extraordinary bravery during the Russian-Japanese War, over board and cried: "I got it on the sea, and now I give it back to the sea!"

The same day, he left Sevastopol and never came back.

Now Kolchak was high commander of the White Army in Siberia, to which the Czech legion also belonged. In the spring of 1919, it was decided that Denikin's army in the south and Kolchak's army in the east would be joined together and meet on the way to Moscow. Vrangel was to march via Saratov, Pensa, Nishny Novgorod, and Vladimir; Sidorin via Voronesh and Ryasan; and finally General May-Mayevsky via Kursk, Oryol, and Tula. Saratov was to be the seat of government for future coordination of the volunteer movement. For the time being, everything looked successful:

In May 1919, Kolchak, approaching from the east, stood before Kasan.

Vrangel reached Vyelikoknyasheskaya on 19 May, 320 kilometers north of Yekaterinodar.

On 4 June, May-Mayevsky took Slavyansk, 450 kilometers northwest of Yekaterinodar.

On 29 June, Shkuro held Yekaterinoslav and Novocherkassk.

From 20 June on, Vrangel was in Zarizyn.

On 30 August, Kiev was considered to be "in White hands." The same was true of Kursk on 20 September, and of Voronesh ten days later. Kutyepov had polished off 700 kilometers with his army in a short amount of time. 98,000 Whites faced 160,000 Reds. Denikin's unified armies controlled a territory of 1.4 million square kilometers (about three times the territory of France).

On 13 October, Kutyepov marched into Oryol, 180 kilometers southwest of Tula. The army was now 300 kilometers from Moscow.

From the west, Poland's Pilsudski had established a flank from Chernigov to Minsk; from the northwest, Yudenich was approaching Petrograd. In October, he was in Zarskoye Syelo.

neral Kornilov.

General Markov and a captain of the
Drosdovsky-regiment.

Kornilov-regiment.

Pioneer battalion.

The Czar's cavalry regiment.

ssacks.

ssacks from the Kuban region.

The father of Georgiy Guenishta.

Georgi Guenishta.

The younger brother of Georgiy Guenishta.

Georgi Guenishta's sister.

a Burova (extreme left) in a group of partisans in Caucas, around 1919.

General Kutypov in Gallipoli.

Count M.N. Grabbe, Ataman of the Don-Cossacks.

Symbol of the 1st Kuban-campaign i 1918.

lonel Levitov of the IInd Kornilov at-
k regiment.

Members of the IIIrd company of the
Kornilov attack regiment.

ter Varvara S. Levitova.

1st Sister Lena of the Kornilov attack
regiment.

"All the News That's Fit to Print."

The New York Times.

THE WEATHER
Fair, warmer today; tomorrow fair, somewhat colder; westerly winds.

VOL. LXVII...NO. 21,942.　　　　NEW YORK, TUESDAY, MARCH 12, 1918.—TWENTY-TWO PAGES.　　　　TWO CENTS

WILSON PLEDGES OUR AID TO RUSSIA; EXPRESSES SYMPATHY, AND HOPES SHE MAY BE FREED OF GERMAN POWER

MESSAGE TO SOVIET CONGRESS

Consul General at Moscow Will Deliver It to Great Meeting Today.

HELP JUST NOW IMPOSSIBLE

But President Will Lose No Chance to Promote Aim of Complete Independence.

COUNTER-BLOW AT ENEMY

Message Will Offset Attempt to Rouse Fear of Japan's Action in Siberia.

Special to The New York Times.

WASHINGTON, March 11.—President Wilson took steps today to counteract any feeling that might have been aroused in Russia against the Allies. He sent a cable message to the people of Russia through the Soviet Congress, which meets in Moscow tomorrow, expressing the sympathy of the American people toward the Russian people over the manner of their treatment by the invading Germans. While regretting the inability of the United States Government to render direct aid at this time, the President gave assurance to the Russian people that it "will avail itself of every opportunity to secure for Russia once more complete sovereignty and independence in her own affairs and full restoration in the life of Europe and the modern world."

Through this cordial message President Wilson serves notice to the whole world that he still regards Russia as a party to the war against Germany and a co-belligerent of the United States and the other nations engaged in the effort to put an end to German autocratic methods. At the same time he brings to the minds of the Russian people that the allied purpose is remote from any desire to make a conquest of Russian territory.

Although no interpretation of the President's reasons for sending this message is offered in any authoritative quarter, it is obvious that it was the outcome, in part, at least, of a desire to counteract as far as possible the attempt to make it appear that the Japanese proposal to place armed forces in Siberia meant dismemberment of Russian territory at the hands of Japan. The representations made in response to Japan's invitation for a statement of the American view showed that the President was fearful that the presence of Japanese soldiers on Russian soil would lead to anti-Ally feeling among the Russian people. There has been evidence that the attempt to arouse this feeling is being made. Officials in Washington do not doubt that German agents in Russia will spread the report that Japan contemplates seizing Siberian territory and retaining it permanently.

President's Consistent Policy.

From the very beginning of the Russian collapse President Wilson has been insistent that it should be kept plainly before the Russian people that the United States Government was in sympathy with their democratic aims, and did not intend to permit the condition of chaos in which the country found itself to sway the firm friendship of America for Russia. He has voiced this policy before Congress, and to an extent consistent with the circumstances has emphasized it in the American communication to Japan concerning the suggestion of Japanese intervention in Siberia. He has taken occasion to show his lack of sympathy with the declaration of Mr. Lloyd George, the British Prime Minister, indicating that Great Britain expected nothing more from Russia. In these and other ways the President has made it manifest that the United States still has faith in the ability of Russia to " come back."

Today's message is the most pronounced example of the President's attitude toward demoralized and shattered Russia. In a measure it is a more important declaration than the "conversational " note to Japan in response to the invitation for a statement of American views as to the suggestion that Japanese troops should take possession of Eastern Siberia, for it is a public declaration delivered at a time when Russia is agitated over Japan's contemplated action.

It is quite evident to observers that the President wishes to keep before the world in the strongest possible light that he holds consistently to his view that nothing should be done by the allied powers that would seem to be at variance with the purposes of the Russian revolutionaries to gain complete freedom for themselves and recognition of their right of self-determination within the limits of what was once the Russian Empire.

His message to the Congress of the Soviets calls to mind that the danger in Russia results from the German invasion, which suggest that the people of Russia should concentrate their energies against the Teutonic conquerors and not against the Japanese. The President also promises that the United States Government will stand by the Russian people with the purpose of obtaining for them again "complete sovereignty and independence" and restoration of their standing as a first-class power.

This appears to mean that the United States, as a co-belligerent of Japan, will use its influence, should necessity arise, to bring about the withdrawal of Japanese troops from Russian territory and take every other necessary step to preserve the administrative and territorial integrity of Russia.

The President's message, to the Congress of the Soviets is in line with his policy of holding before the peoples of the perturbed countries of Europe, including Germany and Austria-Hungary, that the main aim of the United States in the War is to produce a condition which will insure all peoples such a measure of participation in their own government that the autocratic military power which was able to throw the whole world into a bloody conflict will be unable to do its will without popular approval.

Following the practice adopted with the entrance of the United States in war, it is expected that efforts will be made to have the President's message circulated in Germany and Austria-Hungary, so that the peoples of those countries will be reminded that the United States has not swerved from its declared sympathy with the democratic ideas that are shared by many liberals of enemy allegiance.

The message appears to put an end to speculation as to whether the President would revise his policy of disapproval toward suggestions that Japanese troops be sent to occupy parts of Siberia. There have been signs that the statements of Lord Robert Cecil, defending British indorsement to Japan's proposal, have made interested persons here see the situation in a light more favorable to Japanese intervention, but the President's words of sympathy to the Russian people indicate that his attitude has not changed.

AMERICAN TROOPS, TAKING OFFENSIVE, MAKE 3 BIG RAIDS

Sweep Over Foe's First Line in Lorraine and Reach Second, 600 Yards Back.

GUNS CO-OPERATE FINELY

Germans Flee Before Shells, So Prisoners Are Few—French Aid in Two Operations.

SECRETARY BAKER IN PARIS

WITH THE AMERICAN ARMY IN FRANCE, March 10, (Associated Press.) —American troops on the Lorraine sector carried out three raids last night and this morning. They swept past the German first line and penetrated to the enemy's second line, 600 yards back.

Two of the raids, made in co-operation with the French, were started simultaneously, one northwest and one northeast of ———— (deleted,) after tense artillery preparation, lasting four hours, in which the German position were leveled.

The two forces, each one of —— (deleted,) with small French forces their flanks, moved upon the enemy objectives at midnight behind a creeping barrage, each on a front of —— yards. When the Americans reached the German first lines the barrage was lifted so as to box in the enemy positions at both points.

The men dropped into the trenches expecting a hand-to-hand fight, but found that the Germans had fled. Continuing the advance, they went forward 600 yards to the second German line. All the time American machine guns were firing on each flank of the two parties to prevent the enemy from undertaking flanking operations.

One French flanking party found six wounded Germans in a dugout and took them prisoner. The Americans found none.

The Americans remained forty-five minutes in the enemy's lines. They found excellent concrete dugouts, which they blew up, and brought back large quantities of material and valuable papers.

While they were in the German lines the enemy artillery began a vigorous counterbarrage, but it was quickly silenced by American heavy and light artillery, which hurled large quantities of gas shells on the batteries.

An American trench mortar battery, the homes of most of whose men in —— (deleted) participated in the artillery preparation preceding the raids, helping to level the enemy position. The artillery, both light and heavy, was manned by soldiers mostly from —— (deleted).

Soon after these two raids had been completed, the Americans staged another at a point further along the line to the right. They went over the —— after artillery preparation of forty-five minutes, in which the enemy's position were obliterated for the most part.

At this place the dugouts were found to have been constructed principally of logs. Engineers accompanying the raiding party completed the work of destruction. The American infantrymen who took part in this raid are from —— (deleted) and the engineers from ———— (deleted).

The raids were carried out skillfully and but for the fact that the Germans fled more prisoners doubtless would have been taken.

The American gas shells are believed to have caused many casualties among the enemy. No Americans are unaccounted for.

A "Bold Raid," Says Paris.

PARIS, March 12.—Today's statement by the War Office includes this statement: " American troops in Lorraine carried out a bold raid into the German line.

Their motto was: "For holy Russia to Moscow, the heart of the country."

The Bolsheviks were getting nervous.

In a secret report, Trotsky made a warning that was not published until five years later:

> Previously, the biggest danger seemed to be a unification of Kolchak's and Denikin's armies at the Volga. Today, General Denikin seems to be our most serious opponent.

Lenin believed that a defeat was close. Among his comrades, he stated: "However, we have endured longer than the Paris Commune!" *Izvestiya* made a call for action:

> Comrades! One of the most critical, perhaps *the* most critical moment, has come for the socialist revolution! Foreign capitalists are striving desperately to reestablish the yoke of the capitalists through an invasion by Denikin. All workers and peasants and forces in the Soviet Republic must unify and concentrate their strength to throw back the intruder Denikin!

The mention of "capitalist help" from abroad proved to be fatally untrue for the Whites. Despite their intervention, the British refused to support General Yudenich's army in the Russian northwest, as he was being beaten back by the Red fleet a short distance in front of Petrograd. The British fleet did not budge. Yudenich lost.

The same thing happened in the northeast. Now that the Germans were considered defeated, the British no longer considered it necessary to protect Archangelsk. The Russian General Miller could not hold out much longer.

In the East, the Czechs began to lay down their weapons. The Soviets manipulated army positions, filling the fighting units facing Kolchak's feared army with motivated proletarian workers and peasants. The Russian soldiers of the Whites now began to succumb to their propaganda more and more. At the decisive moment, the Czechs themselves delivered General Kolchak to the Bolsheviks.[12] They were supported by their French allies—specifically by General Janin—and also by the allied Japanese. As expected, Kolchak was shot by the Bolsheviks.

In the south, Denikin found himself confronting unexpected problems. His telegrams to Kolchak had been going through French-held Odessa and fell into the hands of the Bolsheviks when French troops in Odessa began to mutiny and leave Odessa, essentially giving it to the Reds. The Russian governor had just enough time to shoot himself before the Bolsheviks took over, but he neglected to destroy the papers concerning Denikin. The plans for the unification of the armies and the planned seat of government of the Whites in Saratov were made public in the Bolshevik press, along with Denikin's criticism of the behavior of the French. The Bolsheviks now mobilized appropriately concentrated units against the Whites in Saratov.

Meanwhile, Denikin's own cossacks were giving him trouble. As mentioned earlier, the population of the Kuban and the Caucasus, supported by the separatist movement in the Ukranian Rada, wanted to have guarantees for a territory independent of Russia. But no such guaranty was possible from a general who was leading his armies under the motto "For a unified Russia." Moreover, Denikin refused to sanction anti-Semitic excesses and pogroms; within his own circle, this brought him the reputation of being soft on the Bolsheviks: The Bolshevik government and the administrative commission of its subdepartments were full of chiefly Jewish names. Many cossacks deserted after the cities in their own territories had been militarily defended. Denikin was forced to leave Yekaterinodar. For the time being, he made Rostov on the Don his headquarters.

Poland disappeared as a partner. It turned out that General Pilsudski had merely wanted territorial guaranties for Wolhynien, Lithuania, and White Russia, which Denikin could not give him.

But there were even problems on the way to Moscow itself. Communication between the southern and northern flanks of the army approaching from below no longer functioned reliably—hardly astounding in view of the huge extent of the territory, which made it hard to control.

Railroad workers were open to Bolshevik propaganda, and the Whites were unable to hold the railway lines.

Supplies were becoming worse and worse. Shipments from the allies were now arriving only in small quantities. Whatever did get sent from England or France to the White Army disappeared along the way to its destination—not surprising in view of food shortages and inflation. In 1900, one ruble cost 2.7 francs. In 1920, one had to pay 150 rubles for one franc.

Denikin's army now had almost no money. While Kolchak had been able to save a relatively large amount of money from the Russian treasury for his armies, there were four different editions of the ruble in circulation in Denikin's armies: from the czarist ruble through Kerensky's ruble and the Bolsheviks' ruble to the ruble of the Don government. Not one of them was protected by guarantees.

Now the French disappeared even as financial supporters of the White Armies. They wanted to give money only in response to guarantees concerning the czarist loans, which, as has been mentioned, had been repudiated by Lenin's government.

Through Lloyd George, the English government openly articulated what had already become a reality:

> I dare to predict that Bolshevism and its dangerous doctrines will not be defeated by the sword alone. We have already sent help in the amount of 100 million.[13] I do not regret a single penny we have spent, but there is no doubt that we no longer have the necessary means to continue an intervention which is so costly in this unpredictable Civil War.

Unabashed, Lloyd George declared to the House of Commons a week later his intention to drop support of the Whites:

> Denikin and Kolchak are aiming for two different goals. The first is the destruction of Bolshevism and the establishment of a good Russian regime; we are in agreement with this goal. But their second goal is the reunification of Russia. This policy cannot be viewed positively by the British Empire. One of our great statesmen, Lord Beaconsfield, has already expressed the view that a large, unified Russia would roll down like a landslide on Persia, Afghanistan, and India, thus posing the greatest imaginable threat to the British Empire.

C.E. Bechhofer, an English war correspondent stationed in Taganrog, the city where the Whites had their headquarters at the time, saw how this speech struck the White Army:

> It was like an electric shock. The battle troops had gotten their morale from the idea that they would last through this last phase of the Civil War with the help of the allies. Suddenly, they understood that Great Britain considered its war to be over, and that their war was thus merely a vulgar Civil War in the eyes of the British. Within a few days, the atmosphere in southern Russia changed completely. The fact that Lloyd George had sentenced their cause to failure seemed to sentenced them to failure in

their own eyes. No matter what reasons he may have had to let the
Volunteer Army fall, I still have to say that this change of behavior with
respect to an ally occurred in a most dishonorable way.

In late August 1919, General Denikin wrote to his wife:

The situation on both the outer and the inner front is difficult. It
appears that our breath is running out right at this moment.

Two months later:

In Rostov panic has broken out. I'm living in the train.

And in January of 1920:

The most recent period has hit us with brutal blows of fate. But I will
fight on to the end.

On 27 February 1920, Denikin had to admit:

There is no more Kuban army. I am living in a train car in Yekaterinodar. Some do not want to go to the front, others are giving up. A curse
on these agitators from the extreme right! The Don cossacks are fighting
bravely, but they are losing their nerves, because no reinforcements are
coming; the Kuban cossacks come and act like soldiers in an operetta.
They sing, "We are marching forth, adieu," and stay where they are. The
demagogues who are leading them are playing a game that is pleasing to
the Bolsheviks. Even among the officers, there is decay. What are they
hoping for—won't they ultimately land between two chairs?

On 30 March, the mood was hopeless:

Such a mass of unhappy circumstances and events! My feelings are
overwhelming me, and I am hardly able to think any logical thoughts.
The cossacks of the Don and the Kuban gave up Yekaterinodar too
quickly. They didn't even bother to keep the Kuban River occupied, and
the Bolsheviks were easily able to penetrate their line. The retreat has
begun. One army corps has joined up with the Greens![14] Some have laid
down their weapons; others are refusing to fight. The atmosphere in

Novorossiysk is tense. The retreat began in an orderly fashion, and my heart bleeds when I see the morale of the troops, the pitiful transportation. When I think of the treasures that we left behind! Our entire artillery, all our horses! The army has been bled dry.

Nina Burova agrees with other eyewitnesses in her report of the remains of an army which embarked for the Crimea in Novorossiysk:

It was a terrible moment. The ships, of which there were not enough, were too full. Those who succeeded in going along had to leave practically everything behind. Horses swam after their officers, who had to shoot them.

General Vrangel still ruled as undisputed commander of the Whites in the Crimea to whom Denikin's army now went. Soon, however, the last strongholds of the Whites and the civilian populace that had fled there would fall—partly as a result of disputes among the generals. Just as before, when a political setback sufficed to bring about the fall of a disunified government, so, too, in the area of military planning disunity hit the White opponent at a moment when he was not only not getting any support from the outside but had also become weak due to the decay of forces that had previously been unified for a single goal.

Trotsky did several things to improve the strength of his Red Army, which was now getting ready to deliver the final blow. In order to establish better discipline, he now disposed of the committees and soldiers councils that had been formed by the Social Revolutionaries during the February Revolution. Their main function had been to weaken fighting morale and strength. Before, Trotsky had tried to find czarist officers and shoot them. Now he tried to woo them as leaders for his army. Many Russians saved their lives in this less-than-honorable way, but many of them went back to the Whites again. Major General Alexander Alexandrovich Drenteln, former commander of His Majesty's Bodyguard of the Preobrashensky Regiment, found another way to escape Trotsky's call. His daughter remembers:

One day, a telegram came from Trotsky to my father. It said that my father had been named commander of the southwestern army (of the Bolsheviks), and he was ordered to go to Moscow immediately for further orders. First of all, he should go to the recruitment medical station in Vologda for a health test. My father was deeply faithful, but nevertheless he decided that—if he could not get out of this shameful order—he would immediately put an end to his own life.

That was when he got the idea. Before he went to the station for a medical examination, he went to an insane asylum several versts[15] from Vologda. There, he explained to the chief doctor that he was suffering from attacks of insanity, and occasional losses of consciousness and memory, which must be the result of an injured nerve in his ear. Apparently, the doctor understood the situation and actually wrote out a certificate for my father testifying to periodical insanity, adding all sorts of symptoms and terms to the ones my father had mentioned, and submitting it all to the leadering commissar of the asylum for his signature. When my father arrived at the medical station, the doctors there were so shocked by the contents of the certificate that they immediately wrote a resolution on his inability to take over any kind of responsible command position. But they demanded that he should come back to the commission for examinations every six months. This sword of Damocles hung over him, but it did not fall on him in the five years before his death.

During the same period, Whites who had not retreated to the Crimea with the Volunteer Army acted as partisans. There were rarely women among them. But Nina Burova, who had ridden horses since her childhood, seized the initiative after her husband died:

Somehow, things had to go on even after the disintegration of the Whites. I had learned a lot from my husband before, when he asked me to correct essays that he had to write as a teacher for war tactics. So I also knew about the tactics of partisan groups in wars. I was able to convince friends to form a group of partisans together. I could ride and shoot well. Thus my fighting existence in the Causasus began. After a while, I was even elected to be an Ataman.[16] I commanded the group for an entire year. I became so well known that women kissed my feet when we came into a village—I was sitting on my horse, of course. Songs were sung for me.

The Bolshevik fighters were cowardly. When they fled, they threw away all sorts of things—food, bags. I gathered all of it and took it into a cossack village that we were just coming to, because no one had anything to eat there. Even the wounded were virtually without medical attention

and medicaments. I frequently helped care for wounds with my mani-
curing scissors. The flies that the climate brought with it were dangerous.
The horses suffered from that, there were bodies all over everywhere, the
flies were infected. Cossack children had festering wounds. As a disin-
fectant, we drank Raki, vodka made from corn.

Sometimes, it seemed to me that I looked like Joan of Arc. I remember,
for instance, one scene near Tverda, a mountain in the Caucasus. We
were in a long gorge. The Reds were above us on the mountain. They
were shooting at us. While riding, I was hit in the breast and fell from
my horse. My people had to go on. So the Reds found me. I was laid on
a stretcher and taken to Rostov. The Reds cared for me, however, so that
they would be able to cross-examine me about who was riding with my
group. I was sitting in jail under unimaginable circumstances, but I was
not shot.

Sometimes the Red Army used old tricks, as Vladimir Bulgakov
reports:

It happened that we fell into an ambush. Reds had disguised themselves
in cadet's uniforms. Because of this, of course, we suffered great losses.
Our general, however, did not have all the people whom we had taken
prisoner shot, though we had been put on our guard by this event. We
took some of them into our regiment on probation. Our division was an
excellent shock troop, and gradually they began to take on this fighting
spirit too. That was important, because we needed reinforcements. Many
had left the front—an entire regiment—and in the Samira region the 37th
Division had surrendered completely to the Soviet regime. When soldiers
marched by with the banner of their regiment, they were shot immediately
by the others.

The civilian population was forced to fight for its survival every
day. It was not just former members of the old regime, the so-called
"Ownership Class" and the nobility who, as "enemies of the
revolution," were open game for robbery and murder. Even merely
potential opponents were persecuted—a process sanctioned by the
slogans of the Soviets. The rule of law had disappeared, and in the
resulting chaos terror groups could move unpunished from door to door.
Possible opponents of the regime were officially disposed of. There were
separatist terrorists in the Ukraine. And simple criminals acted

wantonly. All of this meant that survival during the years of the Civil War depended on chance. Varvara Mandelstam lived in Odessa:

The Bolsheviks declared that the White Guards were shooting workers, and that they should take revenge. Even today, I cannot forget the sight of the many corpses that lay around. They had been shot without knowing why. A friend of our family, a well-known surgeon, jumped from his window when the Bolsheviks took Odessa.

Tatyana Neklyudova's memories illuminate a typical Russian situation during that period of time.

After the revolution bands were formed and one of them came in on a machine gun wagon to the Gagarin's estate. They pushed their way into the house and explained that they were going to kill everyone. The eighty-year-old grandmother answered, with utter serenity: "Wait, I've got to change my clothes for death." They sat down and agreed. The grandmother returned wearing her best dress and the appropriate head covering and stated: "I'm ready, I only ask to be killed in the church." The members of the bands also agreed to this. So the grandmother, her sister Yulya Gagarina, the Vadbolskys—a man, his wife and two of their sons who were 14 and 15 years old (the youngest, Schura, had hidden under a bed in the house and had not been discovered)—the neighbor, the countess Henrikova and her companion, an English lady named Miss Cecily, who were all visiting the Gagarins, were murdered in the private chapel of the house.

Afterwards the bands went to another estate, which belonged to Katya the granddaughter of old Mrs. Sadonskaya. She was just 25 years old, very beautiful, could play the piano magnificently and sing and was married to the considerably older Nikolay Michaylovich Neklyudov (our uncle), by whom she had had five or six children. A domestic servant from the neighboring estate had called her up to warn her about the approaching band. But she did not lose her wits. She quickly set the table on the terrace and brought out food and drink, even the upright piano was dragged out. When the wagon arrived with the men, she received them, bowing deeply, and invited them to the table. As hungry as they were, they ate and drank until they were full, and Katya played and sang for them. Somehow after dinner they had lost the desire to kill anyone and they left again. This is how Katya saved the lives of her family. During the retreat of the Whites from Novocherkassk, many died when they fell into the hands of the Reds, but she survived since she was sick with typhus and the Reds passed over those who were sick with typhus.

Nina Sergeyevna Patrick remembers how unbridled propaganda gave free rein to pent-up aggressions. At least with members of the old regime who were subject to persecution by the new rulers anyway, the methods of killing apparently become a form of bestial pleasure:

> Even ordinary citizens who just tried to go with the evacuation ships were considered enemies. My uncle and aunt were unable to reach the last ship. They were shot on the Feodosiya Beach. Officers were frequently tortured beforehand. My father-in-law was lying sick in his house near Chernigov. He had been wounded during the war and crippled for the rest of his life. The men from the Red Guard—or from the Cheka—came and threw him still alive to the pigs to eat.
>
> It was a completely dehumanized crowd. In order to understand that, one has to read *The Demons* by Dostoyevsky.

Yekaterina Volkonskaya, however, also remembers an episode which saved the life of her husband Boris Dimitriyevich Volkonsky and reveals the Russian mentality:

> As a young officer, my husband was supposed be shot. Shortly after the local commissioner of the new ruling power—it was early 1918—came to the village, my husband was picked up by a young member of the Red Guard and led out of the village. On the way, this young fellow noticed the watch on Boris' hand and clearly admired it. Meanwhile, other Red Guardsmen were already gambling for his boots. The farmers had collected two thousand Kerensky Rubles for his life—for nothing. Facing his near death, Boris took off his watch and gave it to the lad. Suddenly the Red Guardsman felt some sympathy towards my husband: "It's a pity for you—only 22 years old, and I'm supposed to shoot you? I'm not going to do it today, but get out of here immediately, or someone else will do it!"
>
> Boris rode day and night towards the south and joined a regiment of Cossacks in the volunteer army. He fell here a short time later.

Maria Kusnyezova:

It was not just actual or potential opponents of the regime who were shot. Even members of what, according to the name of the state, was the ruling class, were shot: peasants. When they refused to give up their supplies of food, they were shot. For every Chekist shot by the Whites there were hundreds of retaliatory murders. That got worse and worse after the unsuccessful attempts to assassinate Lenin. The climate kept getting hotter. From time to time, one had the feeling that they were just wild children running rampant.

A scene that Maria von Meiendorf remembers seems to confirm this. Fully conscious of the danger this posed in an area that was already controlled by the Bolsheviks, her two sons had wanted to break through to the Whites at the front. But they fell into the hands of the "Greens," a separatist terror organization operating in the Ukraine and southern Russia. They were taken to a prison for cross-examining. Before they were shot, they had the opportunity to write to their loved ones. Maria von Meiendorf received this farewell message from her sons:

> The band's messengers—their commander looked like a wild animal —came into our house. Joking scornfully, they informed me of the death of my sons. The commander took a note out of his pocket and began to read:
> "Dear Mother!
> I wanted to give you joy by coming home, but instead I must bring you pain. But I can do nothing; it is surely the will of God. It is said that things are looking bad for us, and that we will be shot. I do not regret my life. It must be that my death will serve the good cause better than my further life. When I am not there any more, do not thrust the children away from you. Take them under your protection. They will not be a burden to you. They will cheer you up. Forgive me if I am in your debt for any reason. I also beg forgiveness from all relatives and those who are close to me. Christ be with you.
> May God protect you. Yuri."
> What followed were words to the children:
> "My beloved children!
> Maybe we will never see each other again in this world. Forgive me, my loved ones—I wanted to bring you the joy of being together again, but instead of this we will be parted forever. This is God's will. Do not be too sad about this. Rather, bear your pain with patience and submission.

Increase through your lives the good and the true on this earth. Do not take revenge for my death, either in deed or in thought. This is the way the Lord acted. Only pray that He will forgive my sins. I do not fear death. I go before the Lord in the deep hope that when I stand trial before Him for my life he will accept my offering. I am asking your grandmother to take care of you. Be obedient, good grandchildren, and give her comfort in her pain. I bless you and lead you to everything that is good.

Your father."

The bandit had started reading in an amused tone. But in the course of reading his voice became more serious. Gradually, the other men left the room in silence. The commander brought out the last words haltingly. When he was done, he ran out.

Later, he came back alone. He offered to take us away the next day. I was silent. I do not know whether he came back the next day.

We were not there anymore either.

NOTES

1. "Rus" is the old name of the first medieval Russian feudal state (from the ninth to the thirteenth centuries), which resulted from the unification of the eastern Slavic tribes. It was concentrated around Kiev.

2. Here the speaker is evidently referring to the fact that the revolutionaries, their helpers, and agents were acting in German interests.

3. What is meant here is evidently the Bolshevik propaganda against defense of the fatherland. This propaganda had destroyed morale at the front.

4. Mass desertion from the front as a result of propagandistic promises of land.

5. Here Lenin forgot to mention that the same capitalists had supported him and were still supporting him.

6. i.e., a council government.

7. General Alexey Kaledin was Hetman (i.e., chief) of the Don cossacks.

8. Only a few years earlier, the Kuban cossacks had received a new military school, where artillery, infantry, cavalry, and war technology were taught in the French way.

9. Caucasian swords were less bent than cossack swords, and hence they resembled large daggers.

10. In the direction of Moscow.

11. During the period when names connected to the Czar were being eliminated, Zarizyn on the Volga was renamed Vogograd, and after that Stalingrad.

12. This act brought the Czechs the bad name which they have borne ever since among Russian emigrants. In analogy to "Czechoslovaki" (i.e., Czechs), they were now called "Czechosobaki" (Czech dogs).

13. Probably English pounds.

14. The "Greens" were a separatist anarchist group in the Kuban and the Ukraine.

15. A verst is the equivalent of about 1.067 kilometers.

16. Hetman, or Cossack leader.

Chapter Eight

//

Farewell Forever

Postrevolutionary reality, escape and emigration—a kaleidoscope.

The political revolution had been set in motion, and administrative measures had been taken throughout the country in order to carry it out. There had been a radical break with everything that was old, and no system arose to replace the order that had ruled previously. In its place, there was chaos, wantonness, and raw violence. The network of local Soviets instituted by the Central Committee all over the country was not yet completely effective. In certain places, there was an interregnum in the frequent change of rulers—such as in Siberia and the Ukraine, where Reds and Whites took turns ruling a territory. The fronts of the White Volunteer Army gradually broke apart. When the Polish General Pilsudski surrendered to the Red Army, he freed up the Red Army on the Polish front, which could now concentrate on putting down the regime established by General Vrangel in the Crimea. In 1920, this last stronghold of the Whites and the civilians who had fled there broke apart; with the help of the English, the general was just able to evacuate his army to Constantinople, and some civilians were able to take refuge on some of these ships.

Russia between 1918 and 1920 and even later—that was a kaleidoscope of many colors: the gradual seizure of power by the Bolsheviks throughout the country, the shedding of blood, violence, resistance, resignation, and flight. For those who wanted to escape there were hardly more than three possibilities: in the south one of Vrangel's

189

ships, in the northeast trying to get through to the Chinese border and spending lots of money to be led across, or slipping over the Finnish border in similar night-and-fog circumstances. A dramatic journey, which succeeded only in a few cases, as will be seen in what follows.

In Petrograd and later Moscow, the two centers of power, calculated planning, rather than wanton excess, reigned supreme.

Yevgeniya Kvyatkovskaya remembers the first phase of the new Soviet state, during which expropriation actions are being carried out by the local Soviets. Naturally, those who had something to lose tried to save their valuables from expropriation. Yevgeniya Kvyatkovskaya was living on her grandmother's estate forty versts from the Tuma train station (east of Moscow):

> I had moved from Moscow to my grandmother's estate, since it was said that these were times in which one had to be on one's guard. I myself heard speakers at assemblies in front of the Historical Museum[1] curse and make terrible threats against the "Burshui."[2] My brother explained to me that they were Leninists.
>
> One day, we learned that there would be house searches. We had sold most of our animals; we tried to hide our food supplies and preserves as well as we could. We hid the wine bottles in the snow—chiefly in order to prevent the Red Army people from drinking too much and getting violent. I sewed money and financial papers—and that was what was essential for our existence—into a belt of rough linen, of which there was a lot in the house. I did the same with my grandmother's gold coins, since it was lethally dangerous to own something like that. I made a complete slip of linen and sewed all the large papers and coins into it, as well as a neckerchief that an aunt of mine had once gotten from the Czar—I still have it. Then I gathered the silverware into a cloth bag and put my grandmother's revolver in, too, after I had greased it down. My grandmother owned a whole collection of revolvers, which she carried along on trips or during the evening. But when the Red Guards found a weapon like that, one was compromised and exposed to immediate execution.
>
> When my brother saw one of the Red Army men from my window, I quickly put on the slip, took the suitcase with the things, and swung myself with it through the rear window into the garden. I ran to a place where there was lots of undergrowth and tree stumps from felled trees. That was where I hid the bag with the silver and the revolver. When I returned to the house, several of the men came toward me and asked where my grandmother—Sinaida Vladimirovna Batasheva—was. I ex-

plained that she had gone away—she was out buying hay for the horses. I had to lead the Red Army people into our rooms and my grandmother's rooms. One of the first things they discovered and took immediately was another suitcase with the silver coins; when they got close to my brother's boots, where I had hidden the belt with the gold, I distracted them with a protest about something else, which they took along. They actually went into the next room. When I got the chance, I ran back into my brother's room and put on the belt. For the next few days, while the Red Army men were in our house, we were being watched.

Tobolsk, the end of 1917: The ex-Czar Nicholas, his wife, and his children had been brought here from Zarskoye Syelo without being told where they were being taken, and they were under house arrest in a building determined for them. While leaving the palace, Nicholas had requested a confidante of the family:

> Take care of the children in case anything happens to us. Explain to Alexey that one does not need a crown! I know that mother does not understand this, but tell him one does not need a crown.

With her brother, Tatyana Botkina had followed her father to Tobolsk, where he lived across from the imprisoned family of the Czar, also under house arrest. She recalls:

> At Christmas, the Czar's family made presents for each of us, and also for the members of their guard who had duty on the holiday. Because of the authority of their officer Kobylinsky, the rebellious Red Guards were kept somewhat in check in the way they treated their prisoners. At that time, life in this small Siberian city relatively far away from the capital proceeded somewhat the way it had before the revolution. At that time, there was not any hunger there yet, and many peasants brought presents, especially food, which then reached the Czar's family via the few people who could still get into the house without being checked. This changed drastically at the beginning of 1918, though. The guards were replaced by relentless Red Guards, and a completely different atmosphere ensued. The snow mountain that the Czar had built for his son in the garden was destroyed during the night: It was feared that otherwise the former Czar might be seen from the rise by passersby. The guards had little patience with the fact that many passersby had kneeled down at the fence of the house and crossed themselves. Finally, the new Red Guards ordered that

the ex-Czar's epaulets be taken off his uniform. For the first time, he grew angry and refused. Finally, when the officer on duty privately asked him not to resist the directives of the Central Soviet, he found another solution: From now on, he wore a cossack uniform, which did not even require epauletes.

Petrograd: prisoner of war transports arrived, and wounded prisoners were taken to nearby hospitals. The Austrian Count Xaver Schaffgotsch was one of the prisoners who actually ought to have been sent back to his homeland after the peace treaty. Because he could communicate in Russian and enjoyed a certain authority thanks to his personality, he took on the role of representative for the Austrian prisoners among the Russians. While his squad was standing at the Petrograd train station, he went without hesitation to the Smolny, which was still the seat of the Bolshevik government:

> It was not hard to get into the Smolny at this time. I told the guard in the little wooden shelter in front of the building that I had to go to Commissar Trotsky. Without further ado, I was allowed in. I knew Trotsky from Vienna through my friend, the psychologist Alfred Adler; his wife was a Russian and a cousin of Trotsky's wife.
>
> As directed, I went to room number 67. He sat behind his secretary's front room: the minister for foreign affairs. He was wearing glasses, and his hair was slightly graying. There were no signs of rank on the jacket of his uniform. I went up to him and addressed him in German: "I believe we know each other from the Cafe Central in Vienna, through Alfred Adler."
>
> At that he jumped up and said, "What's happening with Alfred Adler, what's happening with the Cafe Central?"
>
> I explained that I couldn't tell him a thing, because I had been a prisoner of war since fall of 1914 and probably knew less about Vienna than he did. Despite that, we chatted for a bit, until he said that I must certainly have come with some sort of request. Then I explained the situation to him: "You see, for us prisoners of war it is a catastrophe when we have to imagine that we must go to Siberia or God knows where again, instead of finally going home. Many of us probably wouldn't survive it, because we have invalids among us. On the one hand, since The Revolution officially there are no prisoners of war anymore; on the other hand, we are not allowed to go home."
>
> "Do you have a useful suggestion to make?"

"The Danish Embassy, which represents our interests, has assured me that it will guarantee that any trains, personnel, and locomotives that you may put at our disposal for the trip home will be sent back again unharmed." I showed him the paper I had prepared.

Trotsky: "We can talk about this. But I am not the only one to decide on this. You must also speak to Comrade Lenin."

So I had to go on and look for Lenin. He was not in the Smolny or in the office of the chairman of the Soviet of the People's Representatives. Finally, I did run into him at the Smolny, and I presented my request and the paper to him.

"Agreed," said Lenin. "I will give you a letter to the General Staff for transportation, and the necessary means of transportation will be put at your disposal."

So on that same evening I went by sled to the General Staff, which frequently worked day and night at that time. Thus, I was immediately able to present the colonel on duty with my papers, and I really did get three hospital trains immediately. They were ready to go at the train station. The very same night, I accompanied the first squad with about eight hundred to one thousand invalids, and we went in the direction of Moscow. We were told that from there we should go via Kiev to Lemberg.

Things wound up happening differently, but this was part of the confusion of the times, in which people were never certain where they could even be safe. The Ukraine, for instance, was first under German protection, then it was disputed territory, changing from Bolshevik to Polish to "White" and then back to "Red" hands. First it was a place of refuge, then it was a dangerous place to be.

Xenia Alexandrovna Giovanni—at the time she was still called Drushinikova—remembers:

The times were uncertain and unpredictable. Before the Bolshevik uprising, my future husband had been active politically. He was a Social Revolutionary and worked on the Preparatory Committee for the Constitutional Assembly. This democratic instrument, which was supposed gradually to realize the reforms necessary for Russia, was boycotted by the Bolsheviks, and its followers were persecuted. Thus, many people simply disappeared without a trace. We lived near Novgorod, and though I had only just been proposed to we married in a rush in order to escape later together.

The day of the wedding promised good luck: It snowed. I remember how the coachman who took me to the wedding said that. But, in fact, everything almost went wrong. I sat down in the simple, open coach with my cousin next to me—according to an old custom, the mother of the bride is not allowed to be present at the wedding—and her son, who was holding the icon. The horse was old. On the way, we had to go by a circus tent. Loud music was coming through its open gate. Suddenly, the horse stopped and refused to go any further. It stood in front of the entrance to the circus and pricked its ears; evidently, it could hear and smell the horses dancing to the music inside. Despite the coachman's desperate attempts to get it moving, the horse just stood there for quite a while. After some time, it suddenly went on again. We were late to the wedding. My bridegroom and the priest were not there any more. They had assumed that something had happened. But we sent for them immediately, and it all worked out after all, very quickly.

We learned that citizens born in Odessa could get legal papers that would make it possible to leave Petrograd for the Ukraine. My husband was in possession of a birth certificate that affirmed he was from Odessa. But the problem was that it was illegal to stop working; this was considered an action against the Soviet state and punished with exile to Siberia or execution. So my husband went first, going underground at his brother's house in Leningrad for a while. In the meantime, I stayed with my mother. On the very next day, they arrived at his original apartment to arrest him. His domestic came to tell us about it. So he had escaped that. But right after he got the visa for the Ukraine from Petrograd, he was to send me a telegram to follow him. But there was no telegram. A week went by, and still there was no news. I got sick with the Spanish flu, which many people died of during the epidemic. In the second week, I had still heard nothing from my husband. Had he been denounced and arrested there? In the third week, my sickness reached its height. I was coughing and had a high fever. At the end of that week, finally, I got word: "Everything ready. Come immediately! Giovanni."

The next day, I was still sick. I went to Petrograd. The day after that, we were already sitting—or better, lying—on the wooden benches of the freight train that had been put at the disposal of the Ukrainians who wanted to go home. It was the last train. After that, even this possibility for getting away no longer existed.

We needed a whole month for the trip, because in the meantime new battles had begun between the communists and the supposedly independent Ukraine. Again and again, the train simply stopped right in the middle of a gunfight. We could hear the shots. They were using artillery.

The only thing we had to eat were potatoes from Petrograd. There had been no bread. Once the train stopped for a whole week. That was in the vicinity of Mogilyev. We were frequently told that the train could only go on if we managed to come up with some fuel. So we went out to get wood from fences or trees. Near Mogilyev, we hoped to find something edible in the city. But the people here were already starving, too. We could find nothing but apples from fruit gardens. But when we got back to the place where the train had stood, it wasn't there anymore. We were shocked to death, because we had left everything that we still owned behind. But then we found out to our relief that the train had simply been shoved somewhere else.

We rode on, and after more day-long stops along the way we finally got to Usa, the border city to the Ukraine. At the crossing point, we learned that Prince Subov and General Dimitrov had ridden along disguised in our compartment. That fact had only come out once we got to the Ukrainians. If the Cheka guards before Usa had noticed this, these gentlemen would not have had a good time. They took one student along and shot him. We never learned why. Subov and Dimitrov showed us later how they had sewed their valuables into pillows and boots.

The Ukraine—that was a different picture from what we were used to: well-dressed officers with epaulets and monocles. Flowers at the train station, food stands, life. And yet even here life was not peaceful. We were able to stay with my husband's sister, who still had an apartment with her husband—a lawyer—and enough to live on.

Nevertheless there were seventeen changes of power in the Ukraine. Whenever there was shooting, we hid in the bathroom. The walls were strongest there, and we were safest. There was lots of shooting, from the Reds, the Whites, the Germans and the Poles. It didn't really matter. Most of the house searches happened when the Reds were there. They were not just looking for possible resistance or representatives of the "enemy" class like aristocrats—in Kiev almost the entire aristocratic quarter was decimated and its inhabitants shot on the edge of the city— they were also requisitioning everything in the house. One had to give up one's gold, everything except one necklace and one wedding ring, as well as clothing, except for two pieces per person. If one had hidden something and it was found anyway, one could be shot. Later on they punched out people's teeth in order to get to their gold fillings.

When the Whites came, there were pogroms against the Jews again. We always had a kind of guard duty in front of the house in shifts, because besides all the occupying soldiers there were also bands of men roaming around, even if they were more frequently in the smaller cities and villages. So my sixteen-year-old niece had guard duty once, when she was asked about Jews by Caucasian White Guards. And though she knew that across from us there was the family of a Jewish dentist, she was brave enough not to betray them and to answer the question concerning them with no. "Truly not?" asked the soldiers. "You can believe me," she replied steadfastly. "The house belongs to my grandmother, and my grandfather was police chief of the city." They rode away—evidently they did not want to begin at the police chief's house. The times were dramatic. The house was soon empty. We had soon traded away everything that the family owned, right down to the last piece of furniture and dishes, in order to survive.

Count Ivan Stenbock also saved himself by going to the Ukraine. He waited out the events at an estate of his uncle's. But the already-mentioned bands—whether acting in the name of the separatist Ukrainian independence movement or simply using the vaccuum of law and order to carry out robbery and booty-taking unpunished—made everyday life in this country area a daily struggle for survival:

We heard that the men who had sneaked onto our estate were simply the advance guard of the Maruska band.[3] The whole band was supposed to come the next morning. I explained to my uncle that we had to hide. But my uncle answered, "I was born in this house, and if it is my fate to be killed in this house, then I will die here." I argued with him: "But uncle, you will be killed, but beforehand Maruska will torture you all, torture you to death." It was pointless trying to change the old man's mind. We, on the other hand, decided to flee.

The evening before, we had a farewell dinner at which we also celebrated my twenty-first birthday. We drank champagne. The old servant who had already been serving my grandmother in the same house when she got married was also there. He had chased my father away from the table with a wet towel when he was being naughty. He was really a part from the past. At our house, he had long since gone into retirement, but when this farewell dinner took place he put on his old uniform and wanted to serve at all costs. Andrey Alexeyevich—that was his name—held the plate with the goose so shakily that we were afraid he would let it fall at any moment—but it would have been unthinkable to say even a word to him about his not being able to serve anymore. He would have died immediately out of hurt pride.

saryev Bicherakov in Cossack uniform.

Iwan count Stenbock-Fermor and his parents.

Count Stenbok's father with his brothers.

Боткинъ

Евгеній Сергѣевичъ

Къ достопримѣ...

Комиссеа Времен...
Правит...

r. Yevgeniy S. Botkin, the Czar's doctor.

Typical Russian grand family, with French nurse and German teacher.

Count Stenbok's estate in Kamenka.

neral Nicholas Baratov in Caucasian Cossack uniform.

Yevgeniya Kvyatkova with her parents and her brother.

Kvyatkova's estate.

ossacks setting up a camp.

ossacks rode their horses differently from other Russian soldiers.

General Vrangel.

General Alexeyev.

General Drosdovsky.

General Denikin.

rvara S. Levitova.

Those who accompanied the Imperial family to Tobolsk.

tter handwritten by Maria Nikolay-
na.

One of the last letters by Olga Nikolay-
evna.

Grand Duchess Leonida Georgyevna
Romanova, born Bogration.

Grand Duke Vladimir Kyrillovich Ro
manov.

Former members of the Kornilov attack regiment (Paris, 1967) at a memorial servic
for the fallen white army and the end of Russia.

That same night, we bade farewell to everyone and the house. We ran through the park into the open steppe to the water reservoir. We had a rifle with us, but we were confident that we would not be attacked on the open steppe, since it was clear that we could shoot back. Suddenly, we heard the beating of horse's hooves. We were already thinking that someone was following us. Only the night watchman had noticed our flight. He was an Austrian prisoner of war. Like thousands of others, he had surrendered because he had Slavic blood himself and did not want to fight against the Russian Slaves anymore. Had he told anyone anything?

It turned out that he had only told our coachman that we were going by foot. The coachman had immediately hitched up the horses and ridden after us. He brought us to a cottage about twenty kilometers from our house. Then he returned to the estate. Though he never drank, that night he imbibed as much alcohol as he could, so that he would be completely drunk and unable to speak. That way the bandits would not get anything out of him.

But the bandits found the wine cellar themselves and drank so much that they could not move from where they were for two days. That is what saved us, because it gave us a start. Another peasant, meanwhile, had learned that we were hiding in this cottage, and he got his coach ready and took us to Nikolayev. This city had already been in Austrian hands, but meanwhile the Reds had come. Then came artillery reinforcements from the Germans, who took Nikolayev. On the way there, we met loads of Bolsheviks who were fleeing from the place. Finally, we came to a German guard. After four years of war against the Germans,[4] they were no longer our enemies. Rather, they were our hope. Now we knew that we were saved.

Tobolsk, spring 1918. The new guard detachment was less compromising than the Red Guards of the first year, and there was an unsettling atmosphere in the house where the Czar's family was being kept prisoner. Back when Kerensky had told the ex-Czar Nicholas that the family must be taken away "for reasons of security" (without, of course, naming the destination as Siberia), Nicholas had looked at him and said "I trust you."

But he probably sensed what he could not know for sure: that Kerensky, who had just told him that he had saved the ex-Czar from suggested execution during a debate the day before, had really been the one at the same debate on the death penalty[5] to plead:

The only person whom I would except from the abolition of the death penalty would be the Czar!

For a long time after Kerensky's brief exercise of power and Lenin's seizure of power, there were no negotiating partners to give (and break) their word. Directives arrived from the Moscow Soviet and were ratified and carried out by the local Soviet. The Czar's family was taken away. This time it turned out after two difficult weeks of travel that Yekaterinburg, the center of the platinum industry, was the destination. The house of Governor Ipatyev, who had to give in to the Bolshevik Soviet, was intended for the family—and its guards. The Grand Duchesses slept on the floor, since there were no beds. The rooms could not be closed off, and the Red Guards were free to enter day and night. The man who took care of Alexey, the son, was no longer allowed to accompany the family. Later, he was shot. Now, only Doctor Botkin and a chambermaid were allowed to stay with the family. In view of the coming journey from Tobolsk, the ex-Czar Nicholas had turned to the doctor and said (perhaps guided by premonitions): "Now I relieve you finally from your duties."

But Botkin had replied, "I will stay in your service until the end of my life."

The Czar is said to have taken his hand spontaneously and argued, "But you have to think of your family." Tatyana Botkina remembers:

> For my father, it was no question, no matter how difficult the decision was. He, too, had a premonition; when we bade farewell to each other he told me to marry Melnik if he made me an offer. "He is a decent person and loves you." I did it later on. My brother and I requested to be allowed to follow our father to the next place of exile, but the Soviets in the city refused us.
>
> I will never forget that moment: As the tiny caravan moved on around two o'clock in the morning—I had stayed up and was watching from my window, which was across the way—I saw my father look up as he passed our house. With his right hand he made the sign of the cross in our direction.

The letters that came from the "house for special purpose," as the Ipatyev house in Yekaterinburg was called, did not sound very hopeful. Even if they did not say what was going on here: toying with the family that had represented the old Russia. Those faithful to the Czar collected money to free the Czar's family, wrote letters that raised hopes—but nothing happened. The Red Guards, meanwhile, made fun of their prisoners, hit utensils out of their hands while they were eating, and took away the icon over Alexey's bed. This one house now became a reflection of what was happening all over the country. Wanton destruction manifested itself in archaic ways, giving vent to centuries-old aggressions. Destruction took place with childish joy.

The British journalist Philipp Price was in the interior of the country at this time, journeying to the southeast of Moscow. He summarized the chaos between the old Russia and the new Soviet regime in the following picture:

> The governor's house in Ryasan was destroyed. People say that furniture and art objects inside the residence, worth millions, were burned, that storage rooms were broken open and robbed or destroyed; farmer women took the French porcelain vases and used them as containers for sour cream; robbery and drunkenness are spreading, some peasants are attacking their own people.
>
> Pogroms and acts of destruction resembling the unrest in March are the order of the day in the districts around Tula[6] and Samara. Not a single estate was spared from partial or complete destruction. The loss of agricultural machines, animals, and grains is as high as thirty million rubles.
>
> In administrative district Sibirsk, things look similar. Among the destroyed art objects are those that belong to the house of Karamsin, a respected historian; one building was saved from destruction thanks to the intervention of Austrian prisoners of war. In Pensa, the excesses went so far that the mob set almost all the villas and palaces on fire.
>
> In other parts of the country, however, the farmers have joined together to protect the land and the estates. This is true above all in the areas where cossacks live.[7]
>
> Our train is traveling through Siberia. We have already gotten used to the phenomena associated with communism in Petrograd, but what is happening along the railroad tracks and in the train stations in the provinces is unbelievable. This chaos, this anarchy perpetrated by freed criminals and bands usually operating in the name of the Bolsheviks is indescribable. In the cities, the militia has been disbanded and replaced by members of the Red Guard. Their appearance is inevitably connected with violence, robbery, and murder. Passersby have their fur coats ripped off. This is usual especially in Siberia.
>
> It is horrible how the uneducated masses are being stirred up against

everyone who does not want to identify with the Bolsheviks. In every assembly, one comes to one can hear insults and threats against Mensheviks and Social Revolutionaries, who are being called "blood suckers" or "fat bourgeois." Usually, it is not even clear here what these newly appointed Bolsheviks really want. All one can hear is wild insults against people who think differently.

Grain is being used almost exclusively for vodka. In almost every village, there are at least ten to fifteen distilleries. Rye is being sold for prices between forty-five and fifty-five rubles per pud,[8] but it brings twice as much when it is used for home distilling. There is so much alcohol that there is enough for consumption and export. Everyone is earning money off of it, even the members of the Executive Committee. Again and again, one hears justifications like this: "What kind of freedom would it be if one couldn't even brew a bottle of vodka for home use?"

Under the influence of this alcohol, men are plundering estates and destroying public and private forests. Frequently, deserters from the front are involved in such plunderings and acts of violence. When the commissars of the government take directed action to locate and arrest criminals, soldiers in their brigades usually wind up taking part in the debauches themselves.

Village expeditions are sent out from time to time to secure the "national treasure," as vodka is often called; they set out armed with revolvers and rifles and run up as often as not against expeditions from other villages. Then there are full-blown battles. Taking part in the wild orgies of drinking are old and young men, women, and underaged people; children are put to sleep with alcohol so that their parents can go on drinking undisturbed. Lasciviousness and gambling accompany the drinking; venereal diseases are spreading; and in every village there are cases of typhoid, and wonder drugs are being sold at exorbitant prices everywhere without any kind of control. The villages are swimming in paper money, and since no one knows what to do with it the peasants gamble with it. The most popular game is "Twenty-One." Thousands of rubles can change ownership in one evening.

The lack of order opens the gates wide for bands of rowdies and thieves. The "Burshui" are blamed for all of this and for the lack of salt and sugar.

Along the train stations are piled the museum treasures of the evacuated former capital city of the Czars, Petrograd. Other trains are filled to the brim with refugees. Homeless soldiers, peasants—all looking for a place to stay. Among them, men of the Red Guard. In every station, the train station directors or the workers' Soviets give their own orders without worrying too much about the ones issued by the central Soviets in Petrograd and Moscow. It sometimes happens that a Red Guard commando takes over an entire train, making it go in the direction it desires. After the peace treaty of Brest-Litovsk, some units of the Red Guards had stopped recognizing the Central Committee of the Soviet in the capital city as their highest authority. They began a guerrilla war against the Germans in the western territories. Among those units was the one directed by Dybenko, a member of the Baltic fleet.

Everywhere one can sense the spirit of rebellion. Now it is no longer just estate owners or cadets against whom one must fight but also invading Germans, for whom their own peace treaty is nothing more than "a piece of paper."

Aggressions that have been building for centuries have now come to the surface. The age-old instinct for revenge against supposed oppressors is now being lived out.

Revenge is sanctioned by the highest authorities; indeed, it is prescribed, after the German ambassador, Baron Mirnbach (a symbol of the German financing of Lenin), and then the chief of the secret police were murdered and Lenin wounded in an assassination attempt, all in the middle of 1918.

Lydiya Vasilchikova describes scenes from southern Russia:

Most of the people who had gone to the Crimea actually managed to save themselves—with the exception of the unfortunate officers of the Black Sea fleet—but our relatives and acquaintances in the Caucasus, for example, experienced terrible things. Most of them died. The Crimea Regiment stationed in Livadiya tried to throw off Soviet rule. But it was in the minority, since the tartar population had no serious political convictions and always sided with whomever was strongest. So the uprising was unsuccessful, and the Crimea Regiment disintegrated completely afterward. Several escaped to the North, others were killed immediately, and still others fled into the mountains, where they led guerrilla battles against the Soviet regime.

The consequences for the Navy officers in Sevastopol were fatal. Many of them were beaten to death, others were shot, and others were thrown still alive into the heating tanks of the ships; some of them had weights tied to their feet, and they were thrown into the ocean alive. When the

Germans came, divers were sent out after the victims. One came up to the surface again shortly after the action had begun and screamed that he had lost his mind.

The enemy's hatred was strong. When General Kornilov, symbol and leadership figure of the Kuban campaign, was hit by a shell near Yekaterinodar in the south of Russia and died, he was secretly burried on the private estate of his General Staff headquarters. The seizure of the city was put off. Meanwhile, the Red Army arrived. When it got to Yekaterinodar, it had all the new graves searched. When Kornilov's body was found, it was carried through town with the head down. The body was burned, and its ashes were spread to the wind.

This did not change the fact that there were sometimes conflicts of conscience when young Russians faced each other as enemies. Varvara Levitova, a nurse in General Kornilov's combat patrol, remembers:

> I will never forget that moment. We were supposed to take the village Novo-Dmitriyevsk. It was a rainy day, and the rain froze into ice. While waiting for the other units to finally arrive, the freezing soldiers lit a camp fire to warm themselves. In the light, they became aware of a "Red" soldier who had hidden himself in a nearby cottage. When he came running out, I screamed. Because of my scream, our soldiers rushed toward him and caught the fleeing man with a lasso. A moment later, I heard a shot—evidently they had killed him. Although this was to be expected, my responsibility for this fratricide troubles me to this day. Back then, neither side spared the other.

Saving one's own life meant that one could not be particularly concerned for others:

> During the night, we started the retreat. We were forbidden to speak, smoke, or make any kind of light. The Reds followed us with cannon shots. From time to time, we cared for the wounded. We could only take along lightly wounded people—we put them into carts and took them with us. As for those with serious wounds, we could only give them first aid and leave them in a cottage, since we had to go on so as not to lose contact with out regiment, which we were supposed to be caring for. This all meant lethal danger for us and the doctors. At one point, we were just about to move on when we suddenly discovered a few Reds across from

us in the darkness of night, right in the middle of the steppe. "Who are you?" we heard. What kind of a question was that?! Our doctor replied, "A doctor and nurses." "From which regiment?" The doctor must have guessed the worst, because they gradually began to surround us. He named the number of a regiment that did not even exist. There was a horrible silence. It was clear that they understood that we were "Whites." Suddenly, the doctor pulled his revolver and began to shoot at them. "Run, nurses!" he cried to us. Tanya and I started running, with the doctor after us. But the Bolsheviks—others of them, probably—shot after us. They hit the doctor fatally.

Alexandra Neklyudova reports on the fate of her family at his time:

My brother Sergei was killed in these bloody battles of the White Army. He was 23 years old. My other brother Vasily had fled to Yugoslavia. There my mother was, alone with me and my younger brother Alexey, after the death of my father years before. We were already in the Caucasus and had somehow managed to get our hands on some valid exit permits. Some of our relatives had fled, except for our cousin, who was a revolutionary and had thousands executed, till he was later shot under Stalin. Other families related to us were completely exterminated, such as the Prince Vadbolsky's eleven-member family, who were murdered on their own estate; others died of typhus while fleeing through the area around Novocherkassk. My mother could not, however, make the decision to leave. Even though an eyewitness, who had ridden with my brother Sergei, and when faced with the attacker, was able to roll down the river bank and thus escape, had told my mother of Sergei's death. My mother simply could not believe that he was no longer alive. She was convinced that he would one day return. So, instead of leaving, she retreated with us back to our village and remained there. The house had been confiscated in the meantime, and she owned nothing. She sold a little jewelry, which she had, so that she could trade it for a couple of sacks of flour. Looked down on as a 'socially alienating element,' she wanted to bake bread and build an existence for the three of us that way. It turned out though, that only the top of the sacks were filled with flour and really contained mostly plaster. It looked like everything was falling apart. Then our former family doctor, who was in the meantime head of the local hospital, took me in as an assistant nurse, and so we were somehow able to keep going.

Yekaterinburg, the night from 16 to 17 July 1918. The seven-member family of ex-Czar Nicholas II was shot to death, followed two days later by six other members of the Czar's family in Alapayevsk.

A scene in Siberia, sometime between 1918 and 1919—the experiences of a soldier which give insight into the failure of the Whites:

> Fear of being captured by the enemy was worse than fear of death. But this was precisely the kind of situation that I almost fell into during one catastrophic operation. Our division consisted of four regiments. It received the order to attack the Reds at night. According to the plan, the forward members of the regiment were supposed to attack, while the regiment itself was supposed to surround the Reds with the artillery group to which I belonged. While they were busy trying to defend themselves, we were supposed to attack. It was a cold, rainy night, and the roads were so soft that we got stuck in the mud with every step we took. It was particularly difficult for the horses to pull the artillery.
>
> The operation was supposed to begin at two o'clock in the morning. Because of communication problems, the regiment began the action too early, thus forcing the Reds to retreat to precisely the place where we were in the process of trying to surround them! Meanwhile, four hours had gone by, but it was still dark, and the rain was pouring even more heavily than before.
>
> At that time, the uniforms of the two opposing regiments were quite similar, so that it was conceivable for the Reds to mistake us for their comrades. Ten of my comrades and I suddenly found ourselves sitting in a cart with a couple of Reds exchanging "jokes." It is easy to imagine that such a situation did not last long, because we were soon discovered, and the terrible news that we ourselves were surrounded spread like wildfire. That was the longest night of my life, because it was clear to me that we did not have much longer to live. In the gray of dawn, we had a spirited fight trying to escape from our predicament. In the meantime, the other three regiments had figured out the situation and attacked with a new front in order to save us. This was successful, though there were heavy losses. We had to leave a lot of wounded soldiers behind, and we lost all of our horses as well as four pieces of artillery. My friend had one of his ears cut off during the battle. Meanwhile the fifth column[9] intensified its activities, and so they were successful in getting a whole series of "Whites" to go over to the side of the "Reds." Our moral weakness became evident when the order for a front-on attack was given to the infantry. The people in front refused to obey, thus influencing the rest of the regiment. Several

times, our battery had to explode shells over the heads of our own infantry in order to get them to leave their trenches and attack the enemy! The Red Army was growing constantly. At the end of 1918, there were already 800,000 soldiers marching against Admiral Kolchak's 125,000 men. Trotsky's appearance at the front brought the Reds even more recruits. There was above all a lack of leadership personalities among the "Whites"; there were unclear political goals, bad communication, poor equipment and supplies—all of these things contributed to the failure of the "Whites."

In addition, there were the weather conditions, especially in Siberia, which helped out the "Reds," who were far better equipped and supplied. The communists requisitioned what they needed violently from the peasants and inhabitants, while we bought everything—as long as we had money. The peasants were doubly hard hit, and we usually had inadequate and frozen food that we had to smash into tiny bits with our axes. Finally, the "Reds" succeeded in winning over the peasants with propaganda and promises.

The presence of the international troops in Siberia was actually a drawback for us, since they were considered enemies of the Bolsheviks, too, especially the French, British, and five thousand Americans under the command of General Graves. We believed that the "allied forces were fishing in muddy waters," as people say around here. The only effective help in fighting against the Bolsheviks came from the Japanese troops. Not only were they stronger than the other units, they were excellent fighters and demonstrated iron discipline.

Toward the end of 1919, Kolchak's army in eastern Siberia began to fall apart. Our retreat now had only one purpose: to make use of our one-day advantage over the "Reds" for the defensive battle that we would be forced to fight the following morning. Finally, the high command informed us that every unit was being given the right to choose its own fate: either to take part in the retreat or to go over to the "Reds." The extremely hard climatic conditions, insufficient nourishment, unbearable tiredness, the agony of defeat, and the appearance of the typhoid epidemic all cost a great price in terms of human lives. I saw hundreds of dead bodies being taken away on sleds—no one knew where.

During the winter, the situation became catastrophic. The temperatures sank twenty-five and thirty degrees below zero (Celsius). All troops were ordered to keep marching; we were forbidden to sit down even for a moment of rest. This command went unheeded again and again, not

because of insubordination but because the men were completely exhausted and could not go on any further. Inevitably, this meant that it
was their last rest, because they met the painless death of freezing. One
could see many macabre figures there under the snowy trees. Now they
felt no more pain and no suffering.

Yekaterinburg, 1918, 1919. The only people now able to speak for
the Czar's family were their murderers. Admiral Kolchak appointed
Sokolov investigative judge, and he, along with the family's former
English teacher Gibbes, helped to shed light on the last details and
identify the bits and pieces that have not been burnt. The few remains
were kept in a box that managed to get out of the country under
adventurous circumstances. Grand Duchess Tatyana's blue diamond
ring was found among (shreds) of clothing that belonged to the
murdered people (evidently, it had not been seen previously by the Red
Army men). A short while later, it was seen sparkling on the hand of
Trotsky's sister. When Sokolov asked the English high commissioner in
Harbin to take receipt of the tiny box and send it to England so that its
fate would not be the same as his own uncertain one, he was refused:
The English government viewed such a last honor for the Russian
ruling house as "inopportune." (Only the French high commissioner was
willing to take the shipment. However, the box's whereabouts are now
unknown.) All this did nothing to change the fact that among the few
possessions of the Czar's family that escaped the Red Army a diamond
tiara and a diamond necklace that had belonged to Czarina Alexandra
Fyodorovna—now form a natural part of the British crown jewels.

In Omsk, uprisings were stimulated by agitators. The French
helped the agitators rather than Kolchak's Whites, whose seat of
government was there. Kolchak surrendered in Siberia. Though he had
been guaranteed free passage to Harbin, he was handed over by the
French and Czechs to the Bolsheviks. Now the armies' retreat began to
look like a long series of escape adventures, with both soldiers and
civilians involved. A fight for survival was now occuring—in both the
south and the northwest.

A soldier of Kolchak's army was able to fight his way through to
Irkutsk, the capital of Siberia. There he managed to find his sister and
her husband. As can be seen in his report, the Bolsheviks were slow in
taking de facto military and political posession of these far-flung
territories of the empire, even though it was now years after the
October Revolution:

I went to the city square, where "Red" speakers were trying to entice people with their promises. A commissar was riding on horseback through the square and shouting propaganda slogans to the crowd. I can still remember his red beard and red hair, which shone out from under his military cap with the red star.

But the situation in Irkutsk soon became dangerous for me. Meanwhile, my brother-in-law had secretly been negotiating with members of the Japanese High Command. It was agreed that we would get onto the Japanese train on the east bank of the Angara River. Our escape had to take place at night, so as not to arouse any suspicion among the communists, who were already in control of the city. Dressed in a bum's clothing that had been made specifically for this purpose, I went to the owner of a ferry. This was the only possibility for crossing over the river to noncommunist territory and getting to the train. I made an appropriate agreement with the owner. At around eleven o'clock in the evening—it was so cold that neither human beings nor animals could have stood being on the street—the twelve of us—my sister, my brother-in-law, friends, and their dog—got onto the boat. The ferryman seemed surly when he looked at the bulldog before we took off: As far as he could remember, proletarians did not usually own a dog like that. Despite his obvious discomfort, he eventually did start in the direction of the east bank. Each one of us counted the minutes; never did time drag on so slowly.

It seemed that hours had gone by, but in fact it had only lasted half an hour when we finally got to our destination and were received by Japanese soldiers with rifles with fixed bayonets. They led us to the train. Now we were safe, because the Reds were not interested in fighting against soldiers like that. When the train started moving, we joined in a grateful prayer.

The train set off in the direction of Harbin, the central connecting link of the eastern Chinese railway. This was a thin strip of land that the Chinese government had leased to Russia for ninety-nine years in order to make possible a connection to Siberia. Between Irkutsk and Harbin was the railway link Chita, which was under the command of General Semyonov. We were afraid that the train would be searched, but we were pleasantly surprised that the General evidently had no need for "Whites," and we were able to continue our journey to Harbin.

There were guerrilla fights in this area. Red partisans were murdering civilians—not only Russian but also Japanese. Under the command of Red guerrilla leader Tryapizyn, seven hundred Japanese were killed in Nikolayevsk on 20 March 1920. He also ordered all children under five years old to be murdered, so that later they would not be able to remember what they have seen and entertain thoughts of revenge. Scenes in the south of Russia, winter 1919–1920. Lydia Vasilchikova reports:

During the winter—the Germans had gotten out of Russia in the meantime[10]—a contingent of Red army men arrived in Nemirov. They surrounded the estate and arrested its inhabitants. They specifically chose a day when there was a market in a faraway village, so that the peasants nearby would be absent and would not be able to protect the Sherbatovs, my relatives. The old princess was told that she would be shot the next day. They offered Sandra her freedom, but she refused to leave her mother and decided to share her fate. During the hours that still remained, my aunt calmly gave her last orders to the household staff. She was not allowed to say good-bye to her grandchildren, but she got a promise from the English nanny to remain with the children until they were grown up. Arm in arm, their prayer books in their hands, mother and daughter went to their deaths together.

Olga Grigoryevna Nyesvitzkaya came from Poltava in the Ukraine. With the help of her husband, the officer Karmilov, she managed to get to Siberia, and she was with Kolchak when his army retreated:

When I left my mother in Kremenchug, she blessed me and gave me our family icon, which was always given to the oldest daughter. The icon dated back to the last year of Czarina Catherine's reign, and later I gave it to the Russian Orthodox church in Jerusalem. I promised my mother that our family would be reunited some day. I kept my promise. We saw each other again in Honan, China.

I should have seen it as a sign: As we left Kremenchug, the battles between the Reds and Whites were just beginning there. General Yudenich had been in the northwest, just five miles from Petrograd, and had to give up because of lack of munitions and replacements.[11] The same sorts of things happened to the other parts of the White Army. The munitions that were sent from the United States, England, and France did not even fit into the rifles, and the tanks were already rusty. These countries hated czarist Russia, just as they hate the Soviet Union today. They did not want there to be a strong, large Russia again. In Siberia, we saw parts of Kolchak's retreating army. Soldiers near Aral Lake had already melted into tiny groups in the steppes near Orenburg—because of lack of food and water. The lakes were too salty.

My husband had been promoted to captain and had been designated an intelligence officer. He was with General Dutov from Kolchak's army. Dutov had left Omsk in the direction of the Chinese border with forty thousand men. He had reached it with hardly more than eight hundred. Most of them had frozen to death, starved, or died of typhoid. As for desertion, there was no place to go.

Every day, I experienced with them how bad the situation really was. My husband was very pessimistic, too. After the fall of Omsk, the retreat began in great chaos. The Czech soldiers robbed and stole from the Russians wherever they could. General Hyda took the Siberian gold with him before he left—he simply expropriated the reserves of Kolchak's government. The French general Janin and his staff organized a special train for themselves to Vladivostok. Kolchak had been arrested by the approaching Reds. The French had broken their agreement with him and given him to the Bolsheviks. None of the allies intervened in any way when Admiral Kolchak and his interior minister were shot in Irkutsk and sunk in Lake Baikal. The admiral died a hero. Siberia was lost. Thus there was no more hope for going back to Russia.

My husband got more and more nervous about getting us to safety. We roamed through Siberia for a total of two years—on horseback, on foot, sometimes by train, sometimes in the carts of helpful peasants. Then we stayed for a few weeks in the mountains, lived with the Kirgis in their Yurts,[12] slept on the ground. Whenever we crossed a retreating column of the Whites, we saw terrible pictures: deserted carts with dead horses next to them, dead soldiers and refugees strewn around, and frozen people, some in the process of dying.

Occasionally, we had guides who knew the area well and could show us peasant cottages where we could be given shelter even in the most deserted areas. When we got close to the border, we saw destroyed mills. The millers had not wanted to leave them for the Reds to use. In one of these border towns, Makanchi, a certain captain Arbusov had named himself general, marshal, and many other things and had confiscated money, wagons, and even people. Thank God, his men let us pass. They only confiscated my horse and my husband's revolvers. We avoided territory held by the Reds, and on 23 January, 1920 we reached Bachty—the last Russian village before the Chinese border. My husband found a ruin where we were able to sleep on the floor that night. Our horses had gotten as thin as skeletons. Sick and dying people were lying around without help. The next morning, my husband bought sixty pounds of oats, and sixty bails of hay for three thousand Romanov rubles. A pound of flour cost fifty rubles. We found a guide who promised to take us to Chuguchak—a border crossing—for ten thousand Romanov rubles. It was a dangerous undertaking, since the police might arrest us and take us back to Bachty. Our first attempt failed: We were seen and shot at. But we drew back in time. A few days later, we tried it again, and we succeeded in getting to China.

Scenes in the north of the country. Andrey Borisovich Nolde[13] reports on the situation in Petrograd:

When my father was arrested for the second time, it was clear to us that we had to think about going away. The first time, my father came back, even though it was unusual for the Cheka to let anyone go free again. But they had needed my father—who had previously worked in the Ministry for Foreign Affairs—to figure out some documents. No one had any idea about the materials or about foreign languages. Many papers had simply been burned or been lost, and so it was decided to get former civil servants as instructors. So they let my father live.

Later on, the Cheka's activities against "enemies of the regime"—and that, after all, meant every average bourgeois, even if he was not interested in politics—became more and more drastic. Streets and roads were blocked at both ends, so that no one would escape during house searches, requisitioning, and arrests. Of course, often the owners of large mansions were able to escape through the servants' entraces into rear courtyards, coming from there to neighboring houses. But none of this was bearable anymore.

My father was released a second time. Now we had firmly decided to leave. In order to go away, though, we needed to solve three problems: to find a way to leave the city without being noticed, to figure out how to get over the border, and finally to take care of how we would survive in an unknown foreign country.

At first, we hoped that perhaps there would still be something left at our estate in Nikitino near Ryasan, which we could convert into money. We sent our maid Natasha there. Eight days later, she came back in tears and reported that on the day she arrived the town had been taken over by the local Soviet. All the furnishings in the house had been dragged into the yard, and there had been a lottery. Also in the lottery had been the agricultural equipment and furnishings as well as the farm animals. Since the "profits" were necessarily distributed very unequally—the men of the Soviets could get a book just as easily as they could get a horse or an armchair—there were soon arguments and fights. Eventually, they decided on a solution that treated all the players of this macabre game equally: They locked the animals and the desired objects into the stall and simply set it on fire. What pointless destruction under the motto "Steal what was stolen!" and the demand to divide the land!

How to escape from Petrograd now? The only possible routes for emigration—through the Ukraine or the Ural, through the Caucasus, Poland, or the Baltic—were no longer accessible to the inhabitants of the old capital. The few trains were closely checked.

The border to Finland, which ran about three hundred kilometers through forests and swamps, was traditionally the most closely guarded one in the Russian Empire. After all, most anarchists, revolutionaries and terrorists had come into the country through this territory, and they had contact with middlemen in Finland and Sweden. Lenin himself had frequently hidden in the forest before the October Revolution, since the area was closely watched. This was most certainly true now, too. The border units of the Red Army had taken up strengthened positions a good fifteen kilometers in front of the border, where they formed a closed circle.

Nevertheless, there were guides. They came from border villages, and usually they were not happy about the new regime, or they simply wanted to improve on their meager earnings. My father succeeded in making contact with a man like this, and he confided in him, telling him about my family's fate. First, however, he had to try to get his hands on some hard currency—which was practically impossible at that time—so that we would have a necessary minimum at our disposal in Finland and Sweden. This led to my father's third arrest.

He had already bought a couple of Finnish marks and Swedish crowns at exorbitant prices on the black market. Then a friend offered him a certificate for a franc account in Paris. He himself evidently had no intention or ability to leave the country. My father wanted to back himself up for such a high sum, and hence he went to the French consulate in Petrograd to notarize the friend's signature for the bank in Paris. They both went in together. Hardly had the door closed behind them than they were seized by two Cheka men, who asked them the reason for their visit. Without waiting for an answer, they declared that both were arrested. On the way to the registration office that the Cheka had set up in the French consulate, it became clear to my father that the paper which guaranteed him a credit of thirty thousand francs would be found in the inevitable body search and would suffice for an immediate execution. At the spur of the moment, he came up with an idea which seemed the only possible way out of this situation: He simulated strong stomach cramps and begged for permission to go to the toilet. The Cheka men had a debate, during which my father felt that his death was near, but finally they allowed him to do what he had asked for. A guard accompanied him and waited outside the door, which was not supposed to be closed. My father had to react with lightning speed during one of the brief moments when the guard was not paying attention, throwing the compromising document into the water and flushing the toilet immediately. He was so relieved that his face regained some of its color, thus confirming his previous simulation after the fact.

Despite this, the two were sent to jail. My father may well have been one of the very few people—if not the only person—to have been arrested but not executed or sent to a prison camp. My mother's attempts to get him free, and above all the fact that as a former civil servant he was, as already mentioned, useful to the Bolsheviks, since they were not prepared for their administrative tasks in the ministries—all this saved him from the worst, and there was a miracle: He came home. His friend, though, died in a camp to which he had been deported.

Two days after my father's return, we left Petrograd. My parents dressed us in raggedy clothes and gave us each a bag of potatoes. My younger brother did not know that besides toys and teddy bears there were also bank checks in one of the bags. We went through the rear door into a tiny street, following the man who was helping us. We went to a train station in a tiny suburb of Petrograd, which was filled chiefly with peasants who came here during the day to sell their goods. We were put into one of those train cars and sat on the floor in the middle of peasants and little animals: my mother with me and a brother in a wagon, my father and the man who was helping us with another brother in the next wagon. We had also walked separately, so that we would not be seen as an entire family.

At one point, a militia man wanted to check one of our bags, and we thought this was the end. But before he had made his way to us in the crowd, he lost his grip once and gave up. From the final station of the suburban train, we followed our guides to a peasant farmhouse. There we walked through his backyard, which led directly into the forest, and set off through the night. It was midnight, but not completely dark.[14] The peasants went first, carrying our bags, and the five of us followed them. Behind me was another guide. Not a word was spoken here, just as in their house. After about three hours of walking through the forest, we stopped. We were told that the most dangerous part of the journey lay before us. We now had to go over a clearing through which a tiny stream ran, and from there back into the forest. We were told that this was a shortcut to the border, but the guards who patrolled the border area were standing right there.

The guides in front helped my parents over the steep incline to the bank. My two brothers climbed after them on their own. After that, they crossed over the river in the same order with a third guide, using branches that had been carved into staffs. They had already arrived on the other side, in the clearing, where there was a wide meadow with a little haystack, everything covered with morning fog. Just as I was getting ready to cross over the river, followed by the guide behind, the tense quiet was broken suddenly by a wild volley of shots. At the same moment, I was able to see two soldiers rushing out of the haystack, stopping from time to time to reload their rifles. They ran toward my parents and brothers, who fled to the right along the riverbank, while the two guides in front disappeared to the left.

The guide who had been about to go over the river in front of me jumped into the water, which came up to his chest, and he swam back to the incline from which we had come. The guide behind me, who was acting as a rear guard, did the same.

I could see my parents throw themselves onto the ground under the hail of shots. Then the smoke from the shots and the fog cut off my view of the clearing. Deathly afraid, I climbed back to the path which we had used to descend from the incline, just as the two guides in front of and behind me had done. As I reached the path, I could see one of them disappearing between the trees about fifty meters away from me. I ran after him but soon lost sight of him. The men had run through the forest; I had no chance of finding them. I stopped, out of breath and crazy with fear. I was absolutely alone! I could hear no more shots.

What should I do?

My parents must be dead—or they would be at any moment. And my brothers? I could not imagine that they, too, would be shot, but it was clear to me that I would never see them again.

At all costs, I must try to get through to Petrograd! I would certainly find the way back to the peasant farmhouse, and from there I would somehow find a way. My grandmother, aunt, and other relatives were there, and they would know what I should do.

But could I leave my parents in the lurch? Without really knowing what had happened to them? I couldn't! First I had to be certain.

I turned around. I began slowly and quietly to crawl back to the incline on my belly. From there, I would be able to see the valley. But it was still foggy, and I couldn't see anything.

Suddenly, I heard a sound to my left: "Pst!" I was lost. I was looking into the face of a soldier, who motioned for me to come closer. I was a prisoner. Escape! He will kill me! Should I try to fight him? Pointless. Perhaps I could discover something about my parents! I come closer to him.

"Walk in front of me and watch out!" he whispers to me.

So he will shoot me from behind! But I had no choice. I obeyed.

Again I climbed down and crossed the river, followed closely by my unknown companion. On the other bank, I had to run toward the cottage. Another soldier was standing in front of the little door. He shoved me inside.

My parents and two brothers were there! Looking well and unharmed! But there was no time for outbursts of feeling. Already we were being pushed out again and pointed in a direction that led further into the forest:

"This way! Walk quickly, quickly!"

We tried as hard as we could to keep to the direction they had indicated. Our luggage was getting heavier and heavier, and we inspected it along the way so as not to throw away anything absolutely necessary. Meanwhile, I heard the story of what had happened explained to me in a whisper. Lying on the ground, my parents had soon been caught by the soldiers. They brought them and my brothers to the cottage in order to cross-examine them. Right at the beginning, my mother explained coldly that we wanted to go to Finland, and she asked how much the two wanted for permission to pass. They named a relatively modest price, which my mother immediately paid. But they had to leave immediately, since the neighboring guards would inevitably have been alarmed by the shots. That was when they noticed that I was missing. It was out of the question for my parents to go on without me. Whether it was because the soldiers did not want to have any major problems with their catch or because they actually did have sympathy with my mother—at any rate, one of them looked for and found me.

After a few hours, we came to a group of peasants. It turned out that we had gone in a completely different direction and were near a Russian village but hours away from the Finnish border. Would they take us to the border?—No, that was too dangerous, because there were patrols of the Red Guard everywhere in the forest.

"We would pay you generously."

"Russian money has no more value here."

"Do you want Finnish marks?"

"How much can you give us?"

"This much."

"Oh! That is not enough. We are risking our skin."

"So take twice as much; it's all we have."

Finally, they reached an agreement. It was three times as much as the Red Guards had gotten, who, after all, had let us live! So the peasants were greedier than the soldiers! But the main thing was that we now had help; around ten o'clock in the morning, we finally got out of the forest. In front of us, there were fields, and in the distance, once again on the other side of a river, I could see tiny houses: That was Finland already.

"This way, and good luck!" With that, our guides disappeared into the forest. We found the crossing they had pointed out.

It was over. We were free!

Southern Russia—Feodosiya, Crimea, around 1920. Andrey Sedych:

In the Crimea, the regime changed several times within a few years. First, there was a tartar republic, then came the Whites, then the communist, the Germans, the anarchists, the Petlyura bands. Each one of them forced the population to obey its rules and fought against its enemies. In addition, there were soldiers roaming around in masses. Since the peace treaty, they had been coming from the front, and they had nothing to live on anymore. I could see no future for myself here. I left Russia the day I finished school. I was hired as a sailor on a freight ship. That was possible back then. It didn't bother me at all to clean the floor. I got off in Bulgaria and set out for Constantinople—like most of the people who had been evacuated from Sevastopol or Feodosiya Novorossiysk in the White Army's ships.

Lydiya Vasilchikova was on one of these ships:

We had left on the Saturday before the Russian Easter. Inasmuch as possible, we gathered between decks on the ship to sing the songs usual in the orthodox church during Holy Week, and to celebrate mass at midnight. There were a lot of singers. Among them was the famous gypsy woman Masha Suvorina. We were given new courage and strength by the beautiful church songs. It was as if we would always carry the essence of our country with us, no matter where we went or what fate had in store for us.

Our uncertain future had begun at this moment. Russia lay forever behind us—deserted and forgotten by its former allies and left to walk the path of suffering in the future.

Vladimir Bulgakov:

I was lying in the hospital sick with typhoid when we heard that the Red cavalry was coming en masse. They far outnumbered us, and we had no more reserves. Our commanders walked through and declared that we would be evacuated—whoever wanted could stay at his own risk. We did not want to stay under any circumstances.

Andrey Nikitin summarizes:

Why did the Red Army outnumber us? Very simple. They went from village to village and took men with them. Whoever didn't want to go was shot on the spot. In this way, even women and children went with the Bolsheviks. They were promised virtually everything. And the Russian peasant never bothered with political questions. He simply lived as he lived, well or badly, but he was never interested in particular political questions. His motto was "For the Czar!" or "Honor the officer." The leaders of the White Army never made political considerations; they simply fought as well as they could, and that was their mistake—or drawback. Finally, the allies never really helped us—it was only a put-on: The fourteen or fifteen tanks the English did give us were long since useless and ready for the dump. They sent us things like this and said, "There you have it, in exchange give us Baku, the oil." Of course, Denikin refused, and we got no more help. Not to mention the French, who actually helped the rebels and gave General Kolchak to the Bolsheviks. The entire world did not want our army to achieve a unified, strong, great Russia again. They helped the Bolsheviks, because they thought this would weaken the country so much that it would not be powerful anymore. The Bolsheviks themselves built their empire on the ruins of the old one and raised new people on the bodies of the ones they had murdered. Does anyone really know how many millions of people the Bolsheviks killed during the Revolution and the Civil War? And then there was starvation, which was brought on artificially in the Ukraine in order to decimate the unruly population: in the Ukraine, which had fed the world, so much starvation that even human flesh was sold beside horse meat and people ate their own children!

In order to understand how all of this was even possible, one must read Dostoyevsky. He was the only one, much earlier, to foresee what would happen. In *The Demons* he showed everything that would happen: They come and promise the people paradise, the end of an unjust world. And, in fact, everyone had the same chances. Where people worked, the cities bloomed; where they drank, people remained poor. Everyone is to blame, all the countries that helped the Bolsheviks.

The archbishop of the Russian Orthodox church in New York, Vladimir Grabbe:

> I think that for an effective defense we were lacking not just leadership personnel but also ideology. There was only a negative ideology—against something, against communism. But there was no real positive ideology that would have brought the population along. Then one thing added onto another, whether it was supply or other problems. They all had political consequences.

Vladimir Semyonovich Averino:

> There were no inspiring mottos in the White movement. Lenin said, "Land for the peasants, the factories for the workers!" The Whites said, "We promise nothing in advance. We will liberate Moscow, call in the Constitutional Assembly, and we will not make any decisions until then." Thus the Bolsheviks had an easier time winning over the population, at least those who were uneducated. When they got to know the Bolsheviks better, it was already too late. Some then went over to the Whites. They were not just aristocrats and landowners but also simple people, peasants, and cossacks.
>
> In addition to everything else, organization never functioned very well with the Whites. As a soldier, I hardly had enough to wear.
>
> Finally, Russia had no real friends. England was relieved that we were out of the running for Constantinople. Without the revolution, we would have ended the war victoriously in Berlin and conquered Constantinople, and that is exactly what the others did not want.
>
> Why weren't the Reds stopped on their march to the south? Because there were not enough competent leaders and replacements among the Whites, even when one does not take into account the lack of support by

the allies, which I have already mentioned. The personnel question had already been the reason that Czar Nicholas had not given the appropriate answer to the revolution of 1905. It was the wrong people who were determining the decisions.

When I left Russia I thought of the words of my grandmother, who had said that I should never lose faith in the Russian people, even if this should prove difficult for me. And of a verse by Tyuchev:

One can not grasp Russia with one's understanding—one can only believe in Russia.

Postscript

The revolution eats its children—but not just its children. Also its parents. The subsequent purges of the builders of the Soviet regime, those who fought for it and those who knew about its financing are well known. Not just inside the country, but also abroad, assassinations from both sides against members or leaders of the respective opponent occurred in the capitals of Europe. When the assassins of a Cheka man in Switzerland were supposed to be sentenced, ex-Duma president Rodsyanko sent an open telegram to the defense attorney. His telegram was a picture of the reality in what is now the Soviet Empire at the beginning of the 1920s:

AS EX-PRESIDENT OF THE DUMA OF THE RUSSIAN EMPIRE I TURN TO THE BRAVE DEFENDERS OF MY COUNTRYMEN AND CANNOT STOP MYSELF FROM MAKING THE FOLLOWING KNOWN STOP WHILE RUSSIAN PATRIOTS ARE BEING SENTENCED FOR KILLING ONE OF THE BOLSHEVIK COMMISSARS WHO HAVE FOR A LONG TIME BEEN COMMITTING COUNT-LESS CRIMES WITHOUT PUNISHMENT STOP BEHIND THE RUSSIAN BORDER A TERROR UNPARALLELED IN HISTORY CONTINUES TO REIGN STOP AC-CORDING TO RELIABLE REPORTS, MASS ARRESTS ARE BEING CARRIED OUT IN MOSCOW AND PETROGRAD STOP EXECUTIONS WITHOUT SEN-TENCING ARE INCREASING AND ARE THE ORDER OF THE DAY STOP THE BOLSHEVIKS COMMIT MURDER NOT FOR CRIMES BUT SIMPLY TO DESTROY THOSE WHO DO NOT SHARE THEIR UTOPIAN AND IMMORAL IDEAS STOP RUSSIAN CIVILIZATION IS NOW EXPOSED TO DESTRUCTION AND THE RUSSIAN PEOPLE SUBJECTED TO BLOODY TERROR IN THE PART OF THE USURPERS OF POWER STOP I DESPISE IN THE DEEPEST DEGREE THE PAID WITNESSES EX-GENERALS WHO DARE TO DEFEND THE CAUSE OF THE SOVIETS WHO ARE DESTROYING MY HOMELAND STOP I BEG YOU TO GIVE

MY DEEPEST SYMPATHY AND REVERENCE TO MESSRS. CONRADI AND POLUNIN STOP EX-PRESIDENT OF DUMA M RODSYANKO

NOTES

1. This is located at the entrance to Red Square.

2. Russian pejorative form of the word "bourgeois."

3. Maruska was the leader of a band in southern Russia. It is said that in her youth she had been raped and subsequently developed sadistic tendencies.

4. As is well known, the Germans had not been satisfied with their rights over Ukraine as a protectorate, and moreover they feared that Bolshevik agitation would spread over the border. Hence they marched into the Ukraine again. Among other things, this was also in order to secure its reserves.

5. In 1906, Czar Nicholas II had gotten rid of the death penalty—except for murder of the Czar and triple murder. In 1918, Lenin reinstated it again, and under Stalin the age limit for the death penalty was taken down to twelve years.

6. Tula was a center of the metal industry and hence had a larger proportion of industrial proletariat than other regional centers. It was more receptive to revolutionary propaganda.

7. Cossacks were bound up in tradition and thus not particularly receptive to Bolshevik ideas. Moreover, the peasants in southern Russia were relatively well-to-do and could not identify with communist tendencies toward appropriation. They were loyal to their lords.

8. 1 pud equals 16.38 kilograms.

9. Term for Bolshevik agitators.

10. What is being referred to here is the occupation of certain areas of interest in southern Russia by the Germans after the peace treaty of Brest-Litovsk. After the outbreak of revolution in Germany, however, the Germans left these areas again.

11. This was also due to the failure of the English fleet to act. It stood by and watched as Yudenich was pushed back.

12. Nomads' tents.

13. At the time of these experiences, Nolde was about fourteen years old.

14. It was June. At this time of year, it never becomes completely dark in Petrograd and to the west of it. People refer to such nights as the "White Nights."

Chapter Nine

———*//*———

An Interview with Grand Duke Vladimir Kyrillovich Romanov[1], the Current Pretender to the Throne

E.H.: Your Royal Highness, what significance do you attach to the assassination of Prime Minister Pyotr Stolypin in the year 1911 and the subsequent discontinuation of his reform plans? Would the revolution not have happened at all, or do you see the revolution as a historical necessity that the war merely served to ignite?

V.K.: Certainly a continuation of Stolypin's reforms would have taken away the main basis for revolutionary arguments, and it is certainly imaginable that the revolution could have been put off at least for a while. However, I do not really believe that historic developments can be stopped. They multiply through decades and centuries, and at some point they ultimately lead to a crisis. This is what happened with the French Revolution and other moments that changed history.

As for reform activities in the social area and Russia, there had already been attempts to do this, and they were interrupted again and again. For instance, Alexander I did important things to improve the situation of the peasants. The decisive steps to remove bondage from the serfs were then taken in the consequent reign of Nicholas I, whom liberal publicists like to present as a reactionary. But he was the one who put the machinery into motion that ultimately led to the emancipation of the serfs. When they were given equal rights in 1861, a whole epoch of reforms was ushered in. This went all the way from the organization of the land for the peasants and their entry into peasants' groups to legal, judicial, and military reforms, from changes in the educational system all the way to local administration. These achievements were good until 1917. As for the process of democratization, there was a movement toward self-administration by elected representatives already present in outline during Alexander II's reign. He was able to realize these plans only because he did not have to answer to a parliament but could take on responsibility for such a decision himself. He knew that very well when he gave the program for self-administration his full support in 1862, at the same time, however, that he opposed the creation of a central body to represent the people. At the time. But a mere two decades later, when the changes were already taking root, he signed a decree for the creation of a central representation for the people, which was at first supposed to support the government in an advisory capacity. One day later, he was fatally wounded by a terrorist bomb, and his plans had to wait for realization.

E.H.: Among the many factors that led to the October Revolution of 1917, the main one was the manipulation of events by the revolutionaries, who were given generous support by the Germans. Which other country, in your opinion, was interested in destabilizing and weakening Russia that much and also helped in some way?

V.K.: I think almost all the great powers bear a certain portion of the blame. For the simple reason that our empire—Russia, that is— was not just a monarchy but also a political and territorial unity that was feared by most of the Western powers. At that time, Russia was developing its economy with extreme rapidity and was also in the process of expanding further territorially. England was afraid for the eastern provinces of its empire as well as for its ability to compete industrially, but there were also other, minor circumstances that led to the fact that in the West people wanted to stop the expansion of our industrial and military power.

One cannot put the blame on one person alone. The situation was very complex. Unfortunately our allies in the First World War were not one hundred percent honest. It is obvious that Germany's support of the Bolsheviks was a desperate maneuver to get rid of its opponent. But those who supported the Bolsheviks after their seizure of power bear an even larger portion of the blame. It was this that influenced world history to the great disadvantage of all of us, leading to a danger that threatens us even today.

E.H.: As long as we are talking about guilt, how do you view the role of the Czar during these decisive years, and what about the role of the Duma? Who failed?

V.K.: The Duma. Autocracy in the Russian sense—in contrast to its meaning in German—was never in conflict with the idea that people's representatives could help decide the future of the country. Such a democratic institution can already be seen at the time of the Muscovite Empire. Back then as well—at least in the Russian czarist empire—this was not meant as an alternative to government by a monarch, as was the case in European struggles for democracy. Even Ivan the Terrible summoned the first assembly of estate representatives, which existed from the sixteenth century onward. And this was precisely the institution that in 1613 reinstated the Russian monarchy by calling on Michayl Romanov after the time of political unrest and the occupation of Moscow by the Poles, as well as the liberation from the Poles by a Russian People's Army. Czar Michayl was only able to heal the wounds in this battered empire and solve its problems by working together with this body, which is what he did. Its activities later were pushed into the background under Peter the Great, until they were again given form by the Duma, the Russian parliament in the twentieth century—of course, under different circumstances.

After this historical digression, with which I wanted to show the essence of the Russian monarchy, let me talk about the role of the Duma in the events of 1917. There is indeed an accepted opinion that during the decisive spring revolution before the abdication of Nicholas II the Duma gave great service to the country. This is wrong. The liberals in the nineteenth century could claim to be constructive with respect to reforms, but the liberals of the twentieth century could more accurately be characterized as "destructive." Their avowed goal for the Duma was to overthrow the Russian regime. They were not willing to cooperate with any reform policies initiated by the government that would have helped it out. Meanwhile, the members of the Duma—at least "liberals"—made the Czar alone responsible for all the setbacks on the front in the first years of the war, and they demanded the creation of a parliamentary democracy. Nicholas II understandably refused to take on a restructuring of the state during the war, which led to the lowest and most unfair rumors and accusations against the Czar and the Czarina.

Here is a depressing example of how the members of the Duma acted against the government even at the cost of Russian national interests. A decision had been made at the allied conference in February of 1917 in Petrograd to undertake a mutual offensive against the enemy on two fronts. The Central European powers would hardly have been able to withstand this. The supply situation on the Russian side had gotten better again, and the army was well supplied with war materiel. Now liberal circles in the Duma started circulating the consideration that a victory for Russia brought on by its Czarist government would delegitimize the liberals' critique of the government's incompetence, making it seem like a common slander in the eyes of the populace, proving the government's competence and destroying the liberals' chances of ever coming to power. Concessions had to be forced out of the Czar. The ideal time for this seemed to be the unrest, which the liberals used as a lever for depriving the Czar of his power. Nicholas, who was with the General Staff at the front, was bombarded with telegrams in which even the president of the Duma urged him to abdicate. The Czar requested that his ministers hold out until he returned. We know the end. When the Czar was hurrying back to the capital city, his train was stopped along the way, and he himself was confronted with the urgent demand that he abdicate. Meanwhile, the men who were adding pressure to this demand through confirmations from other staff chiefs and generals were hiding from the Czar telegrams from generals urging him to withstand these requests. The Czar was given the false idea that if his reign continued during this critical war situation there would inevitably be a civil war, and this of course had to lead to his abdication on 2 March, 1917—a decision which meant the highest sacrifice for the ruler, who thought it was for the good of his country.

The liberals and radicals in the Duma formed a cabinet with precisely the same structure they had demanded from the Czar, and his final order to the country and the armed forces was to be loyal to the new government. This final address, however, was withheld from publication by the new rulers. In the following eight months, the Provisional Government lost control of the country and the army until Russia, as it had been known for centuries, no longer existed.

E.H.: What do you think about the line of reasoning that holds that at least the February Revolution was, among other things, a delayed reaction to the harsh attitude of the government toward the demonstrators of the 1905 Revolution?

V.K.: It is true that for a long time the February Revolution was considered an act of liberation from an oppressive reactionary regime. But the monarchy was nothing of the sort. Revolutionary movements were put down only in response to terrorist activities. The monarchy never used terror itself as a method in its politics, nor was it ever in its interest to keep the population subservient by means of a low level of education. On the contrary, illiteracy was quickly disappearing. Even the educational level of members of the army rose, with the percentage of people with a high school degree going from thirty-eight percent at the end of the nineteenth century to seventy-three percent in 1913. By 1922, all-encompassing educational program for all of Russia was supposed to be completed. Finally, the accusation that the monarchy was nothing but reactionary must be rejected. It is well known that—at least until 1917, though not afterward—there was variety in politics an ideology, and there was freedom to express one's opinions, as one can see in the plethora of newspapers representing various worldviews. Moreover, there was freedom in the exercise of religion, even for sects. Every class and each segment of the population was completely free in its search for its own individual realization—that was what the Czars had been fighting for, what my great-grandfather Alexander

II died for, and what Nicholas II, his wife, and their five children and faithful servants had to suffer a terrible death for.

E.H.: What do you think about the situation in Russia—or the Soviet Union—today, seven decades after the revolution?

V.K.: I do not view the revolution as the end, but rather as one phase in a development. Nothing is final, and neither is the result of the revolution, the Soviet regime. After all, the Russian Empire has remained an empire even in its new form, and it seems significant to me that ever since Lenin, in analogy to earlier times, there has always been a leadership figure—whoever that may be. The Russian people are used to being ruled by one leader at the top, and it seems to me that nothing will change in this. Perhaps you can still remember the noteworthy dispute between Alexander Solzhenitsyn and Andrei Sacharov, in which Sacharov pleaded for a democratic form of government for Russia, while Solzhenitsyn viewed only an authoritarian government as the adequate form of government for Russia.

What is essential, however, is that despite the lies on which the Soviet regime has built its rule, the Russian people's will to live has not been broken. In 1938, in the most difficult period under Stalin, for instance, an opinion survey was carried out. Based on the regime's assertion that God's existence is scientifically disproved by dialectical materialism, they wanted to prove that most of the people in the country had long since given up believing in God. But in this survey—at the high point of religious persecution—fifty million citizens still found the courage to declare their belief in God. This result was declared invalid, and no such survey was ever carried out again. But this shows that the people are still unbroken and able to survive even after all these years.

E.H.: Your Royal Highness, you grew up in the West, outside your country. Do you still feel yourself to be a Russian?

V.K.: Of course. My parents brought me up in this way. As a member of the Russian Imperial family and today the head of the family, I feel completely bound to my fatherland. Of course, it is my dearest wish one day to have the opportunity to serve my country. That is the meaning of my existence. My parents raised me not only with the French language but also with Russian, English, and German. In general, they tried to give me a practical education in the Boy Scout sense of "Try to be prepared."

As much as possible, I am trying even now to be concerned with my country, to ask myself how this or that problem could be solved. Moreover, whenever possible I have contact with the Russian emigrés, try to keep them together, and make sure that they do not lose their national consciousness. I am in correspondence with practically the entire world, from Australia to Canada, and North, South, and Central America. Many emigrants teach their children the Russian language and culture, thus carrying on the heritage of their country even after they have long since taken on another nationality.

I also try to pass along to my own children my philosophy of life, above all, my belief in God. I believe in God, as I believe that there is such a thing as good and evil. Belief is not an obstacle on the path to a modern future. Rather, it is an aid to people in difficult moments, and it inspires them to accomplish better things and to overcome difficulties.

E.H.: You bear the title of a regent. Do you believe a return of the monarchy is possible?

V.K.: I make no pretenses whatsoever. I was born a member of the dynasty, which gives us legitimation. If we do not relinquish the role that falls to us by virtue of this fact, we will at least be in a position to preserve and pass on certain values.

Of course, there is no turning back in world history. Hence I do not believe in a restoration of the old regime—which, however, does not mean that Russia will never again have a monarchy. Back then, not only the Russian but also the German and the Austrian empires fell apart. Our society had reached such a level of inertia that it was no longer able to cope with reality. The First World War triggered the catastrophe.

Today, however, one must admit that monarchy was always a form of government that kept a nation together in its dealings with the outside. And domestically it acted ideally as a sort of last resort in social and national conflicts. While England, for instance, was protected from enemy attacks by virtue of its insular position, Russia was plagued from its earliest times with invading enemies from the east and west. In the thirteenth century came the tartars, in the seventeenth century the Poles, in the eighteenth century the Swedes, then the French, etc. But in despite it all, the Russian monarchy lived on unharmed and undivided as a symbol of the country's unity. In contrast to ideas that are popular in the west, the Russian people viewed their monarch as the protector of their freedom—freedom from foreign rule and the rule of group interests as opposed to the interests of the nation. Every country with a monarchist past may sooner or later wonder whether it has not lost some of its national values and does not long again for its historic roots. The head of a dynasty must be in a position to act on such desires.

The period of waiting may last a long time. My dynasty has not been on the throne for seventy years now, but the French royal house has waited even longer. And today, after such a long time, it is still there—and ready to heed a call, if one should come, and fulfill its duty. This does not mean that I see this hour at hand for Russia, but in view of the current regime I believe it to be possible.

NOTES

1. Grand Duke Vladimir Kyrillovich Romanov is the great-grandson of Czar Alexander II and is currently first in the line of succession to the Romanov throne.

IMPORTANT DATES

─────//─────

(The dates until 1918 are given according to the old Russian calendar.)

1850: Marx writes The Communist Manifesto, formulating the concept "Dictatorship of the Proletariat."

1864: The first International is founded.

1873: End of the First International.

1875: The first South Russian Federation of Workers is founded.

1879: Stalin is born.

1881: Trotsky is born.
Czar Alexander II is murdered by anarchists.
The Ochrana is founded (originally a personal body guard for the czar).

1883: The first factory workers' law in Russia.
Plechanov, Axelrod, and Sasulich found the first Russian Marxist emigration organization: Federation for the Liberation of Labor.
Kamenyev is born.
Sinoviev is born.

1885: Radek is born.

1887: Lenin's brother Alexander Ulyanov is executed as punishment for participation in an anarchist conspiracy.
Lenin is arrested and expelled from the University of Kasan due to participation in Marxist student rallies.

1888: Bucharin is born.

1889: The Second International is founded.

1890: Lenin is permitted to continue his studies.

1892: Lenin is admitted to the bar in Samara.

1893: Lenin moves to Petersburg.

1894: Czar Nicholas II ascends the throne.

1895: Lenin, Petresslov, and Martov found the Petersburg Fighting Front for the Liberation of the Working Class.

1897: Lenin is exiled to Siberia.

1898: Founding party congress of the Social Democratic Workers Party in Minsk.
Lenin marries Krupskaya in Shushenskoye, his place of exile.

1900: Lenin returns from exile and emigrates to Switzerland.
The magazine *Iskra* (The Flame) is founded.

1901: A new wave of assassinations by anarchists in Russia.
The party of the "Social Revolutionaries" is founded again.

1903: Second party congress of the Russian Social Democrats in Brussels and London—the party splits into the Mensheviks and Bolsheviks (which is the more radical group)
Czar Nicholas II formulates a plan to conquer Korea and Manchuria.

1904: Outbreak of the Russo-Japanese War after a surprising Japanese attack on Russian positions in the Far East

1905:
1/9: The first Russian Revolution ("Bloody Sunday")—a line of demonstrators is shot by the police without the Czar's knowledge.
6/14: Uprising on the battleship *Potemkin*.

10/17: Czar Nicholas II approves the constitution.
Trotsky becomes chairman of the Petersburg Soviet.
Lenin returns to Russia for a short time.
At the party conference in Tammerfors (Finland), Lenin and Stalin meet for the first time.

1906: The first Duma (Russian parliament) meets and is disolved (5/10–7/22).

1907: The Second Duma (3/15–6/17).
The Third Duma (11/14–6/22, 1912).
London Conference of the Pan-Russian Social Democratic Workers Party.

1910: Rallies during Tolstoy's burrial.

1911:
9/14: Prime Minister Pyotr Stolypin is assassinated.

1912: The Bolsheviks form their own party—later the Communist—party—in Prague.
The Fourth Duma (until 1917).
Pravda is founded.

1913: Celebration of three hundred years of the Romanov Dynasty. Czar Nicholas II gives a large number of political prisoners amnesty.

1914: In May, there are strikes in the navy arsenals.
The murder of the Austrian successor Archeduke Franz Ferdinand and his wife in Sarayevo.
8/1: Germany declares war on Russia.
Petersburg's name is changed to Petrograd.

1915:
9/5–8 Conference of the socialist pacifists in Zimmerwald (Switzerland). Lenin formulates his theses on the transformation of the "imperialist" war into a civil war.
In the middle of 1915, the Russian exile Parvus makes contact with the German foreign office, presenting an extensive organizational program for a revolution in Russia.

1916:
4/2–9 New pacifist conference in Kiental in Switzerland.
12/16: Rasputin is murdered by Prince Yusupov.

12/17:   Temporary suspension of the (Fourth) Duma.

1917:

2/13–2/14   Demonstrations on the Nevsky Prospect: "Bread, Peace."
Strikes for food and higher wages.

2/23–2/24   200,000 workers go on strike. General Strike in Petrograd.

2/24:   Rodsyanko convenes an extraordinary session of the Duma.

2/25:   Czar Nicholas II orders a postponement of the reconvening of
the Duma, which had been scheduled for 2/26.

2/25:   5:40 P.M.: General Chabalov, commander of the Petrograd Military District, sends a telegram to General Alexeyev (in the
headquarters of the general staff); in it he reports on the unrest
of 2/23–24 and demands reinforcement by front troops.

2/25:   in the evening: telegram from Czar Nicholas II to General Chabalov with the order "to liquidate the unrest immediately."
Postponement of the Imperial Duma's meetings.

2/26:   1:05 P.M.: telegram from General Chabalov to General Alexeyev
reporting on attacks by the population against soldiers and police.

2/26:   several hours later: The Volhynian bodyguard regiment shoots
into the crowd.

2/26:   9:50 P.M. Telegram from Duma President Rodsyanko to General
Alexeyev with the urgent request for him to communicate to
the Czar the necessity of a reorganization of the government and
the appointment of a new prime minister.

2/27:   Telegram from Rodsyanko to the Czar with the request to be
entrusted with the formation of a new government. Telegram
from General Chabalov to the Czar with the following contents:
It is no longer possible to restore order in the capital city, since
the Wolhynian Regiment is fraternizing with the rebels and the
Pavlov Regiment is disobeying the order to shoot.
Telegram from General Alexeyev to War Minister Belyayev, assuring him that his request for three reliable companies of the
Georgian battalion will be met. Also to be sent to Petrograd: the
newly appointed commander of the Petrograd Military District,
Adjutant General N.Y. Ivanov, a brigade of the Fifteenth Cavalry Division and an infantry brigade from the northern front.
The Duma: A provisional Executive Committee is formed (its
members: Rodsyanko, Kerenskly, Cheidse, Shulgin and Milyukov).

A delegation of rebel soldiers enters the Duma. Revolutionary troops with the Red Guard (and armed civilians) reach the Duma and are received there by representatives; their leaders replace the previous guards at the Taurian Palace and occupy the post and telegraph offices of the Imperial Duma.

The Soviet of Workers and Soldiers Deputies is formed. The Peter-Paul Fortress is taken. The Palace of Justice burns. Executions.

2/28: The Executive Committee of the Imperial Duma and of the Workers and Soldiers Soviets calls on the population to maintain order.

Telegram from Military District Commander General Mrosovsky to General Alexeyev about the situation in Moscow. The Czar appoints Prince G. Y. Lvov to be the new chairman of the Council of Ministers.

Recognition of the Provisional Committee.

The first issue of *Izvestia* appears.

3/2: Provisional Government under Prince G. Y. Lvov; the first "bourgeois ministry."

3/3: Abdication of czar Nikolay II in favor of his brother Michayl

3/3: Abdication of Grand Duke Michayl (he renounces his claim to the throne).

3/6: General amnesty for political crimes.

3/7: The Czar's family is arrested.

3/12: Stalin arrives in Petrograd.

4/3: Lenin returns from exile in Switzerland.

4/4: Lenin's "April Theses" on the continuation of the revolution in Russia. He distances himself from other parties and groups.

4/24: The first Pan-Russian Party Congress of the Bolsheviks in Petrograd.

5/4: Trotsky returns to Russia.

5/5: The first coalition government.

5/12: The leftist parties, with the exception of the Bolsheviks, enter the Provisional Government.

6/3: First Congress of the Soviets.

6/18: Beginning of the last major Russian offensive on the German front.

7/4: An uprising by the Bolsheviks in Petrograd fails (the "July putsch"). Lenin escapes to Finland.

7/6: German counteroffensive breaks through the Russian line.

7/7: Prince Lvov resigns. Kerensky becomes chairman of the Provisional Government. The Red Guard is disarmed.

7/18: Lenin, Sinoviev, etc. are charged with high treason and incitement to revolution.

7/22: Trotsky is arrested.

7/24: The second coalition government.

8/29: Kornilov-Offensive.

8/29: General Kornilov's putsch attempt fails.

9/1: Proclamation of the Republic—Kerensky rules alone.

9/23: General strike by railroad workers.

9/25: Trotsky becomes president of the Petrograd Soviet.

9/26 and 10/1 Lenin demands that the Petrograd Bolsheviks start an uprising.

10/7: Lenin returns to Petrograd.

10/10: The Bolshevik Central Committee decides to attempt to seize power.
Military Revolutionary Committee forms under Trotsky's leadership.

10/19: The Minister of Justice orders Lenin's arrest.

10/24: Beginning of the October Revolution.

10/25: Kerensky's government falls by the storm to the Winter Palace. Kerensky escapes from Petrograd. Pan-Russian Soviet Congress opened in Petrograd.

10/26: The formation of a provisional "Workers and Peasants Government" of the "Council of People's Commissars." Lenin takes power. Chairman: Lenin. Foreign Affairs: Trotsky.
Decrees on appropriation, peace, etc.

10/27: Kerensky marches on Petrograd with a unit of cossacks.

10/29: The Bolsheviks shoot at bases held by seargeants in Moscow.

10/30: Battles on the outskirts of Petrograd (near Gachina).

11/1: Kerensky escapes to England, later to the United States.

11/7: The Russian high commander Duchonin is ordered to begin immediate negotiations for a cease-fire.

11/9: Duchonin refuses and is shot.
Krylenko is appointed high commander.

11/12: General elections for the Assembly. The moderate Social Revolutionaries achieve a majority.

11/18: All non-Bolshevik and non-Social Revolutionary newspapers are banned.

12/3: Military ranks and decorations are abolished in the army.

12/7: The Cheka is founded. Lenin orders Dzherzhinsky to prosecute people of the "bourgeoise" and the "counterrevolution".

12/13: Decree Number 112 of the Council of People's Commissars on support for revolutionary movements outside Russia.

12/17: Formation of a volunteer resistance army, the "White Army" in southern Russia.

1918: Civil War, 1918–1921

January Formation of the Russian Socialist Federated Soviet Republic (RSFSR).

The Gregorian calendar is no longer used.[31] January starts the calendar like the western tradition and is followed by 14 February.

2/10: Trotsky, the leader of the Soviet peace delegation in Brest-Litovsk, declares that the war between Russia and the central powers is ended, but he refuses to sign a peace treaty ("Neither War nor Peace")

2/18: The German offensive begins again on the eastern front.

2/21: Decision to found the Red Army.

3/2: German troops occupy Kiev. The Ukrainian national "rada" is formed.

3/3: The peace of Brest-Litovsk is signed between Russia and the central powers.

3/8: The party of the Bolsheviks names itself the Communist Party; however, the name CPSU is not formulated until the ratification of the new constitution of the Soviet Union.

3/10: The Soviet government moves its seat to Moscow.

3/13: Trotsky becomes war commissar (previously commissar for foreign affairs).

3/15: In protest against the peace of Brest-Litovsk, the leftist Social Revolutionaries walk out of the government. The Bolsheviks rule alone.

3/18: The first official issue of *Pravda* appears.

4/6: The Japanese land in Vladivostok.

5/25: The first battles between Bolshevik troops and the Czech legion in Siberia.

6/8: Anti-Bolshevik "White" governments in Samara and Omsk under Kolchak.

7/4: Pan-Russian Soviet Congress opened in Moscow.

7/6: Uprising by the leftist Social Revolutionaries. German ambassador Count Mirbach is assassinated. Uprising in Yaroslavl under the leadership of the Social Revolutionary Savinkov.

7/11: General Muravyev rebels against the Soviet government on the Volga front; he is shot by his soldiers.

7/16: The Czar's family is murdered in Yekaterinburg.

7/17: Six more members of the Czar's family are murdered in Alapayevsk.

7/21: The uprising of the Social Revolutionaries is put down in Yaroslavl.

7/30: Colonel General Eichhorn, German high commander in the Ukraine, is murdered by the Social Revolutionary Donskoy.

8/2: British landing in Archangelsk.
An anti-Bolshevik government is formed in northern Russia.

8/6: Kasan is conquered by the Czech legion.

8/14: Baku is occupied by British troops.

8/30: Assassination attempt on Lenin in Moscow by the Social Revolutionary Fanya Kaplan. Lenin is severely wounded.
Petrograd Cheka chief Uritzky is murdered.

9/3: Proclamation of the Red mass terror.

9/8: State conference of anti-Bolshevik Siberian Governments in Ufa.

11/12: Declaration of the Republic in Austria.
Communist putsch attempt in Austria fails.

11/13: The peace of Brest-Litovsk is declared invalid by the Soviet government.
The High Allied War Council represents allied spheres of interest in Russia.

11/8: Admiral Kolchak is recognized as the "High Ruler" of the Siberian government in Omsk.

11/27: Provisional Soviet government in the Ukraine.
Kiev is conquered by Ukrainian nationalist separatists under Petlyura.

1919:

1/19: Communist electoral defeat in Germany.

2/6: Kiev is conquered by the Red Army.

3/2: Founding party congress for the Third International in Moscow. Founding of the Comintern (Communist International).

3/21:   Bela Kun's council government in Hungary.

5/16:   Cheka chief Dzherzhinsky becomes people's commissar for domestic affairs.

5/19:   The White Army under General Denikin breaks through the Soviet southern front near Yusovka.

6/9:   The Red Army conquers Ufa. Kolchak's retreat.

6/25:   Denikin conquers Charkov.

6/30:   Denikin conquers Zarizyn (later Volgograd and Stalingrad).

8/23:   Denikin conquers Odessa.

10/11:   The White Russian General Yudenich marches on Petrograd.

10/14:   Denikin conquers Oryol and reaches the high point of his military success.

10/20:   Oryol is won back by the Red Army.

10/22:   Yudenich is pushed back near Petrograd; Trotsky is in command of the Red Army.

11/14:   Omsk is taken by the Red Army.

12/12:   Charkov is taken by the Red Army.

12/16:   Kiev is taken by the Red Army.

21/27:   A leftist counter-government is formed against Kolchak in Irkutsk.

1920:

1/3:   Zarizyn is conquered by the Red Army.

1/4:   Kolchak resigns in favor of Denikin.

1/15:   Kolchak is betrayed to the Army by Czechs and French in Irkutsk.

1/18:   A Bolshevik revolutionary committee takes over in Irkutsk.

2/7:   Kolchak is shot in Irkutsk.

4/4:   General Vrangel takes over after Denikin in southern Russia and the Crimea.

5/2:   Polish-Russian War.
       The Polish Army conquers Kiev.

6/12:   Kiev is retaken by the Red Army.

7/11:   Minsk is conquered by the Red Army.

7/12:   Vilna is conquered by the Red Army.

8/1:   Brest-Litovsk is taken by the Red Army.

8/15:   Polish counteroffensive on the Vistula.

10/12:   Polish-Soviet peace treaty signed in Riga.

10/20:   The Red Army begins its offensive against Vrangel.

11/14: Vrangel leaves the Crimean peninsula with the last White troops. Some of the civilian population is also evacuated.

1921:
  2/27: The Red Army marches into Georgia.
   3/1: Strikes in Petrograd.
        Uprising of the sailors in Kronstadt. Sailors and workers claim the fulfilling of Lenins promises of his "revolution"
   3/8: Tenth Party Congress of the CPSU.
        Lenin proclaims the "New Economic Policy" (NEP).
  3/17: The uprising in Kronstadt is crushed.

1922: Lenin announces the resumption of mass terror against any counterrevolutionary activity.
Stalin becomes secretary general of the CPSU.
Radek now a Comintern agent in Berlin.
Comintern agent Borodin is expelled from Great Britain.
The Patriarch of the orthodox church, Tichon, is arrested and charged with counterrevolutionary activities.
A new constitution declares the Union of Soviet Socialist Republics (USSR).
The Cheka becomes the GPU.
Lenin suffers two strokes.

1923: The beginning of mass terror against the orthodox church.
Patriarch Tichon is released from prison and subordinates himself to Soviet power.
Eighty-four bishops and about one thousand priests are relieved of their duties.
Terror starts against Catholics.
Archbishop Zepliak and Prelate Butkevich are sentenced to death.
General Goriev is Comintern agent in the Ruhr—communist unrest in Germany.
An armed communist uprising under Dimitrov in Bulgaria is put down.
Lenin suffers another stroke.
Lenin dictates his political will.

1924: Lenin dictates a postscript to his political will, suggesting that Stalin be removed.
  1/24: Lenin's death.

GLOSSARY

———— // ————

The transcription of Russian names and words was done according to
popular spelling conventions, taking authentic pronunciation into account.

Bolsheviks: Fraction of the Russian Social Democratic Workers Party
(RSDWP) that distanced itself from the Mensheviks during the split in
London in 1903. Because the Mensheviks were boycotting the meeting,
the Bolsheviks formed the majority (bolshinstvo—Bolsheviks). Lenin
was already the leader. In contrast to the Mensheviks, this party held
that its members must be professional revolutionaries who were not
allowed to make compromises with other parties and who must be
centrally organized. Among the Bolsheviks were Kamenyev, Sinoviev,
etc.

Bund (Federation): Jewish Social Democratic Workers Party, founded in
the European part of Russia in 1897. It played an important role a year
later when the Social Democratic Party came into being in Minsk, but
it only existed until 1917.

Cadets (from the initials "C.D." for "Constitutional Democrats"):
Political party of Russian liberalism with bourgeois point of view. They
were striving for reforms and the creation of a constitutional republic
or monarchy with England as their model.

239

Cadets: Military pupils in the Corps of Cadets, with officers training.

Constitutional Assembly (also "Constituante"): Legislative assembly demanded by various political groups in order to create an elected parliament to determine the actual form of government—independent of the question as to the preservation of the dynasty; in the course of the February Revolution in 1917 it was promised by the Provisional Government and scheduled for November of 1917. It was dissolved by Lenin when he saw that his party of the Bolsheviks did not achieve a majority and thus had no chance to take power legally.

Cossacks: Border population organized militarily. They proved themselves to be particularly loyal to the regime and were thus used to combat unrest; as elite troops they provided personal escorts for Czarina Catherine on her trips through the country. Later they formed the cavalry for the Czar's army.

Duma (Thought): Russian parliament with legislative powers; opened in this form by Czar Nicholas II in 1905 in what was then called Saint Petersburg. Its members were elected. Those elected in 1913 were replaced by the "National Assembly." In large cities, there was an analogous city Duma, a kind of city council. There had been city and district Dumas as advisory organs for the Russian czars and princes since the tenth century, though they were largely composed of aristocrats. The Boyar Duma was dissolved in 1711 by Czar Peter I and replaced by the Senate. After the Duma was dissolved in 1917, the Soviets ruled.

Dyelo Naroda (The People's Cause): Press organ of the Social Revolutionaries, edited among others by Sorokin.

Intelligentsia: Traditional name for the educated, usually progressive middle classes in Russia.

Iskra (Flame): Revolutionary newspaper founded by Lenin and Plechanov around 1900, printed in Germany and brought to Russia.

Izvestia (News): Daily newspaper put out by the Petrograd Workers and Soldiers Council after the 1917 February Revolution. It represented the moderate line of the Social Revolutionaries.

Kiental: In this tiny Swiss town south of Thun Lake there were pacifist conferences from 24–29 April 1916 following the Zimmerwald Conference in which the foundation of the Third International was discussed.

Leningrad: From 1924 on, the name for Petrograd (until 1914 St. Petersburg).

Marinsky Palace: Seat of the Provisional Government from spring until August of 1917, when it moved to the Winter Palace; during the latter period, it was the seat of the preparatory parliament until it was dissolved by Lenin in the fall of 1917.

Mensheviks (Minority): Moderate group of the Social Democratic Workers Party of Russia after the Second Party Congress in 1903. Its leaders were Martov, Axelrod, and Sereteli around 1917; Trotsky at first belonged to the Mensheviks: he viewed the centralized form of proletarian government that Lenin was trying to achieve as posing the danger of a personal dictatorship by Lenin.

Military-Revolutionary Committee: In October 1917, this was founded by the Executive Committee of the Petrograd Soviet in the Smolny Institute— in order to control the city and its garrisons and organize the armed putsch planned in October by Trotsky.

Militia: People's soldiers functioning as police after the end of the czarist forces of order in March 1917.

Monarchists: Party wanting to keep the dynasty as the highest government power, supported among others by Duma president Rodsyanko and some of the Constitutional Democrats under the leadership of Foreign Minister Milyukov.

Nyevsky Prospect: Central Street in Petersburg, where business life was concentrated (Gogol called it "all of Petersburg"); among other things, it goes past the great palaces of the leading aristocrats, past the Kasans Cathedral, and leads to the bridge over the Neva on Admiral Square next to the Winter Palace.

Peterhof/Petrodvovyec Summer palace northeast of Petersburg on the Gulf of Finland.

Peter-Paul Fortress: Fortress on the Neva across from the Winter Palace. Founded by Czar Peter the Great and used as a prison (whether for Decembrists under the czar in the nineteenth century, for members of the czarist government after the February Revolution, or for members of the Provisional Government and of the ancient regime or of the bourgeois class under the Bolsheviks after October of 1917).

Petersburg (Saint Petersburg): Also called "Pieter" by the people in everyday language. The Russian capital and residence of the Czar from its founding by Czar Peter the Great until 1918. In 1914 it was renamed Petrograd at the beginning of the war, and in 1924 it was named Leningrad.

Petrograd: See Petersburg.

Petrograd Soviet (Petrograd Council): Took on national powers in 1917 until the formation of the Pan-Russian Soviet Congress in June of 1917.

Pravda **(Truth):** First a monthly magazine published in Moscow from 1904 to 1906 as the press organ of the Social Democrats. From 1912 on, it was published in St. Petersburg as a daily newspaper. Because of its pacifist views, it was banned after 1914 and smuggled by Lenin from Paris to the Russian capital. From March 1917 on, it was the press organ of the Bolsheviks in Petrograd under the leadership of Lenin.

Preparatory Parliament (Preparliament): This body was to exercise legislative functions but was boycotted by the Bolsheviks and dissolved by Lenin.

Provisional Government: An emergency government formed temporarily during the March Revolution from a provisional committee of the Duma. It was one of two government bodies together with the Soviet. It governed in 1917 first with changing membership, and from May on with Kerensky as leader, until it was driven by the Bolsheviks from the Winter Palace during the October putsch. Its cabinet consisted for the most part of liberal cadets, with the socialist Kerensky as mediator between the radical forces and the Soviet, which kept a watch on the cabinet and controlled the police de facto. When several members of the Soviet entered the cabinet, there was a shift of power in favor of conservative forces—which was, in Lenin's eyes, "compromising betrayal."

Red Guard: Volunteer armed workers (from 1905 on) who supported the Bolsheviks.

Ryech: Daily newspaper in Petersburg from 1906 to 1917. It was the central organ of the Cadet Party. Among its editors and authors were P.N. Milyukov, V.A. Maklakov, and P.V. Struve.

Selyonye (Greens): Name for separatists in southern Russia during the Civil War.

Smolny: Petersburg instute for the daughters of high-level families. It was created in the eighteenth century from a cloister. In 1917, it became the seat of the Petrograd Soviet and the Central Planning Bureau of the Bolshevik Military-Revolutionary Committee.

Soviet (Council): Created first as the "Council of Workers Deputies" in October of 1905 in Petersburg. This form of organization then spread widely.

Social Democratic Party (RSDWP): Founded in 1898 as the Russian Social Democratic Workers Party, it strove for a socialist development in Russia using Marxist theories. In 1903, the group divided into the professional revolutionaries—the Bolsheviks around Lenin—and the moderate Mensheviks, among whom where Plechanov, Axelrod (one of the founders of Russian Marxism), Sasulich, Martov, Cheidse (after the February Revolution of 1917), Skobelyev and Sereteli. In contrast to Lenin, they wanted the Soviets (councils) to exercise power, and they wanted to work together with other parties.

Social Revolutionaries (SR): Founded in 1902 by revolutionary populists led among others by Victor Chernov. Kerensky was also a member. They wanted socialization of the countryside and were in favor of terror as a political weapon. They too divided into a radical and moderate wing. Members of the moderate wing were represented in the Provisional Government and felt insulted by the October putsch. The leftist Social Revolutionaries welcomed the Bolshevik October putsch and stayed in the Bolsheviks' government until they were excluded because of their protest against the peace treaty of Brest-Litovsk in March 1918. In January 1918, they had achieved the majority in the elections for the Constitutional Assembly, which was, however, dissolved by Lenin.

Svyesda **(Star):** Petrograd newspaper with conservative-liberal views. During the years from 1914 to 1917 it was in favor of a continuation of the war until victory in the name of defense of the fatherland.

Syemstvo: Self-administration in the country to improve conditions for the peasants. Instituted from 1864 on parallel with the city councils; like them, it was consumed by the local Soviet organs after 1917. These organs were subordinate to the directives of the Moscow Soviet after 1918.

Taurian Palace: Baroque palace in Petersburg where the Duma met.

Villa Kresinskaya: The house of a Petersburg Ballerina who had been a youthful love of Czar Nicholas II. The Bolsheviks used the building as their office until July of 1917. Lenin lived here after his return from exile in April 1917. When it was discovered that he had received German help, several of his colleagues were arrested. The office had to be closed down and moved somewhere else. Lenin barely escaped arrest and was able to go underground in Finland.

Winter Palace (also called the "Eremitage"): The Czar's residence on the Neva in Petersburg.

Yedinstvo (Unity): Splinter group of the Russian Social Democratic Party with a moderate domestic and foreign policy program: compromise with the bourgeois parties, the convening of a Constitutional Assembly, the formation of a strong government with broad support, the continuation of a war for national defense, destruction of German militarism. The ideas of the Social Revolutionaries contrasted with this. They wanted to make no compromises in domestic politics, and they were pacifists in favor of ending the war under all circumstances.

Zarskoye Syelo (the Czar's village): Summer residence of the Czar created by Peter the Great twenty kilometers south of Petersburg, later called by the Soviets Krashoye Syelo

Zimmerwald: In this Swiss town near Bern, Socialist pacifists held an international conference in September of 1915, demanding a peace treaty and the foundation of the Third International.

INDEX

A

Abdication
  of Michayl Alexandrovich in
    favor of the people, 67–75
  of Nicholas II (Czar), 63–66
Alexandrovich, Michayl, 61, 63–
  76, 96
  abdication of throne in favor of
    the people, 67–75
  pronounced Czar upon
    abdication of Nicholas, 63–66
Alexeyev, Michayl (General), 50,
  57–58, 63–64, 81–82, 104,
  159, 164
  Guchkov telegram, 104
Alexeyevich, Andrey, 196
Alexinsky, Grigory, 131, 141
Anti-semitism, by White Army,
  195–196
Antiwar sentiment, of Russian
  citizens, 48–49
Austrian Army, 48
Averino, Vladimir Semyonovich,
  75, 217
  account of February
    Revolution, 56–57

B

Barat, Leon, 155, 165
Bechhhofer, C.E., 179
Berthoud, Antoinette, 93
Besobrasov, W.M. (General),
  diary of, 20–22
Bisenko, 148
Black Sea Fleet, 201
Bloody Sunday, anniversary of,
  49
Bolsheviks, 84–85, 92
  Bolsheviks' journey through
    Germany, 88–89
  changing of name to
    Communist Party, 91
  first conference of, 91
  seizure of power in Moscow,
    128–157
Bontsch-Bruyevich, V., 139
Botkina, Tatyana, 95, 191
  account of February
    Revolution, 54–55
  impressions of war declaration
    days, 9–10, 12–13
Boyar Duma, dissolution of, 240
Bryusilov (General), 47–48, 64

245

DATE DUE

261-2500			Printed in USA